THE
TRADING
DESK

BRAD
GINESIN

Outskirts Press, Inc.
http://www.outskirtspress.com

ISBN: 978-1-9772-2757-7

Cover Photo © 2021 www.gettyimages.com. All rights reserved - used with permission.

Outskirts Press and the "OP" logo are trademarks belonging to Outskirts Press, Inc.

PRINTED IN THE UNITED STATES OF AMERICA

To Lucia, Zack & Petra

To my mom, an old soul who is greatly missed

And, of course, to stock traders everywhere

AUTHOR'S NOTE

I wrote *The Trading Desk* with the hope of telling an entertaining and authentic tale of Wall Street, while also imparting some trading wisdom and history for another generation to retrace. The fictional public company featured in this story is loosely inspired by elements of a handful of actual companies. Some of the characters are real people, including well-known financial journalists and hedge fund managers—most written with direct assistance from their real-life counterparts. The fictional characters may, at times, bear a resemblance to people I've met during my career on Wall Street since 1992. But in all instances, *The Trading Desk* is a work of fiction.

Part I

Chapter 1
IN A FLASH

May 6, 2010

Three Molotov cocktails were carefully secured in a pouch across Stavros Christoulas's chest as he stepped out into the streets of Athens. He could smell the kerosene as he strode down a cobblestone lane, overwhelming the sweet scent of the orange trees that lined the street. He stretched his lanky body to pluck a few blossoms from a branch and gently deposited them into his pouch.

Neither their sweet scent nor the Mediterranean breeze could cool his seething anger. Despair for the future and a longing for the past consumed his sleepless nights, and the rhythmic thumping of his old military boots on the cobblestones helped measure his roiling thoughts. Finally, he would act.

"Stav, please stop," Maria cried as she ran to catch up to her brother. Her dark brown eyes, matching his, were wide with fear and rimmed red from grief. He ignored her and kept walking, but she kept pace with him.

"Baba would not have wanted this," she implored. Stavros snorted and still he did not stop.

"Our father died to make a statement." Stavros forced his voice not to tremble. "He would not have tried to stop me—he would have been proud!"

Only a few weeks earlier, their 77-year-old father had shocked his family and the nation when he shot himself with a handgun in front of the Parliament building in Syntagma Square. His note had simply stated that he refused to be a burden on his family. Stavros felt the familiar knot in his stomach while thinking about his father.

The Greek people had been hit hardest in the two years since the start of the 2008 global financial crisis. The importer where Stavros had worked as a stevedore reduced its imports by almost two-thirds and laid off over half its workers. Stavros had been unemployed and living with his younger sister's family for 22 months now, and his father's death only fueled his rage at the government's continued belt-tightening. He would not allow his father's death to be disregarded, and he knew his father would approve of protesting, even violently, against the growing austerity measures.

Stavros spun around. "Go home, Maria." He wrapped an arm around his pouch, his resolve hardening even further. He could see the stubborn set of her jaw as she prepared to argue with him, but he continued before she could open her mouth. "The protests yesterday were violent. Your kids don't need you to get caught up in that."

He could see her wilt; she knew he was right. The Hellenic Parliament was prepared to ratify the third round of unprecedented austerity measures demanded by the Germans and the European troika. This was the last straw for many in Greece. Hundreds of thousands of protesters were already gathered in Athens due to a nationwide worker strike. Outrage at the latest planned cutbacks quickly turned to violent clashes between protesters and riot police.

"People died yesterday," said Stavros. "Innocent people. Please, go home and be safe."

"You be safe." She folded her arms across her chest. She looked like their mother, he thought before he could stop himself. Maria's gaze settled on the pouch he carried, and her expression tightened even more. "Don't do anything too stupid."

He nodded slowly, as though he wasn't planning to commit arson, and left his sister standing in the street among the orange blossoms.

Stavros took a deep breath and continued walking, the streets growing busier as he approached the city center. Stray cats paced skittishly, as if on edge, awakened from their usual afternoon naps. As he strode past the Mitrópoli, he made the sign of the cross and said a silent prayer. His eyes narrowed as he marched steadily by restaurants and closed shops on the garbage-strewn Ermou Street, heading toward Syntagma Square and the Parliament building.

He focused on Marfin Egnatia Bank's charred facade, where the riots yesterday had taken a deadly turn. Three people had died after the bank had been set ablaze, one of them a pregnant employee. Today, flowers and stuffed animals were piled high at the foot of the building. Sobered by the events of the day before, many protesters vowed to remain peaceful, but the most strident among them—Stavros included—marched on undeterred.

In the earlier hours of the morning, both protesters and police had staked their territorial claims on the square. After the previous day's casualties, police had orders to step up the use of force to control unruly protesters. Riot police had barricaded the stairs that led to Parliament. Behind the barricades stood stores of flash bombs, smoke bombs, and tear gas launchers with innumerable canisters. Shields, batons, and gas masks were assembled on top of the barriers.

Protesters positioned themselves on the outskirts of the square in front of the Parliament building. Well behind the front lines, young men gathered ammunition in overturned dumpsters while peaceful protesters slowly filled the streets.

Stavros placed his Molotov cocktails into a protester-annexed dumpster. He walked to the edge of the square and reached into his pouch as he looked to the place where his father had taken his life. Taking the orange tree blossoms in his hand, he tossed the flowers into the breeze, whispering a prayer for his lost parent. The wind lifted the petals, and Stavros watched them for a moment but continued staring toward the sky as they scattered across the stone of the square. He eyed the riot police guarding the Parliament building, then faded back to a makeshift ammunition depot.

"Are you ready, Stav?" asked Nick, a friend and former colleague. He too wore all black, with the same bandana around his neck and the same stony expression carved into his face.

Stavros nodded. He and Nick waited into the evening for the protest crowds to grow more raucous. They stood smoking among a group of young men, beneath the awning of a closed shop. Some of the men were anarchists and anti-capitalists taking the opportunity to wreak havoc, but most were like Stavros, overwhelmed by hurt and the need to lash out at their government.

"Do you see the cameras up there?" Stavros pointed to reporters and camera crews atop buildings all around the square. "We're big news."

Nick glanced upward. "Of course we're big news. Or haven't you heard? The euro is ready to collapse. They're here to see whether Parliament will reject the austerity measures."

"Who cares if the euro collapses?" Stavros bent down to retie his boots. "We're all struggling anyway. They're just trying to scare us into more cuts. Fucking Germans."

Nick squinted to get a clearer look at the crowded rooftops nearby and let a low whistle escape his lips. "BBC, Al Jazeera, Reuters. The world is watching, my friend."

"Good." Stavros eyed the crowd, hearing their chants grow steadily to an angry crescendo. Yells erupted across the square, where riot police had deployed tear gas to disperse some of the wildest clusters. "It's time. Let them see."

Stavros flicked his cigarette butt to the ground and stomped it out under his heel. He slipped a bandana over his face, grabbed a Molotov cocktail from the dumpster, and walked purposefully into the fray. Unlike many of his fellow rabble-rousers, he lacked a gas mask, but he was undaunted as his heavy boots crunched over broken glass.

His nerves were raw and his heart pounded as he took a lighter to the kerosene-drenched cloth. When the flame caught, he broke from the crowd and ran directly into a cloud of tear gas toward the Parliament building. Half-blinded, he skirted the thickest of the gas clouds and held his breath as his lungs scorched. Like a javelin thrower at his Olympic debut, he hurled the bottle high toward the building.

He glimpsed a flash and felt the distant heat of the erupting fireball, but he turned to retreat without watching the effects of his work. Through burning eyes, he squinted as he stumbled toward a group of shadows in the street. The crowd ensconced Stavros protectively. People screamed as helmeted, baton-swinging police shoved and struck their way through the crowd of protestors. Already straining to breathe, Stavros felt the wind leave his lungs entirely as a baton connected squarely with his ribs. He fought the searing pain in his side and struggled to get away, but two policemen wrested him from the crowd, while others beat back those fighting to pull him free.

The crowd jeered at the cops as a dazed Stavros was hauled off to a police truck. Sickened by the tear gas, he heaved forward and retched violently over the pavement. Stavros turned to wipe his mouth on the shoulder of his jacket and gazed toward the sky. Tears streamed from his eyes and he thought of his father. He had made his statement. He hoped Maria would forgive him.

Chapter 2

CRASH COURSE

The day of the protests in Greece started unremarkably on the stock trading desk of Glacial Capital, where Brandon Shuster worked as an equity trader and principal. The Midtown Manhattan firm was a hybrid between a hedge fund and a prop shop.

Just over a year had passed since the biggest housing bubble of all time had burst, precipitating a tumultuous 57% drop in the S&P 500. Skepticism remained high among traders and market participants about the steep rally that followed. The Federal Reserve's remedies were more like a tourniquet to stanch the bleeding, albeit successfully applied to keep the patient alive and kick the can down the road. Still fresh in the minds of traders lurked the housing crash and subsequent financial crisis that required government bailouts for bankrupt automakers and insolvent financial institutions.

So, on that warm and sunny May afternoon, the traders on the desk continued to sip their second round of coffees as they observed the 60-point downdraft, a 5% pullback in the S&P. For those times, it was routine skittishness stemming from European financial contagion.

From the corner of the trading desk nearest a large overhead TV screen, Brandon casually noted to his seven colleagues,

"You guys see what's going on in Greece? This looks like a serious escalation." He turned to Eli Katsanos, born in Greece, who still had close connections there after 20 years in the States. "What's happening in the homeland? I hope your family's okay."

Brandon had 18 years of stock trading experience and had helped start Glacial's trading desk 15 years earlier. His bespectacled hazel eyes were usually focused intensely on his computer screens, where he sought out trading opportunities like a Manhattan cabbie weaving through traffic in search of his next fare.

Eli appeared completely unfazed yet captivated by the protests. "The demonstrators are still pissed at that austerity vote yesterday. But this just looks like a bunch of punks with too much time on their hands. Same fuckin' anarchists that cause trouble at every protest." After tapping away at his keyboard for a few minutes, he reported, "Just made contact with my uncle. Everything's cool with the family. They're in Thessaloniki. The protests there are mellow compared to Athens."

CNBC's intrepid international correspondent Michelle Caruso-Cabrera was covering the riots live, perched on a rooftop with a view of Syntagma Square. "As evening falls, what we're witnessing are some of the most violent clashes between police and protesters." Cameras panned to rioters who tossed explosives and clashed with police brigades. "There are many, many fires burning. The streets below are thick with smoke and tear gas."

While Eli remained transfixed by footage of the protests, the other traders divided their attention between watching the markets on their computers, which seemed further rattled by the chaos in Athens, and listening to Eli's intense narrative. "Hey guys! You see this action? An officer got lit up by a Molotov cocktail." Eli jumped up and walked closer to the TV.

"The police just stormed into the crowd, whacking people with batons." Eli paused with a hand over his mouth. "*Holy shit*, they're dragging some hoodlum off." They all looked up at the TV just in time to watch a mangled, black-clad man get hauled away by police.

In those moments, the complexion of the sharp market pullback changed—fully recognized on the desk as "opportunity." When anarchy appeared to erupt in the cradle of democracy, market uncertainty flared, turning a rout into a panic. The accelerated selling induced by "blood in the streets" splashed across TV screens seemed like a prime time to buy.

As the S&P slipped lower and the SPY slid through $112 on its fall from $118, the solidly experienced traders on the desk began to scoop up stocks aggressively.

"What the hell does Greece have to do with the price of Bristol Myers?" Brandon shouted the Wall Street cliché, certain that the market was overreacting to the violence in Greece. "Gotta buy this pullback."

"$111 SPY! Ho, S&P's down over 70 handles," he added, wistfully gazing at puts speeding higher like the national debt clock.

Brandon often took the role of calling out stock prices and adding a narrative to the action. He thought it added to the collegiality of the desk and kept him focused on hunting for opportunities. The overworked air conditioning of the Helmsley Building could hardly keep up with the blazing computers packed into their modest office space, as they sat four on each side of their connected desks, a band of eight brothers in trade.

"Cisco just got slammed to a good level. I'm buying some size here," Mitch said in his steely voice. Cisco, a reliable tech stock to buy on weakness, had quickly dropped from $26 to $24.50. Mitch, a young and utterly fearless trader, thought buying Cisco on weakness felt conservative. No company was better known on the trading desk. For over a decade, the traders' most enduring ritual had been staying after hours to tune into Cisco's quarterly earnings conference call led by the CEO, John Chambers. With his West Virginian twang, Chambers would give the most trusted guidance and discuss the company's technology, outlook, and "kay-ash and kay-ash equivalents."

Dominick Cott, a principal and trader at the firm who managed the desk, replied, "I have my hands full with Hewlett—the stock just dropped, like, three points. I'm catching them. Of course I started too early." Like most of the Street, Dominick had confidence in Hewlett-Packard's CEO, Mark Hurd. He figured this was his chance to pick up cheap stock since Hurd had led the company through the financial crisis relatively unscathed.

Brandon rose out of his seat and shouted, "$110 SPY! I'm legging into Accenture, GE, and the SPY. Looks like we're getting capitulation selling. We gotta buy this. A few Molotov cocktails and everyone's in a panic."

The desk routinely took the contrarian side of market action. While others flinched from falling knives, they often tried to snatch the handle at the right moment.

"They're out there panicking right now. I can feel it—they're panicking," Mitch declared in the cadence of Billy Ray Valentine mocking traders worried about affording a G.I. Joe with the kung-fu grip.

Eugene "Goldie" Goldstein, one of the firm's principals, had a knack for finding the most egregiously mispriced stocks. He was a diminutive trading whiz of Korean descent who had been adopted by a West Coast Jewish family, and also had a knack for confusing package deliverymen. Goldie's nostrils flared as he made a show of sniffing loudly. "I love the smell of panic."

Brandon lifted his head. "$109 now on the SPY. Holy shit, my stocks are getting killed here." His urging to buy quickly sounded less certain as the downdraft gathered speed.

"Dom!" Mitch bellowed in a hoarse voice. "I'm down a quick hundred thou' in Cisco. I've never seen this stock come down so fast. I'm catching this panic right in the face."

Dominick oversaw the desk's risk exposure and was well aware of the mounting losses. "I'm getting killed, too. I'm still buying. Just use your best judgment." Dominick consciously ignored the firm's approaching risk capital thresholds for adequate liquidity. "This is crazy," he whispered to himself.

"$108!" Brandon tapped his glasses, his eyes wide. "Just bought more Accenture down $10. This is a crash—the market's *crashing*." Vivid stories from market old-timers burst into his mind about the 1987 stock market crash, when the Dow Jones plunged over 22% on Black Monday. He recalled how the legendary NYSE floor broker Art Cashin liked to quip that, since the crash, "First thing I look for when I walk into a room is the exit sign."

"Apple, anyone buying Apple? Just went from $255 to $220." Goldie glanced around in amazement. After a moment with no replies, he added, "I got my catcher's mitt out."

"$107!" Brandon's voice cracked. "I'm buying more SPY. This is my third average down—I'm so fucked." He knew the desk was in trouble, and his utterance was the best he could muster as the downward spiral continued.

"Uh, be careful buying more stock here. We're not going to be able to hold all these positions." Dominick could no longer ignore the firm's capital situation, which was leveraged well beyond comfort as positions increased and losses escalated.

Confusion set in. Gasps and curses flew around the desk. What had felt like opportunity moments before now turned to fear, frustration, and self-loathing.

The market cascaded down like a waterfall, and the lower it went, the faster it plunged. The traders watched in horror the uncontrollable force at work on their screens. They were a crew barely afloat in a lifeboat with no oars. Brandon wanted to look across the desk at Mitch's bearded face to see if, for once, his unshakable colleague looked flustered, but he couldn't take his eyes off the numbers.

"I'm down $300K. Dom, what do I do?" Mitch ran his fingers through his thinning brown hair.

"I see, I see. I have my hands full here, but technically we really can't buy anything," Dominick answered, knowing the firm was well over its capital limit. He berated himself. "Ugh, I'm so dead—what the hell am I doing long all this shit? I completely suck. Stupid decision-making!"

"Fuck that. Apple just went to $200. We gotta buy this! Apple! Apple!" Goldie scooped up Apple shares, ignoring Dominick's caution about capital limits.

"$106 SPY! Fuckin' look at those puts. We're the ones with no swimsuits," Brandon agonized. He sensed the desk had landed directly in the crosshairs of Warren Buffett's metaphorical red flag: "Only when the tide goes out do you discover who's been swimming naked."

"I'm in with you, Goldie," Mitch called out.

Brandon peered disbelieving through his glasses as every bid in Accenture disappeared before his eyes. "Accenture, oh my God. It was just $30." He paused to take a breath as he sat frozen for a few seconds. "Look at that chart! Traded under a buck!" Brandon's eyes darted from side to side as unfathomable numbers flashed everywhere. "Uh, it's back to $25. What the fuck just happened?" The stock rallied back quickly. Thrilled to see an exit, he unloaded his entire position on the first bid to hit around $30. As the stock raced back over $33 in the next blink, he thought, *What did I just do?!* He sank back into his chair and let all the air out of his lungs. His shirt was soaked with sweat.

Before the market stopped and reversed, the Dow Jones had fallen a thousand points, an unprecedented decline, the last 5% within four minutes. Seven stocks in the S&P, including Accenture, inexplicably traded down to one penny at the market's nadir.

"Cramer just said to buy P&G in the $40s!" Sneaks flicked a finger at CNBC's Jim Cramer on one of the TVs. "The stock just went from $55 to $40. It's already back to $50. Ugh, I missed it already." Sneaks was the youngest and least experienced trader on the desk, yet the only person scrappy enough to have graduated from Glacial Capital's trainee program. He sported a collection of sneakers that could rival any NBA player's, hence his desk nickname.

"SPY $107!" Still eyeing SPY puts and Accenture, Brandon reflexively continued to update.

"That was the bottom!" Goldie waved his arm. "LVS, DOW, GE, haven't turned yet. Buy some shit, and don't worry about the capital right now. Procter is still cheap at $50—it opened at $62!"

"Yeah, but it was just $40." Sneaks lifted an arm and scrunched his face.

Dominick wiped his brow as he glanced at the firm's positions. "Guys, we can't just ignore the capital." His attempt to maintain the firm's exposure within a normal range of risk sounded halfhearted.

"$108." Brandon exhaled deeply. "We're going to be okay. Mitch, how you doin'?"

"Goldie saved my bacon," Mitch replied. "Grabbed some Apple at $205, selling some already at $225. Only down $150K, just need Cisco to keep coming back. Did anyone buy that Cisco in the $22s? I can't believe how low it went."

"Nice job, Cisco Kid." Goldie looked over at Mitch, who gave a modest shrug of his oversized traps. "It took balls to ride that out. Balls like church bells." This was high praise from Goldie, who was notoriously hard to impress.

"$109, thank God. Dom, I'm lightening up, selling some SPY." Brandon felt a wave of relief and relaxed his shoulders. "I wish I hadn't chirped out of Accenture, but I caught a glimpse of my P&L when it went straight to a buck from $40—my career flashed before my eyes. I thought it was the '87 crash all over again."

"Yeah, I'll admit, I thought about how I'd need to dust off the ol' résumé." Mitch winked.

Brandon started to babble as he quickly assessed his decision-making. "Guess I should have tried to buy some at a buck, but it happened so fast I didn't want to put in a market order. I'm okay now, though. SPY and GE are powering back for me. Nice call on the LVS—I put in a limit order too low and got blanked. What a loser." He rolled his eyes. "$110 SPY!" Brandon was still relieved he and the firm didn't get destroyed in the crash. It wasn't until later that the missed opportunity sank in.

"No way those trades down there don't get broken anyway. Even in a crash, those trades are clearly erroneous." Goldie shook his head, referring to the SEC rule of canceling trades executed in error, far away from the prevailing quotes. A few hours later, he was proven correct when all trades below $30 in Accenture were canceled.

"$111." Brandon felt calmer as the market recovered. "Selling most of my longs here; already sold the last of my SPY a half-point ago. Any way we retest that low?" After a heart-stopping day, Brandon fished for an excuse to sell his remaining positions, yet his question was met with the sound of crickets.

"I'm feeding the ducks right here in Apple." Goldie clicked away at his keyboard and mouse. "They swept me!" He leaned way back in his chair, arms outstretched wide. "Killed it."

"Nice trade," Mitch said. "I sold my last Apple 10 points ago—this 20% rally to $245 looks like too much already. I'm almost ready to short some stuff." At once, he reconsidered, "I should really just shut it down. I can't believe I made back $350 thou in 20 minutes. I'm done pushing my luck. Dom, thanks for letting me ride out the Cisco; that was hairy."

"You know, I was so buried myself, I wasn't about to make you bail out," Dominick said.

"I was scared for both of you." Sneaks peered over. "I was so busy spectating your losses, I barely bought anything. Fuckin' Greece."

"Don't tell me you're gonna blame that crash on Greece." Eli jumped out of his chair in protest. "Some stupid rioting in the streets drops the Dow a thousand points? No *fuckin'* way. They riot in Greece all the damn time—how many market crashes have they triggered?"

"What the hell was it, then?" Sneaks looked around, but no one had an answer better than "selling begets selling." For five long years, the traders would be left to wonder until the "answer" arrived: Weeks before the statute of limitations expired, the DOJ would pin the manipulation of S&P futures that contributed to the crash on the spoofing of a 36-year-old who traded from his parents' home in London. Along with most of Wall Street, the desk would come to roundly ridicule the DOJ for charging the least likely culprit. Those who knew better would lay the blame on Waddell & Reed, whose enormous and clumsily executed e-mini market sell order was unleashed minutes before the crash.

When the market closed, Mitch stood up, clasped his hands and pressed his fingertips to his lips as if saying a prayer.

Brandon raised an eyebrow from across the desk when he saw the sweat patches in the armpits of Mitch's snug short-sleeved polo shirt. Although his muscular body and caveman-like hair growth made Mitch prone to sweating in the warm, stuffy office, Brandon took comfort in thinking he was not alone in feeling the day's stress. When Brandon caught sight of Goldie proudly crowing like a rooster over his Apple scoop and bottom call, he had to suppress an envious sneer. Instead, he casually walked over to Mitch, patted him on the back and said, "Strong comeback."

Mitch nodded. Like several of the traders on the desk, he had made an art form of selling stock short during the financial crisis and beyond. He replied in a halting voice, "That was, like, the first time I've been long stock all year. That'll teach me."

"Look, there were only two things to do today: cover shorts and get long. You did the right thing, and you'll be a better trader for it."

"You must have had quite the adrenaline rush yourself." Mitch snapped out of his reverie and turned to Brandon with a smile. "When I looked at Accenture's chart, I did feel a little better that I wasn't such a jackass—things were totally irrational."

"Yeah, I didn't need that," Brandon said. "I'm getting too old for adrenaline rushes. The way I dumped that stock in a panic is gonna leave a mark." Already preparing for some mental repercussions, he gave Mitch a firm pat on the shoulder and sat back down to stare at the day's charts.

Chapter 3

THE ESCAPE

The trying day led to an unspoken but stronger bond among the traders. The firm had survived unscathed the event that became known as the "Flash Crash." For a while, this was all that seemed to matter. It happened so fast, yet left a lasting imprint on the traders' psyches. As a group, the desk considered themselves highly cynical about the stock market—days like this reminded them why.

Out of obligation, in a brief meeting of the desk, Dominick discussed the firm's precarious state, including their meager amount of risk capital. "The desk went way over our overnight margin requirements." He glared at Goldie. "Fortunately, the market rebounded intraday—if it hadn't, we'd have had to sell down many of our positions by the close regardless of price."

Nobody wanted to deliberate hypotheticals for what they instinctively believed to be a once-in-a-generation event. Yet they all knew the capital they'd each invested in the firm would have taken a sizable haircut without the quick recovery.

Brandon stayed late that evening, alone on the desk. Time passed slowly as he sat staring past his computer outside to the cityscape. His glasses askew, he munched on Tums from the communal jumbo-sized container that sat on a windowsill at the edge of the desk. Still, the stress in his stomach remained hard to quell. Between thoughts about the firm's existential risk and his career risk, he replayed the violence in Greece again and again. In his mind, he watched the SPY tank and Accenture go from $40 to $30—then to one penny in a flash—followed by just one flinch of a click on his mouse to sell all the shares he owned at a measly $30. *Fuck.* In every replay, his adrenaline-fueled panic was still palpable. The Accenture sale felt unforgivable, as did his failure to capitalize on the chaos.

He tossed his glasses aside and buried his face in his hands. In the darkness, he pictured the protestor clad in black and the fireball that had seemingly ignited the day's chain of events. He tried to review the trading day to cast it into long-term memory, fearing the details would soon become a blur. But he kept losing concentration and instead imagined himself going home to Lily, his wife. She would be waiting expectantly to hear how, in a day for the ages, he had made a bundle trading the chaos.

How could he explain that instead of scoring big like he should have—like the seasoned trading veteran he was—he had bailed out of Accenture at $30 in a panic, didn't have the guts to buy Apple when Goldie gift-wrapped the call at the bottom, wasted mental energy focusing on puts that spiked after he closed them in the morning, and sold too soon everything he had bought dirt cheap? All this while risking his money in the firm, almost shitting his pants, and barely making it out of the red for the day. *But hey, I kept the desk updated where the SPY traded! And how was your day, honey?* In his easiest decision of the day, he opted to hop on a later train home.

After Brandon finally pulled himself away from his computer, he ambled to Grand Central Terminal with thoughts spinning through his head like a carousel. He walked through the terminal's cavernous halls, expecting to see something different in the faces of those around him, some indication of the fraught day. Yet everyone seemed completely at ease as they went about their evenings. The market had crashed and Greece was in turmoil, but nothing discernible had changed in Manhattan. The city's steady rhythm and routine calmed his frayed nerves.

To help quash his remaining anxiety, he bought an extra beer for his Metro-North ride to Cold Spring in the Hudson Valley. He looked forward to the peaceful sanctuary of his Early American farmhouse surrounded by nature, and the mental diversion of upcoming weekend activities with his wife and kids. Settled into a train seat, he cracked open a beer and wondered how the people of Greece would cope. Their situation seemed dire. Thinking about the trauma of smashed glass, fireballs, and severe austerity measures put the world in perspective, and he felt grateful.

Brandon looked down the aisle just in time to see his neighbor, Jimmy, lumbering in his direction. He cursed himself for absentmindedly sitting in the two-seater as the chatty, too-wide-for-one-seat man slid in next to him. His moment of gratitude was gone.

"Hey, Jimmy." Brandon was in no state of mind to converse with his neighbor and prayed to get away with saying this little. Jimmy had become a doomsday prepper during the financial crisis, with a basement resembling a mini Costco, and spent weekends hunting the local wildlife in season. He and Brandon barely had anything in common.

"Hey, any good buys out there?" the hunter-gatherer asked.

Brandon rolled his eyes behind a long blink at the familiar question. *The last thing I'm going to do is recommend a stock to someone who totes around a rifle.* "There were a bunch at about 2:45 today," he said and took a long swig of beer.

His neighbor grunted, clearly oblivious to the market

action. To Brandon's relief, Jimmy opened the *New York Post* and focused on the newspaper as if it were a porn mag.

As if pulled by gravity, Brandon's mind wandered back to trading, where thoughts of his future as a trader were riddled with self-doubt. *I can't keep taking this risk. Trading is not my forte—18 years is enough to know this. I was always better suited to equity research. If the stress doesn't kill me, Lily will if I lose money in the firm and can't afford the house restoration we're planning.*

Brandon glanced over at the *New York Post* in Jimmy's catcher's-mitt-sized hands and thought, *What could be so interesting? If you read the* Wall Street Journal *with such fervor, you wouldn't be asking me for stock ideas.* The headline "Chaos in Greece" caught Brandon's eye. He gazed back out the train window at the Hudson River and the New Jersey cliffside. While Greece was riddled with uncertainty, he was experiencing the same feeling in his career. His thoughts turned to the hedge fund manager whom he figured must have had a stellar day. Slowly, he formed a serene mental picture, building an ideal life for himself out of trading: the challenge of Wall Street that he loved, without the daily risk-taking. At that moment, he resolved to send letters with his best investment ideas to the two hedge fund managers he would like to work for.

He figured there would be no harm in attempting to make a positive impression that might one day help him land a job doing research. At a minimum, he would consider this a fanciful endeavor to sustain the hope that maybe his future wouldn't always entail the stress of stock trading and putting his own capital at risk.

When Brandon graduated college, he had tried to find a Wall Street job as an equity analyst. After numerous rejections, he sought other Wall Street opportunities. He lacked the natural charisma of a salesman—Brandon doubted he could sell bug repellant in a jungle—so he quickly dismissed brokering as a possibility and settled on equity trading. But 18 years later, he questioned whether he ever had the right temperament for stock trading, and his unfulfilled goal to work as an analyst still beckoned.

Mentally outlining his stock ideas proved to be a pleasant diversion from the self-flagellation about the day's trades and the heat pouring off his neighbor's body. Well into his second beer by now, Brandon finally felt calm.

A few days later, he sent an analysis of his best long and short ideas to David Einhorn of Greenlight Capital, who ran a long/short hedge fund. He also sent his top short idea to Jim Chanos of Kynikos Associates, the manager of the largest hedge fund on Wall Street dedicated to short selling. He repeated this campaign periodically when new stock ideas seemed worthy. More than two years would pass before one of his letters finally received a reply.

Chapter 4

BARRON'S DOES FACEBOOK

May 2012

Wall Street emerged from hibernation in a springtime euphoria, filled with anticipation for Facebook's initial public offering—the largest tech IPO of all time—slated to raise $16 billion. An investor frenzy erupted in the months leading up to the deal since investment banks were perceived to be handing out a big payday to the chosen few recipients of Facebook shares.

For years, Wall Street was forced to watch Facebook's growth from the sidelines as Mark Zuckerberg, its founder and CEO, kept his company private far longer than most Silicon Valley start-ups. The precocious, tech-savvy Zuckerberg was most often likened to Microsoft's founder Bill Gates for their similar backgrounds: Both had dropped out of Harvard to nurture dorm room tech start-ups.

By the time Facebook planned an IPO, the company had almost a billion loyal users worldwide, along with a billion dollars in annual profits. Both were growing at a tidy clip. The years of investor anticipation led to monumental hype, which prompted only one question for Wall Street to answer: What were the shares of Facebook worth?

Prior to Facebook's public offering, *Barron's* assigned the task of analyzing the company to its top reporter, Cliff Ludwig. *Barron's* was one of the most highly regarded publications on the Street. The editorial staff and the columnists, most with decades of experience, adhered to a tradition-bound, process-oriented protocol by which work advanced methodically.

Cliff relished the challenge of creating a comprehensive analysis that would be widely read, scrutinized, and hopefully followed by investors. In the context of the newsroom, his horn-rimmed glasses and graying brown hair seemed reminiscent of a middle-aged Clark Kent. Cliff sometimes came across as more than a little self-righteous, with uncompromising independent reporting and strict valuation guidelines.

He reveled in the history of *Barron's* and enjoyed telling stories of Clarence Barron. Nearly a century after the paper's founding in 1921, Cliff did his utmost to maintain the journalistic tradition Barron intended for his namesake publication. His mission became three-pronged: timely writing about bargain stocks with uncommon value; exposing companies with aggressive or fraudulent accounting; and most importantly, cutting through Wall Street's hype, particularly for companies with suspect business models.

Cliff gave ceaseless thought to Wall Street's inner workings, and enjoyed sharing these observations with fledgling reporters. "There seems to be an inherent faith in markets that there's some efficiency and logic to the price of a stock," he once told one of his colleagues, a recent Columbia University School of Journalism graduate, Aviva Goddard.

"So, you're not a believer in the efficient-market hypothesis, I take it." Aviva had furrowed her brow under loose black curls.

"If I believed that nonsense, I'd be out of a job. I can give you a dozen examples of why stocks can get inefficiently priced."

Aviva nodded expectantly. An attractive intellectual with dark, discerning eyes, her eagerness to learn and write about Wall Street was palpable from the moment Cliff met her.

Cliff grabbed a pen and checked off as he spoke. "Overt mispricing often happens in IPOs with their tiny float of shares or in a short squeeze—and often, the two go hand in hand. Also, market sentiment or macro issues can mask a stock's intrinsic value."

As Aviva gazed around the newsroom, absorbing the lesson, Cliff continued, "Of course, companies can bury business issues through opaque and misleading accounting. Not to mention how few companies can live up to Wall Street's hype. Or the stocks that have their growth extrapolated too far into the future." He laid down his pen and straightened his glasses. "I could go on, but the point is, our job is to cut through a company's business cycle, or expose the overhyped stock and the accounting puffery to find some normalized, intrinsic value of a company's cash-generating ability and growth potential. Fortunately, through the various inefficiencies on Wall Street, our work makes a difference."

Learning from Cliff and other experienced reporters at *Barron's* was one of Aviva's favorite parts of her work. Her interest in journalism had first blossomed as she studied Woodward and Bernstein's investigative reporting; she had always hoped to write about politics and live in D.C. During an internship at her hometown newspaper, *The Oregonian*, Aviva had reluctantly accepted a rotation on the business desk and discovered a place where the world made sense.

When Aviva started at *Barron's*, her youth and optimism contrasted sharply with the skepticism of the seasoned journalists. She drew from the vast knowledge of the newsroom elders, those chronic curmudgeons—a trait she found endearing rather than problematic. In fact, she thought that had Andy

Rooney been a financial journalist instead of a commentator for *60 Minutes*, he would have found a comfortable home at *Barron's*.

Her colleagues quickly came to enjoy and even benefit from the spark of energy she brought to the team. One day while walking across the newsroom, Aviva overheard Alan Abelson, her contrarian octogenarian colleague, declare, "I fully agree we'll get a second-half recovery—it just won't be the second half of *this* year!" She burst out laughing at his quip, which so delighted him that he included the comment in his next column.

Over time, like an oasis that slowly succumbs to the desert sand, Aviva's view of Wall Street would evolve to be as cynical as her colleagues', though her cheerful demeanor would never waver. Cliff developed great confidence in her journalistic ability, and they had a cohesive work rapport. Just that morning, she had offered to help him with his piece on Facebook, and Cliff had accepted.

Cliff pondered this new assignment, the integrity of the Facebook offering, and the current stock market. With over two decades of knowledge and perspective, he was fully prepared to tackle the analysis and deemed he could do it better than anyone on Wall Street. It wasn't arrogance, just an honest belief that his cerebral approach and independent thinking would get the job done for his readers. *Aviva's tenacity and enthusiasm couldn't hurt either*, he thought.

When necessary, Cliff loved to crush Wall Street's hype. Irritated by a touted stock that far outran its fundamentals, in Jerry Maguire fashion, he would shout, "Show me the numbers!" Facebook's IPO was gleefully anticipated by investors as a hot deal. This led to just the kind of hype Cliff expected would need to be reined in. The anticipation reminded him of Netscape's successful 1995 stock market debut when its IPO, priced initially at $28, soared to a high of $75 on the first day of trading and closed at $58. Facebook was the kind of deal that captured the imagination of stockbrokers and cab drivers alike.

In his quest to examine Facebook from every angle, he laid out tasks and schedules for Aviva as she took notes.

"Here's how we need to approach Facebook." Cliff glanced at his pad. "First, we need to read the offering document carefully. From there, we'll set up charts to compare the financial metrics to those of Apple and Google. I'd also like to interview several Wall Street pros with strong opinions on Facebook to flesh out the article."

Eager to work on her biggest stock story yet at *Barron's,* Aviva replied, "I can think of a few people who may have opinions worth quoting, like Fred Hickey from the *High-Tech Strategist*. He knows me from the Intel article. Who else are you thinking of?"

"Fred is always a good source. He's on my list." Cliff nodded. "A couple of funds purchased Facebook in the private market a while back. Check in with Kevin Landis at Firsthand Funds. There's another fund that trades publicly—GSV Capital—that also bought shares, but I think Landis is a sharper manager to speak with. Also, check in with Dan Niles. He's a former tech analyst who now manages money at AlphaOne Capital Partners. He's never shy about going on record with his opinion. Start with those three, but first I want you to know Facebook inside and out."

Aviva quickly scribbled down the information and grabbed a copy of Facebook's IPO prospectus. "I'm on it. I've seen Dan on CNBC; he knows his stuff. I'm curious what he has to say."

Cliff smiled as she walked quickly back to her desk. Then he sighed. He had a long weekend reading Facebook documents ahead of him.

The *Barron's* newsroom was nestled on the fourth floor of News Corp's Manhattan headquarters on the Avenue of the Americas. The space was infused with a constant buzz of typing and conversation. A floating staircase separated *Barron's* from the *Wall Street Journal*. While the latter was in a constant flurry of activity, the *Barron's* newsroom usually remained subdued until Thursday, when the pace picked up prior to the Friday evening publication deadline for the weekly newspaper.

Cliff's desk rested near the center of the wide-open layout, like a seat on the 50-yard line. Aviva's desk sat catty-corner to his, her back to the newsroom with a clear view of a stock ticker and a TV against the wall.

Monday morning, after a weekend reading up on Facebook, Aviva made her way across the newsroom, coffee in hand. She spotted Cliff punching buttons on his circa-1986 HP 12C calculator.

He looked up, his usual even-keeled countenance absent and his voice an octave higher than normal. "Have you seen Facebook's numbers?"

"Sure did." She matched his enthusiasm but wasn't certain where he was heading.

"The valuation that goes with these numbers is completely outrageous!" He gave a backhand slap to his yellow pad. "There's no plausible way to justify where the deal will price, let alone where it might trade after it opens. I know Facebook's a great company, but the numbers just aren't there yet. Way, way too much risk here." He recounted his fear that bankers were mistakenly relying on the thin private market trades—last quoted at $44—for the basis of the deal price range of $28–$35.

Aviva hurried around the desks to peer over his shoulder. "Definitely agree on the valuation issues. What are you thinking?"

Cliff scanned his hand-drawn analysis. "Facebook earned 50 cents per share for the last 12 months on $5 billion in revenue. At $35, Facebook would be a $95 billion company with a P/E ratio of 70 and valued at 18 times sales. Apple is currently growing at a faster clip yet only has a P/E of 15."

"That's not even considering Apple's huge cash hoard," Aviva interjected.

Cliff nodded. "I think this valuation will leave investors deeply disillusioned if they think a stock-pop off the offering price is sustainable. There must be some seasonality in their business, but revenue actually *declined* from the fourth quarter to the first. You don't usually see that in a company growing this fast. It's a *huge* red flag that growth is slowing."

Aviva studied Cliff's notes. "Yeah, the valuation looks sky-high. Everyone thinks it will likely trade at a substantial premium to the offering, no matter where the deal prices." She shook her head bleakly. "But these numbers don't support it. Is there a precedent for this kind of valuation?" In her limited years of experience, technology valuations were mostly restrained after the 2008 recession.

"I get that Facebook is a unique company with unprecedented user reach and engagement, and that it's profitable, but right now, maybe the only precedent is the Nasdaq-bubble-type valuation."

"Hmm. What was it like during the Nasdaq bubble?" Aviva had been in grade school when that occurred.

"Ah, you'll have to talk to Jack." Cliff's scanned the newsroom for Jack Willoughby. "Over ten years later, he's still credited with calling the top of the Nasdaq tech bubble. Jack's article on the massive cash burn rate of many high-flying internet companies came *within a week* of the March 2000 peak." Cliff added, "Part of the bubble stemmed from investors using unconventional methods of valuation, like putting a premium on eyeballs and users without much thought about revenues and earnings." He leaned back in his chair and folded his arms. "I'd say late in the bubble, it became a wanton grab for riches, a mania to get on board before it ran higher. There were many relative valuation arguments—you know, this stock is cheap at 50 times revenue, because this other one is at a hundred times."

"Wow," Aviva said, astonished.

Cliff shrugged. "There were always conversations from non-investor friends and relatives looking to buy, with everyone's crazy uncle handing out stock tips at Thanksgiving." Aviva smiled. "And there were pie-in-the-sky targets, like the call from Morgan Stanley that Cisco was going to a trillion-dollar market cap, as if sprinting to half a trillion wasn't enough. In fact, nearly every mind-boggling price investors were willing to pay for a stock was legitimized by an analyst 'buy rating' and an even more mind-boggling price target—so they were no help. Looking back, the hard questions either got drowned out while the bubble inflated or simply didn't get asked until people started losing serious money. I'm sure I could have done more myself to warn investors. Being the voice of reason in a frenzy like that is always going to be tough, but it's the right thing to do." He sighed. "I was too focused on the value in real economy stocks that were being tossed aside for growth at any cost. Lesson learned, I guess."

Aviva gave a sardonic smile. "Which brings us to the frenzy for Facebook. I've already had a few calls from friends and relatives who know nothing about stocks but want in."

Chapter 5

THE HUBRIS

Cliff took his own words to heart: He decided it would be up to him to act as the voice of reason for overenthusiastic Facebook buyers. He was often vexed when investors imprudently paid too high for a hyped IPO. Facebook, in particular, presented a concerning case. He worried the initial lack of stock supply could cause the shares to trade at an unjustified premium to normal market parameters. The investor frenzy was bound to skew the market to an excessive stock premium.

Cliff stared at his pad as Aviva looked on. "I know it's great that Facebook makes money, but take a look at Google." He scribbled circles around numbers and key points. "When it went public in 2004, Google's revenue had been growing at over 100%, more than twice Facebook's rate, which propelled the stock to $400, up 300% in its first year of trading." He paused. "Meanwhile, Facebook doesn't even have a mobile monetization outlet for users abandoning desktops for mobile phones, plus revenue growth is *already* slowing. The Street needs to sober up with all the hype."

Aviva's anticipation mounted as the deal process unfolded. "I'm looking forward to conducting interviews. It's hard to believe this deal could be a bust, with all the enthusiasm on Wall Street. We'll see if Facebook's investment bankers know what they're doing."

"I'm sure the captain of the Titanic knew exactly what he was doing—right up until that damned iceberg," Cliff replied with a half-smile.

Given the required "quiet period," there wasn't much more information for Cliff to peruse other than Facebook's IPO prospectus and Mark Zuckerberg's brief, hoodie-clad roadshow presentation.

One morning, Aviva pulled a chair up to Cliff's desk to discuss the article. With a week to go before the IPO, Cliff avoided making assumptions of where the shares would price. Together, they looked at the chart Aviva had created and marveled at Apple and Google's lopsided valuation versus Facebook.

Cliff leaned back in his chair. "So, tell me about your interviews."

Aviva sighed. "Well, I spoke with Dan Niles. He's truly bearish. He thinks Facebook is a great company, but cautioned that there's a difference between a great company and a great stock."

Cliff jotted on his pad.

Aviva carefully scanned her notes. "This is telling: His research indicates Facebook isn't making money when a user accesses the website through a smartphone app—they make all their profits from advertising on the desktop. He thinks this makes the valuation comparison against Google much worse." She continued in a hushed voice. "Off the record, he told me he would short the stock—if he could borrow shares—if it trades anywhere in the $40s. He thought the valuation made no sense over $40, yet he had no idea where the stock would open for trading. Overall, his thinking seemed close to ours."

"That's a lot of good info. Interesting that he's looking to short the stock in the $40s." On his calculator, he punched up the market capitalization at $40 and muttered, "Above $110 billion. Yeah, that's crazy." He looked back at Aviva. "That line about Facebook being a great company but perhaps not a great stock is a good quote from him. It's a bit of a platitude but seems appropriate here. Next."

"Okay, next I spoke with Fred Hickey. He was his typical cantankerous self—he digressed and complained about how the Google guys bought themselves a Boeing 747 in 2007." Aviva smiled broadly thinking back to Hickey's Google rant. "But he likes Zuckerberg and doesn't think he's so full of himself to buy anything so extravagant. Naturally, Fred finds the valuation high, but he likes the platform they've created. He did wonder about their ability to monetize its users, though."

"Interesting," Cliff said. "And how did your interview with Kevin Landis go?"

"Landis's fund owns a bunch of shares, so as you'd expect, he was bullish. But he—"

"Bullish! Stop the presses." Cliff grinned sarcastically.

Aviva shrugged. "Well, he seemed a little short on numbers but bullish on the likelihood that, given time, Facebook will figure out how to monetize its 900 million current user base." Aviva paused to look over her notes. "He went on about the value for advertisers, because Facebook has so much more user information—far more than Google, he said. Not too much else that's relevant for the article."

"Well, all three interviews were productive. Nice job. Put together some of their quotes for me, if you wouldn't mind."

"Sure." She nodded and headed back to her desk.

As he drafted the article, Cliff recognized the bull case on Facebook took a leap of faith in Zuckerberg, but he also understood the platform's power. Although negative on the current stock price because of its valuation, he planned to soften the blow by spelling out potential methods for Facebook to monetize its user base to create future value.

Cliff's challenge was to put an appropriate price tag on Facebook. Anywhere within the proposed offering range would leave the stock richly priced, both in absolute and relative terms. The difficulty lay in determining whether the stock would be valued by investors on the same metrics as Apple and Google or more like the richly-priced Amazon, to which Wall Street had given a pass on demonstrating actual earnings due to its online retail dominance and strong revenue growth.

Ultimately, Cliff recommended that *Barron's* readers have fun using Facebook to connect with friends, but his well-reasoned article suggested avoiding the stock—and maybe buying Apple or Google instead. Yet without a final IPO price, he stayed vague about where Facebook's stock would trade. After much contemplation, Cliff predicted the stock would settle in the high $30s after pricing in the mid $30s. As the voice of reason, he made it painfully clear that there were no riches to be found in buying Facebook—valuation issues would put a lid on the share price.

Cliff aimed to present readers with the opportunity to make profitable investments or avoid losses. To see if he'd guided readers correctly, he closely watched stocks of companies he'd covered, especially on Mondays after his weekend articles. But Friday, May 18, 2012, was special: It was the day of Facebook's IPO.

The previous weekend's edition of *Barron's* featured Cliff's negative take on Facebook's valuation at a possible IPO pricing of $35. But during the week, in a stroke of hubris, the lead underwriter, Morgan Stanley, determined demand would be strong enough to price the deal even higher, at $38. They also significantly increased the number of shares offered.

Cliff was highly interested in the market's reception to Facebook. He planned to quickly pen a follow-up article in the upcoming issue once an actual market price for the shares existed. To bolster his case, he formulated additional analysis for his bearish point of view.

A phone call broke his anticipation for the start of trading. An unfamiliar woman's voice spoke on the other end. "Hello, Mr. Ludwig. There's something I'd like to bring to your attention. Do you have time to talk?"

He shifted in his chair. "With whom am I speaking?"

The woman cleared her throat, and when she spoke again, her voice was quiet and shaky. "My name is Holly, and I have some information about a company I believe you would be interested in."

Cliff responded brusquely to her vague answer. "I'm on a deadline to finish a couple of projects. Can you tell me the company and nature of the issues you'd like to discuss?"

"It's about accounting, um, issues at the company where I work. I'm sure you'd know it." Holly's voice was soft, like she was afraid of being overheard.

Cliff's interest was piqued. "I would definitely like to discuss this further, but I don't have time today to talk at length—I'm under the gun for this weekend's issue. Can we talk first thing Monday morning? And can you tell me the company you're referring to? I'd like to get up to speed with some research before we speak again." He glanced over at Aviva, whose eyes were glued to the television on the wall behind him.

"The company is Loony-Life," Holly said. She agreed to call

back Monday morning. After they hung up, Cliff's mind wandered. *Loony-Life*. He frowned, thinking about the burgeoning electronics retailer.

From her desk, Aviva caught his thoughtful expression. "Cliff!" she called, breaking him from his trance. Cliff snapped back just in time to see Facebook open for trading at $42.10. Soon after, Cliff leaned back in his chair with an almost imperceptible smile.

Chapter 6

THE STRATEGY

On the day of Facebook's IPO, Brandon woke at four o'clock in the morning. *No use trying to get back to sleep*, he thought, leaving his glasses on the nightstand as he stared at the ceiling. He had to focus his thoughts first. The last thing he read before falling asleep was the *Barron's* article on Facebook. He'd read it three times that week, and it was the first thing he thought of as he awoke. With a glance at Lily, he quietly slid out of bed and picked up *Barron's* from the floor. He'd been pleased to read their skeptical take on Facebook, which matched his negative view of the IPO prospectus. With Wall Street's surging hype for the deal, he figured rationality would take a back seat. Brandon's mind cranked into gear, now racing down multiple paths as the busiest day of the year lay ahead—a stock trader's dream.

As Brandon listened to Bloomberg Radio in his Prius on the drive to the Cold Spring train station, not a word registered of Tom Keene and Sara Eisen's segment on foreign exchange. Instead, he envisioned various trading strategies to match each possible scenario for the Facebook IPO. Stock quotes ran through his head. The opportunity remained steadfastly palpable. Hype from the impending IPO had the entire tech sector raging higher, especially the shares of any company even remotely associated with social media or Facebook itself.

He arrived at the office at seven thirty. The other traders and one trainee, a recent college graduate, were already chatting on the desk. After years of teamwork and sitting shoulder to shoulder, they often expressed themselves in nothing more than a line from a movie or *Seinfeld,* and were grateful their colleagues knew exactly what they were talking about.

Between arched windows, two painted portraits hung prominently on the wall like revered idols, one of Alan Greenspan and the other of Warren Buffett—two Wall Street icons who would likely reject the desk's trading approach. Glacial Capital's name belied the nimbleness with which the traders moved capital in and out of the market with a strategy of opportunistic trading. Their collective cynicism led to more shorting of stocks than buying long, and produced a history of consistent profitability. All told, they'd scraped together close to $10 million in capital, which they leveraged liberally. This amount, they knew, made them complete small-timers. Compared to the multibillion-dollar funds, the desk nibbled around the edges of the stock market for crumbs but felt no less a part of the feast.

As a group, they had discussed the trading strategy weeks in advance of Facebook's IPO. Goldie, who was the best at articulating money-making ideas, led morning meetings. He also rarely missed an opportunity to point out trader tics, like dry coughing or neurotically pulling up one's socks when stressed in a trade. He even critiqued his own personality flaws: Goldie was a self-admitted, unrepentant asshole.

Nobody on the desk ever found it worthwhile to argue with Goldie. He could rebut any challenge to his logic with a brilliant, long-winded rationalization. Goldie once threatened to fire a trader trainee if he messed up: "If you fuck up this trade, you're gone." Soon after, he dismissed him on the spot when the trade went awry. His words for the abrupt firing—"That's it, pack it up, Skippy; you're done here."—were co-opted from the movie *Boiler Room*. Goldie instantly hopped up to escort the bewildered ex-trainee to the elevator, refusing to consider an appeal. Upon his return to the desk, he justified the action to the other traders, saying, "If he gets flustered on a trade just by my threatening to fire him, he'll never make it anyway. I'm saving him *and* us a shit load of wasted time—this job isn't for him. Case closed."

As he stood up for the morning meeting prior to Facebook's opening for trade, Goldie was all business, upbeat yet serious. "Good morning, fellas. It's finally here, the day we've been waiting for. I just wanna quickly go over the game plan. Today is about *execution*, which means even if your ideas are right, it's easy to fuck up the trade. We know how these days go, but timing and position size are about executing properly, so let's get that right." Goldie looked intensely at the traders. "There are four stocks we've identified that should get crushed regardless of where Facebook trades. By the end of the day, these stocks will be much lower, and you'll probably find the easiest trade was just to stay in the position rather than trying to buy and sell it back and forth. Pick your two or three favorites and look to build some aggressive short positions. Brandon has made the case for shorting GSVC. This idea *will* work. Brandon, you want to go over your case?"

Brandon eagerly rose to his feet. "Sure. First, we've all followed GSV Capital, and the stock is up huge, all on hype—there's truly no rational argument for the stock to stay at these levels. The stock has run up because they own a small position in Facebook. Something like 5% of their portfolio, yet the stock is up 50%. Once people can buy Facebook directly, they'll jettison this crappy proxy stock immediately, if not sooner." He slapped the back of his right hand against the palm of his left.

"I could go on, but you know how I feel about the stock. My thoughts are all out there on Seeking Alpha—it's toast."

For the last two years, Brandon had continued to send his best short ideas to Jim Chanos and David Einhorn. His periodic mailings to them both had gone unanswered, and the futility of the effort was beginning to sink in. Sending his recent idea to short GSV Capital—if it worked—left open a ray of hope for the opportunity of a research job at one of their funds.

"Thanks, Brandon. Toast is totally on the menu today." Goldie nodded. "My two cents on GSVC: This sort of sympathy proxy stock is *one hundred percent* reliable to go down today." He spoke slowly, with conviction. "I've literally never seen this trade not work, and that track record will be completely intact at the end of the day. I'm not being cocky, just confident that this idea is bankable. Zynga should also be on top of the list to short. It's liquid, and nobody will want to own it after the IPO. Zynga has run up because people can access their games through Facebook, and you know what? That reason *sucks*. They sell fuckin' virtual farm animals—'nuff said."

The traders were transfixed by Goldie's words as their already strong resolve deepened. After a pause, he added, "Listen, timing may still be important on these ideas. If Facebook opens way high, these stocks may still try to jam higher first."

Eli spoke up. "My guy from Barclays is telling me that orders out of Europe to buy Facebook are for *size* in the $60–$70 range." Eli, with his slicked-back dark hair, goatee, and deep green eyes, had an unrestrained personality. His loud phone conversations had the other traders well-versed in Greek profanity, which they often repeated without a clue what it meant. He'd proudly divulged that his favorite movie was *American Psycho*, and he quoted from it freely.

With connections up and down Wall Street, Eli often gathered info to which few others were privy. As the lone bachelor on the desk, he dressed sharp, wore a statement watch, and spent several nights a week acting suave while drinking with traders and brokers from all the top investment banks. Since the firm paid for many of these outings, Eli often stretched to emphasize their usefulness.

Goldie bloomed a kiss on his fingertips like a chef savoring a fine dish. "Those European bids are the stuff dreams are made of; I pray it opens up there. The other names we're looking to short are Friend Finder—I know Sneaks likes that best—and Renren, the 'Facebook of China.'"

"That company is *garbage*," Sneaks said in his strong Staten Island accent. Although he was young, the desk had come to trust his instinctive nose for bullshit. He had the unique qualities of being both brash and pugnacious, with a sleeve tattoo scrolled up one of his wiry arms. A steady stream of gripes and snark aired from his corner of the desk.

"Both stocks are fucked. The music stops *today*." Goldie nodded confidently. "Hot money has been buying both of those little shitty names, but that money will flee on the first downtick, no question. There's no rational basis for owning these stocks. It's all greater fool investing, and the jig will be up on the last fuckin' fool today." A couple of the traders chuckled, but Goldie maintained his stoic demeanor.

He continued, "On the flip side of being short all this shit, we're looking to buy Facebook at the opening cross and flip it." Goldie turned to the trainee. "Our strategy to buy the very first trade and attempt to sell higher in short order could be good for a couple of points right off the bat from almost any level."

Brandon cleared his throat and said, "I spoke with Winston last night at that Credit Suisse event. Believe it or not, he was quite bearish on the deal. He thinks it'll trade poorly, maybe somewhere in the $40s. Supposedly, there've been whispers by analysts about Facebook's struggle to monetize their mobile business right now, and the Street's growth assumptions may be too aggressive. His thoughts jibe with the *Barron's* analysis that the stock isn't worth owning above the $38 IPO price, where it's over a $100 billion market cap. It's a crazy valuation, especially compared with Google and Apple. Keep in mind, they're selling *420 million shares* at $38, and nobody really sees upside to the stock."

"It's Facebook; that's the upside," Sneaks boldly interjected. "Nobody's thinking about market cap. If they open it in the $40s, it's a gift to hang on to. Don't psych me out—I've been waiting over a year to buy this deal." Sneaks had been one of the first Facebook users in college, and perhaps that helped shed his unrelenting cynicism. He had completely bought into the hype.

Goldie looked dubious. "Okay, we'll see. Some mixed signals on Facebook. I don't think we want to marry her—we're just in this one for a quickie." Sneaks's head drooped as Goldie continued, "Mitch probably won't last for more than 15 seconds."

Mitch flexed his bulky pecs and narrowed his eyes as he scanned the faces of his snickering colleagues. "If that," he said with a shrug, then joined the laughter echoing around the desk.

After a few moments, Goldie snapped his fingers. "Okay, men. Look, if Facebook doesn't trade well, it just means they'll crush all this sympathy shit even more. Let's communicate, and let's kill it today." He ended with a confident fist pump. He knew the desk was ready.

Chapter 7

FACE PLANT

The hot money Facebook sympathy stocks inched up as word spread of strong bids for Facebook out of Europe. There was still another hour to go before indications were released of where the stock would open.

At ten thirty, Nasdaq posted the first indication of paired-up orders between buyers and sellers. Dominick said, "Opening salvo, indicated to open at $48, paired on 10 million shares."

"Oh damn, $48, that's a steal!" Sneaks shouted. "Anything under $50 has gotta be good."

"It's early. The indication is gonna change big time," Dominick replied matter-of-factly. He was responsible for risk control and worked closely with the firm's prime broker. On bathroom breaks, Dominick dashed through the office to avoid leaving large positions unsupervised.

Within 15 minutes, the opening stock indication went lower. Dominick continued to update. "Looking paired at $46. Wait, now looking $45 on 18 million shares."

Upon the lowered indication, the desk jumped all over the Facebook sympathy stocks, working into aggressive short positions. Just as Goldie had predicted, their inexorable downtrend was underway.

"Friend Finder tanking!" Sneaks crowed. "The last fuckin'

fool and his money have now been parted."

"Nice call. GSV, Zynga getting smoked," noted Brandon.

As the opening indication steadily moved from $44 to $43, then $42, the traders were ecstatic. Short positions worked quickly, and there was even some short covering to focus more on Facebook's opening cross, which they all agreed looked low at $42. At that price, the desk could practically taste the ease of buying and flipping higher for two or three quick points.

"Guys, anywhere around $42, I'm going all-in at the opening," Goldie declared, raising a fist. "This low opening could be seriously *epic*. Best case is that it opens right above the figure." He recognized that if Facebook opened for trading just above $42, there would be little risk due to all the unfilled buy orders at $42, where, if necessary, they could sell to close the trade for a slight loss. Goldie had a keen trading instinct, so the others were quick to follow his lead.

The wait for Facebook to open grew nerve-racking. As the stock looked ready to open, the seconds passed like minutes. The traders were at the start of a race, except no one knew how long they would wait for the starting gun to fire. Since fortunes could be made or lost in the first seconds of trading, they sat frozen, mesmerized, and stressed for what felt like an eternity, their hands hovering over the keyboards.

"It's pathetic that they can't get this stock paired up and opened. Nasdaq should be embarrassed," Mitch jeered in his poised, deep voice. He was a workout freak who never showed an ounce of fear, whether from a huge trading loss or while stalking and smashing the giant roaches that periodically scurried through the office. He was the rock of the desk.

Mitch had once come face-to-face with a knife-wielding mugger on a deserted subway platform. Without hesitation, he'd thrown the cash from his wallet into the thief's face. In a quick burst of confusion, the mugger plunged his knife into

Mitch's side. Mitch immediately responded with a head-butt to the guy's nose, then knocked the stunned man unconscious with a right cross to the head. He had maintained the presence of mind not to instinctively pull the knife from his side. With one hand, he'd held the blade in place to limit blood loss while dialing for help on his flip phone. Mitch and the cuffed mugger then shared an ambulance ride to the hospital. Mitch had fully recovered. The traders periodically watched the NYPD copy of the grainy surveillance video which captured the episode—always in awe of Mitch's coolness.

The desk had grown accustomed to random glitches at IPO openings, which caused a familiar stress and foreboding—except, of course, for Mitch, who was unflappable. With the desk up a quick $250K on their short positions, the pressure eased, so the traders comfortably followed Goldie's aggressive strategy to go all-in on Facebook's opening cross on the appearance of a propitious initial price. They looked to make this a day for the ages, and every one of the traders wanted their part in that glory. Even Brandon, who believed more in the bearish take on Facebook, felt optimistic about the opening price.

Brandon's heartbeat raced as he anticipated the start of trading. He was skeptical of Facebook's valuation and nervous to be long, but he'd seen the quick flip work on hot IPOs too many times not to be fully involved in a deal as big as Facebook. He welcomed the distraction to gripe about CNBC's commentary. "Bob Pisani just said the opening is delayed because of an influx of buy orders placed by investors who didn't expect to get the shares so cheaply. He's going to ruin this opening, goading people to throw in buy orders. They'll never get the stock open."

More than 30 minutes passed with both Nasdaq's system and the traders completely frozen; they began to sense something was amiss beyond Bob Pisani's theory. Yet they found no other reason, because Nasdaq offered nary a word for the delay. At eleven thirty, a full hour after the first indication, the wait finally ended.

Goldie shouted, "There's the opening cross at $42.10! *Perfect.* Holy shit—traded up to $45!" His voice cracking, he almost jumped out of his seat. "Wait. Why can't I sell any? *Where the fuck is my stock*? I should have 25 thou. Dom, what the *fuck* is going on?"

"Something's wrong here—we're not long a share." Dominick gawked in disbelief. "Uh, I'm calling Wedbush right now. I can't tell if the orders were executed or not. Even if we bought the stock, we can't sell any without the shares hitting the accounts. Give me a minute." He hurriedly dialed Wedbush, the firm's prime broker.

"Probably a good thing we can't sell; $42.10 was a sick opening price. We'll sell these much higher," Sneaks said emphatically.

No sooner did those words leave his mouth than the stock crashed down through $42, never to see that price again for 16 months.

The desk quickly shifted into damage control. First, they tried to cancel the opening buy orders, just in case they hadn't been executed, then they assessed risk exposure. The desk was in to buy 125K shares, fully half of their risk capital. They watched helplessly, spitting profanities as the shares plunged lower.

Brandon watched in horror as Facebook sliced through $40. The inability to act made him sick in a way he hadn't felt since the Flash Crash two years ago. "I can't believe I'm loaded up with this shit. Everyone I know was skeptical of the deal. *Barron's* flat-out called it. Un-fuckin'-believable," he said, sounding both exasperated and rueful.

As the stock neared $38, Dominick finally got word that all the buy orders had been filled at the opening price of $42.10. Wedbush advised him to manually enter 125K into position, which finally allowed the stock to be sold.

A gloom descended over the desk when about half a million in paper loss appeared. A collective groan echoed around the room. It wasn't customary risk management that four points would be lost without the ability to sell a position of that size. The saving grace was that the short positions continued to extend on the downside, mostly offsetting the Facebook losses; profits were about $380K at the moment and rising.

"I've been calling around the Street to see what's going on," Eli told the desk. "We're not the only ones—I'm hearing that people have reporting problems all over the place. There's a lot of confusion with positions. UBS has some sort of unquantifiable disaster on its hands." He shouted above the desk chatter, "Guys, listen up. I also heard directly from CS: Some funds were allocated up to 60% of their Facebook indication, which is ridiculously high. One fund of Winston's indicated for half a million shares, thinking they would get allocated only 25–50K, but they ended up getting 300K. Some of their big accounts passed on the deal altogether. He also mentioned a decent amount was allocated to retail, which is always a terrible sign for a deal. So much for 15 to 20 times oversubscribed. Fuckin' bullshitters!"

Dominick shook his head. "Allocated three out of five hundred thousand? That's unheard of."

"Yeah, no shit—this deal blows. Unfortunately, everyone was too busy to get to the phone this morning to tell me what the fuck was going on. Now it cost us a half-million bucks. *Móltas móltas malakas.*" Eli picked up his phone and slammed it back down.

Goldie scowled at Eli. "Dude, don't do that, my fuckin' ears are ringing." In his usual acerbic manner, he belittled Eli's no-tion. "Yes, it would have been helpful to know all the shit you just found out, but the reality is, this traded up to $45. We would have been long out of this thing if not for the tech glitch. That's a *fact*."

In the minutes it took for Facebook to trade back down to its IPO price, Wall Street's hype became exposed as bluster and Nasdaq's technology was deemed to be deeply flawed. The most sought-after IPO in over a decade had no premium to the deal price, and everyone on Wall Street was stunned. Morgan Stanley had some serious explaining to do for the poorly man-aged deal.

"Are you fuckin' kidding me?" Sneaks yelled into his com-puter screen. "Thirty-eight fuckin' dollars? How could this even be? I'm down $40K on this shit. This can't be real." He slammed his hand on the desk. "I clearly won't be getting the new LeBrons, even with Friend Finder getting obliterated."

Meanwhile, Steve Harmon sat quietly in one corner of the desk. He was regarded as a trading animal. A tall, athletic man with a laid-back personality, he had been an NCAA Division III baseball All-American. In addition to being the best and most focused trader of the group, Steve traded the largest size based chiefly on the trading instinct of tape reading. He was the trader everyone wanted to emulate, but none of them had balls that even came close to rivaling the size of his. Yet even the gutsiest trader lost his nerve when the technology he relied on failed, which put him in an unusually awkward situation. Steve was like a rock climber who discovered his safety rope was badly frayed and just wanted the climb to end. "I have to sell. If this breaks $38, it'll drop another two quick points and totally kill my day. They're pounding out stock at $38; I don't think they can hold it in much longer." Steve threw in the towel and hit the bid at $38 with his shares, which booked a fast

$140K loss. "That's it, I sold the piece." His tone was somewhere between relief and disappointment.

"I'm not selling," Mitch cut in. "This is such bullshit—I'm gonna ride it out." The conviction in his voice sounded solid, but it couldn't stop their stomachs from sinking alongside Facebook's shares.

"Steve's right: The floodgates will open if Morgan doesn't hold this in." Brandon knew the lead underwriter had a role in stabilizing the deal at the IPO price, yet they could abruptly step away.

"Hang the fuck in there, Morgan!" Sneaks banged on his desk. "The blocks going off at $38 are unreal. They're not going to let it break."

"Hold the line!" Goldie implored. After a small rally, he said calmly, "That's it, they held the line in the sand."

Profits from the shorts were rolling in when Zynga, the desk's largest short position, suddenly halted trading. Confusion ensued, and audible gasps were heard.

"Oh, shit. Zynga is halted. What could this be, Brandon?" Goldie asked as a wave of panic washed over the desk. "We're short a quarter million shares in-house. This better not be good news."

"Is it possible we get fucked again, back-to-back?" Sneaks shook his head and sank in his seat.

Brandon's stress began growing into anger. "I'm looking, but I don't see any news. Might just be a system issue since there's no news pending. Fucking Nasdaq fucked this whole thing up. Dom, any notifications yet?"

Dominick scrolled through Nasdaq's website. "Yeah, with no news pending, probably a system issue. But no word from Nasdaq on when it'll reopen."

"I'm hearing Merrill has five million Facebook to buy!" Eli shouted, then exhaled deeply in relief.

"Woof!" Sneaks howled, registering his approval.

"The Street's coming in to save this thing." Eli looked upward. "The stock's headed back over $40. Thank the good Lord."

"Um, we're never to speak of the way I panicked out at $38. That was an embarrassment." Dejected, Steve gazed at the portrait of Buffett for inspiration.

"Wasn't just you, Steve. I bailed out of a bunch also," Dominick said in solidarity. "We needed to cut down on our risk exposure."

"At least you hung on to some. I dumped every share. Now, I have to take my revenge out on Zynga when it reopens." Steve hunched over his keyboard, prepared to get back on offense after confirmation that the halt was an error.

Morgan Stanley's support of the syndicate bid was crucial, and Facebook's stock quickly recovered to settle under $41, where most of the traders sold off a good portion of their stock. At that point, profits from their short trades more than offset losses taken on Facebook.

In the meantime, the stock market started a large, across-the-board sell-off. Wall Street became rattled from the combination of the poorly-trading IPO and Nasdaq's glitches.

Dominick stood up. "I'm getting word about what happened on the cross. Nobody on the whole Street got their stock reported. Eli had it right—it wasn't just us. Nasdaq is going to rerun the opening cross and simultaneously report everyone's executions from the opening. It's still going to take a while."

"Wait! What?" Brandon peered agape at Dominick. "Does this also mean that the opening sellers didn't get their report and may have oversold down to $38? There could be a big mistaken short out there. Or maybe just buyers didn't get their fills?" Everyone seemed clueless. He fumed in frustration. "What a cluster clocking by Nasdaq. If no one got reports, they should have halted the stock. Fuckin' Greifeld, ringing open the bell at Facebook instead of making sure the deal goes off well. Fuckin' bullshit. This should have been halted until they sorted it all out."

Bob Greifeld, Nasdaq's CEO, reluctantly and sheepishly disclosed later that he had been mid-flight from California to New York after he rang the opening bell from Facebook's headquarters in Menlo Park. As the debacle unfolded, he was completely out of the decision-making loop. Inexplicably, Nasdaq also disclosed that they "mistakenly" shorted three million shares at the opening cross and booked more than a $10 million profit when they covered those shares lower. "At least someone made money on the Facebook IPO," traders later joked, but they fully expected Nasdaq's serendipitous profits to be redistributed back to them as an accommodation for the opening glitch.

Steve grabbed for his mouse, determined to settle the score. "Zynga just opened back up at $8.80. I'm maxing out my short position—this should get killed." The stock complied promptly.

"Oh baby, don't make this complicated and just go down." Eli rubbed his hands together.

"Yo, Eli, I hope you're talking about a stock," Mitch said with a laugh, trying to perform his customary role of making a joke to ease the pressure. He jumped to his feet to feign a look under Eli's desk.

"Let me tell you, watching Zynga go down right now is better than a blow job." Eli glanced at Mitch, dead serious.

Steve raised his hand. "I'll second that."

"I know what you're saying. If Zynga goes down another half dollar, drinks on me at the Oyster Bar." Mitch snapped his fingers.

"Nobody goes there anymore," Eli retorted with his

oft-repeated line from *American Psycho*.

But mere banter couldn't relieve the tension on the desk.

Around two o'clock, Nasdaq reran an opening cross simulation, which officially executed the opening prints. Instead of the initial opening price of $42.10, the second cross ran at $42, which improved the purchase price by ten cents on all 125K shares.

"That's really weird that they changed the price of the opening cross." Dominick shook his head and shrugged. "They're so messed up at Nasdaq. I guess we'll take it, though."

"Well, this fixes everything; Nasdaq gave us a ten-cent price improvement—now we won't sue them," Sneaks said dryly.

"That's 12 G's Nasdaq just saved us. Drinks on Nasdaq," Mitch said.

Sneaks's sarcasm quickly changed to anger. "Um, cost us a quarter mil, save us $12K—yeah, Nasdaq can still go fuck themselves."

"And I'll second that," Brandon added. "Facebook just lurched lower. Looks like some people only now got the ability to sell the stock and plugged it out. I'm selling the rest of this dog. There's zero reason to cover GSV—down 15% isn't even enough." As GSV Capital also plunged, he was consoled by the idea that it would bail out his day, both monetarily and spiritually.

Goldie clicked away and quickly sold his position. "I'm right with you; the stock is broken. Facebook ain't coming back today—no reason to be long."

Goldie's remark prompted the rest of the traders to throw in the towel and sell their remaining shares just before it broke $40. Facebook restarted its trend lower for the rest of the day.

From the corner of the desk came a roar of anger. The guys turned from their screens in surprise as they watched Steve slam his mouse down and flip his chair back. The chair landed on its side with a loud crash as the traders looked on in shock. "Zynga's halted *again*." He stood up and swung an arm wildly toward his computer screens. "What the fuck is wrong with Nasdaq? I'm way outsized, short a quarter million shares here—this is just crazy."

Dominick shouted above the din, "I think it's the same Nasdaq technical difficulties, not news. Should be back open soon."

Steve rested his hands over his prematurely graying hair and stared blankly as Sneaks retrieved his chair. "Sorry about that, guys. Nasdaq pushed me to the edge. If this stops the downward momentum..."

Nobody on the desk had ever seen Steve lose his cool. They were astounded by the spectacle but completely understood his frustration.

"If I had anywhere near your position, you'd see shit flying all over the desk," Sneaks said.

When Steve sat back down, he said more calmly, "I hope this fucking mouse still works."

Mitch hustled over with a replacement mouse. "Don't worry about it, babe—Greifeld gets all the blame. We'll add a broken mouse to his tab." He patted Steve's back and winked. "And a new chair."

Zynga reopened soon after. The halt was only a brief respite from its continued decline. Facebook also stayed weak; the stock closed slightly above $38. In all regards, the IPO was considered an epic failure. Nasdaq and Morgan Stanley bore the brunt of the blame.

All four of the stocks targeted to short collapsed in price, which salvaged the day for the desk. Ultimately, as horror stories emerged around the Street of huge losses due to Nasdaq's opening cross glitch, most of Glacial's traders felt fortunate to have escaped relatively unscathed, though they were eager to participate in any lawsuit against Nasdaq.

After the closing bell, Brandon sat back and crooned Coldplay in an off-key falsetto, *"No-body said it was ea-sy. It's such a shame we should pa-ar-art."*

Sneaks prodded Bud, the trainee, who'd watched in silence all day. "You still want to be a trader, Bud? You see this bullshit we gotta deal with? And it's fuckin' hot as balls in here to boot."

The latest desk trainee was nicknamed Bud Fox after quoting from the movie *Wall Street* on his first day. Not an hour into sitting on the desk—to the delight of the traders—he'd foolishly paraphrased Gordon Gekko's legendary line by saying, "So... greed is good in here, right, guys?" They immediately determined that he was unworthy of the "Gekko" moniker and should instead be named after his ambitious but not too bright protégé.

Now fully relaxed, Brandon wandered around and leaned over almost cheek-to-cheek with Bud, singing into an imaginary microphone. *"No-body said it was ea-sy. No one ever said it would be so ha-ar-ard."* Bud leaned away and laughed.

"I definitely want to be a trader!" Bud hopped up and walked over to Sneaks. "You guys did an awesome job. You called the action perfectly on the shorts. I learned a lot today."

"Oh, take me back to the sta-ar-art." Brandon drifted back to his chair on the last note, bowing slightly to applause that was only in his head.

"You learned there's no crying on the desk." Steve raised his eyebrows and smirked. "That rule was *almost* broken today."

Goldie guffawed. "Good thing hissy fits are still allowed, though."

Healthy, cathartic laughter rippled around the desk. "At least I can laugh now," Steve said, shaking his head in disbelief at how crazy the day had been.

"Certainly never a dull moment." Eli stood up to put on his

sports jacket. He peered back at a trader chat on his computer. "Speaking of which: Hearing about a flurry of late put buying in Loony-Life."

"Thanks for the heads up; I see it now. Someone snuck some orders in right before the bell." Brandon whistled. "Look at that chart—just cratered two bucks right into the close. Somebody must think they know something bad is coming out over the weekend. Even if I saw that earlier, it's been too crazy a day to get involved. I'll put it on the radar for Monday."

Goldie pushed off the desk, rolling his chair far back before he stood. "Well, that's it for me. Nice work everyone; that was quite a day." He added casually, "I'm so exhausted, I'll need someone else to jerk me off tonight." He walked off the desk while the traders roared with laughter.

Eli was quick to exploit the set-up. "Hey Goldie, when you find someone, let us know *his* name."

Mitch swiftly threw his hands in the air. "Not that there's anything wrong with that."

In his best Al Pacino impression, Eli added a loud "Hoo-ah!" to the ongoing raucous laughter on the desk.

Goldie couldn't help but laugh along as he walked out, one arm curled back over his head for an adieu.

Chapter 8

SAVORING THE MOMENT

On the train home, Brandon relaxed with a beer and processed the events that Facebook's IPO had unleashed. He reflected on the pre-deal hype and found it laughable. Yet he figured Facebook's stock could easily have traded much higher had Morgan Stanley structured the deal more effectively and Nasdaq operated without the snafu. He admired *Barron's* for their caution, impressed they'd taken on the hype and won.

He sipped his beer for a while and mindlessly checked his email. He nearly choked, his eyes bulging when he spotted something he'd dreamed of for years in his inbox: a reply from Jim Chanos. His mind raced and his heart pounded as adrenaline coursed through his veins.

Savoring the moment, he stared out the train window at the Hudson River, the same view he'd had when he conceived the idea to write to Chanos. Clutching the warm, double-sided glass of his iPhone 4, he took a deep, calming breath to little effect, his hands still shaking.

To Wall Street, Jim Chanos was the man who'd publicly declared the accounting chicanery at Enron, Tyco, and WorldCom, but to Brandon, he stood as nothing short of a cult hero. He'd read and listened to almost every interview Chanos had given. There was nothing about the man he didn't admire, but he especially respected his exhaustive research and determination when it came to rooting out fraud.

He'd never forget April of 2001, the first time he saw Jim Chanos in person, light blond and bespectacled. Brandon had attended Jim Grant's conference where the consummate cynic presented his compelling short case against Enron. Brandon had watched in awe as Chanos cataloged a litany of issues culled directly from Enron's SEC filings.

The event remained firmly etched in Brandon's memory due to the cognitive dissonance he'd felt at that moment. Enron had been the toast of Wall Street and the financial press, with analysts and investors wildly bullish about its stock, which performed strongly year in and year out and traded around $60 after numerous splits.

Just months earlier, Enron was named *Fortune* magazine's most innovative company for the sixth consecutive year and ranked 18th on their list of most admired companies. Yet Chanos laid out the most convincing bear case Brandon had ever seen. "Enron is a hedge fund sitting on a pipeline," Chanos insisted in his opening argument. He went on to explain how they only earned 7% on capital, which cost them more than 10% to borrow. Deciphering how they made their reported earnings was an insoluble mystery.

Brandon had long deemed his analytical skills inadequate for understanding Enron's business throughout the stock's meteoric rise in the 1990s, yet after Chanos's presentation, the question *How can this be possible?* had swirled in his head for days. The shock of Enron's bankruptcy filing seven months later taught him that A) things that are hard to fathom are indeed possible on Wall Street, and B) bad things can often be found hiding in plain sight if you're willing to look.

After years of mailing his ideas to Chanos, Brandon was almost too nervous to open the email. He took one last deep breath, then clicked.

The message was short and to the point. "Thank you for sending your bearish thesis on GSV Capital. Your research was well reasoned—as demonstrated by the stock's 20% plunge today—nicely done. For any future ideas, feel free to email me directly. Best, Jim."

Brandon whispered a barely audible "Whoa." He tried to temper his elation, but it bubbled up anyway. At long last, his idol had replied to open the lines of communication. Brandon visualized the opportunity; he was one step closer to becoming a part of Chanos's research team and leaving behind the stress over trading debacles like Facebook.

He reread the email with one thought in mind: *Don't screw this up.*

Barron's published Cliff's follow-up article on Facebook's valuation in the weekend edition, which declared the stock to be worth no more than $30. For the botched deal, he expected other journalists to hold Morgan Stanley and Nasdaq accountable. His sole concern for *Barron's* readers remained in assessing the stock's value and the company's outlook.

As usual, Monday morning on the newsroom floor started slowly. Most of the journalists quietly prepared for their weekly group meeting with the editors to discuss ideas in the works.

After the usual commute from Park Slope on her bright blue Vespa, Aviva strolled into work rosy-cheeked and in high spirits at eight thirty. On the elevator ride up to the newsroom, she ran into Hugh McLaggen, a columnist for the *Wall Street Journal* who had become a friendly acquaintance.

"What's new in Heard today, Hugh?"

The Heard on the Street column, for which Hugh wrote, was one of her favorites. The Heard columnists were a boys' club, but Hugh and his colleagues often joked with Aviva that they were always on the lookout for a female perspective as cynical as theirs to join the team—and they had an eye on her. It was a joking offer that she occasionally wished was serious, but she felt there was still much to learn from *Barron's*. For now, she settled for reading Heard on the Street religiously—along with several other publications and columns she loved—though she hadn't had a chance to read it yet today.

Hugh flashed a smile. He was a Brit built like a rugby forward. "I've done a take on Questcor," he said in his Oxford accent. "And I've had some incisive feedback from my adoring fans on Twitter."

Back at her desk, Aviva grabbed the *Journal* and skimmed through the main sections to get to Hugh's column. It was quite a skeptical take on the high-flying biotech stock and its sole drug, H.P. Acthar Gel. She grinned as she could only imagine the "incisive" ire of those who defended the astronomical price increase for Questcor's 60-year-old drug.

An hour later, Cliff sat at his desk to watch Facebook's stock open for trading. He wasn't surprised to see the shares sink below the IPO price. Content to know his articles had made an impact, he relaxed. He wouldn't rub it in by spiking the football at Wall Street's misery. He'd accomplished his job—to inform and protect his readers. After 25 years at *Barron's*, these victories were still personally significant; it wasn't merely a fleeting feel-good moment. He enjoyed the intellectual challenge of mining into accounting and probabilities, and reveled when he got it right.

Soon after, Facebook's stock plunged through $35, down almost 10%. Cliff knew Wall Street's hype for Facebook was over, and the harsh reality had set in. As he glanced across to Aviva, she flashed him a raised eyebrow and a knowing nod. He mouthed back, "Thank you," and aloud said, "Great work." From halfway across the newsroom, the ever-cynical Alan Abelson gave him a thumbs-up that quickly turned into a swoop downward like a paper airplane. Cliff grinned.

With a last look at Facebook's shares, Cliff turned his attention to Loony-Life, which caught his eye as the stock ticked a point higher, up 2% to $50.

Over the weekend, Cliff and Aviva had scrutinized Loony-Life's financial statements to prepare for a follow-up conversation with Holly, the woman who'd contacted him with a tip. She didn't sound like the typical industry source they were accustomed to discussing ideas with—mostly fund managers talking their book. *I don't know if this Holly person has an axe to grind, or what*, thought Cliff.

Late Monday morning, Cliff's editor, Paul Martin, marched up to Cliff's desk. Paul's wire-rimmed glasses accentuated his thinning gray hair and avuncular disposition. "Nice job with the Facebook write-up. We received only two emails this weekend with complaints about your article, both angry you wrote negatively two weeks in a row. Nothing about the content—nobody's arguing about your analysis. You know that's rare for a negative article."

"Was either one signed 'Morgan Stanley'?" Cliff deadpanned. He was accustomed to receiving some heat for contentious articles. By nature, he knew most investors preferred to read positive stories about the stocks they owned, and some were quick to dispute negative conclusions. Brushing off a barrage of criticism had long ago become second nature to him. "Well, it doesn't seem like anyone is going to step up and challenge my methodology, but there's not much to argue about: The bull case is pretty thin. I'm curious to see where this settles, though. After they report earnings, I'll probably write another update."

Cliff shuffled distractedly through papers. "I'm preparing for a call from a source on Loony-Life, which I mentioned to you. From what I've already read, there's a story here either way. I asked Aviva to give me an assist." Paul nodded and moved on down the row of clattering keyboards.

Cliff walked over to Aviva's desk and asked quietly, "Did you see Facebook this morning? That was something."

"Of course. I've never seen a stock with no news fall so fast." Aviva paused and turned her head slightly to reconsider. "Well, maybe not since Friday after Facebook opened at $42. It's stunning, though. Morgan Stanley's clients must be freaking out."

"No doubt. I'm sure they expected to make a big score. For such a high-profile deal to go awry like this is rare. Investors are already looking for someone to blame, but our readers know it's all right there in the numbers." Not looking to gloat, he moved on to the next story.

Chapter 9

LOONY-LIFE

"So, tell me, what did you get out of Loony-Life's filings?" Cliff asked.

Aviva searched through paperwork. "Let me first say that I shop at their stores. Their sale prices can be pretty crazy, if you ask me; they're comparatively friendly to my lowly postgrad budget." She consulted her notes, which covered pages from her thorough scrutiny of the company's SEC filings. "Moving on to their latest 10-K..."

She glanced at Cliff. "The company sells electronics through its retail stores and website. They started selling through outlets in China a year ago, and that business has ramped up quickly. Their store base has expanded fairly rapidly over the last five years. Profit margins look stable, and most sales growth is from new store openings, both domestically and in China." She paused and looked at Cliff quizzically. "Also, it looks like a lot of insider selling, but that could just be diversification since the founder and CEO still owns 25% of the company. Um, nothing else stands out, except maybe their inventory."

"From what I've read, I see a couple of red flags," Cliff said. "Their auditor looks a bit undersized for the company. Same small auditing firm they've used for years, while in the interim Loony-Life has significantly expanded locations and grown revenues. You're right, though: The insider selling does stand out. They've also spent a lot of cash on expansion, yet the depreciation expense looks somewhat low."

"What do you think of the inventory? In the last three years, it's gone up far more than store openings. Not sure how to explain that." Aviva was curious to see if there might be an obvious answer she'd missed.

"Just one sec—I'm looking at the math right now." Cliff scanned his notes, eyes roving from figure to figure. "Yeah, inventory rose 28% last year, new store growth at 18%. You've tracked that back further than the data I'm looking at here. Can you graph out the last four years since they've been public?"

"Okay, I'll pull the data and set up a spreadsheet." Aviva kept her voice flat but was enthused to find a potentially relevant issue. Cliff nodded and strolled back to his desk.

When his phone rang shortly thereafter, he straightened his notes and picked up. After securing permission to record the conversation to ensure accuracy, he asked Holly about her relationship to Loony-Life.

"I'm the personal assistant to the CEO, Ethan Atlas," she said. Cliff already suspected as much; the employee search he'd done over the weekend brought up results for a Holly Walsh. "He's been my boss for the past three years."

"Okay, Holly, what's going on with the company that you'd like to share?" Cliff leaned back in his chair.

"Well, it's sort of hard to explain," she said slowly. "Here's the thing. Last year, the company expanded to China. I think all the profits reported from there have been made up." She paused for a moment. "They said the company made about $15 million in profit from China, but I don't think they really made anything at all."

"You're saying that Loony-Life fraudulently booked last year's $15 million of reported profits from China?" Cliff hunched over his desk and reached for his calculator. "Are you aware of how the accounting was done to show those profits?"

"Yes, I have a pretty good idea."

Cliff recognized the seriousness of the claim. That $15 million represented about a quarter of Loony-Life's total reported earnings in the prior year. With the stock trading at a 20 P/E, this would potentially inflate the market cap by $300 million. Since audits in China were lax, Cliff could imagine a few ways to book phony profits, but he needed details. He'd seen many accounting scams over the years, and the motive was always the same: Pump up the stock price beyond its worth, manipulate and deceive Wall Street, then attempt to cash out by selling shares.

Cliff grabbed a pen and scribbled a few notes. "Do you have any internal documentation to show the accounting discrepancies?"

Holly hesitated. "I do. I've made copies, but, um, I'm not ready to share them yet."

"Okay, can you explain how the accounting was done to create these profits?" Cliff pressed gently. "I want to understand how the books were doctored."

Holly spoke evenly as she spelled out the scheme. "Every three months, Ethan uses an offshore account to wire between three and four million dollars into the company's bank account in China. That money is booked as sales and profit."

"Whose offshore account is used to wire the money to China? Ethan Atlas's?"

"That's correct." Holly took a deep breath and described the activities she'd witnessed. She went over the outline of what sounded like money laundering, which facilitated a classic pump-and-dump scheme with a notable twist: Proceeds from the CEO's stock sales were transferred offshore, then wired directly into Loony-Life's corporate bank account in China.

Cliff superficially followed the circular money flow with the stark allegations that the books were cooked. Ethan Atlas sold stock, with the proceeds sent to China, then applied to revenue and earnings, bolstering the share price, allowing him to sell more inflated Loony-Life shares. "I see. Atlas has clearly been selling stock, and by what you're telling me, he's funneling that money right back into the company through an offshore entity." He leaned back and tapped his pen on his yellow pad. "Why do you suppose he's doing that? Usually, in accounting scams, insiders are able to cash out, but here the money from the CEO selling his shares just flows back to the company." Cliff sounded perplexed, hoping it would help coax Holly to give up more information.

"I see what you're saying, and I don't have an answer," Holly replied. "But I know he plans to continue selling stock, I think to keep making the transfers. He set up a program to sell."

"Okay. What sort of documentation do you have that you're not ready to share?" Cliff kept his voice calm but sensed the potential for an interesting scoop here—and even more of the story to dig into.

"I need assurance from you first about confidentiality."

Cliff sat up and looked down at the phone receiver. "I can commit to you that if we report on the company, your identity as a source will never be revealed by me or *Barron's*. I will also commit that anything I write will in no way insinuate a source *inside* the company."

"That's all I can ask, I guess. I trust you, based on your reputation. But before I get in too deep, let me ask you: Does this seem like a big deal? I mean, I think what they're doing is wrong, but is it a big deal for the company?"

"Well, what I would say is that if the information you're providing is accurate and verifiable, it's important for investors to know and understand. And that the SEC, which is the government regulator of public corporations, ought to be made aware of it."

"Yes, of course, I know the SEC," Holly said.

"So, back to the documentation."

"Well, what I have are copies of the last 12 months of wire transfers from the account I mentioned to the company's corporate account in China."

"I will definitely need to see those. Do you have the originals generated from the banks?"

"Just the copies."

"I'd like to take a look at your copies as soon as possible, but I'd also like to see the originals if you can get them." Cliff tapped his fingers on his head as he tried to come up with other pertinent questions.

"Copies may be the best I can do, but I'll try," said Holly doubtfully.

"One last question for now: Do you know of any reason why Atlas would send his own money back to Loony-Life other than to inflate profits?"

"None that I'm aware of."

"Well, perhaps just one more question." Cliff squinted. "How did you come to contact me?"

Eager for the inquiry, she relaxed and elaborated with greater detail than anything else so far. "Because of your Facebook article." Holly described how she and her boyfriend had heeded Cliff's advice to avoid buying the stock, which confirmed their instinct that Cliff was a remarkably knowledgeable and well-respected reporter.

Cliff couldn't help but smile. "Thank you, I appreciate that."

After the conversation ended, Cliff leaned back in his chair and pondered the information. He closed his eyes and rested his arm over his head as he often did when deep in thought.

His colleagues knew not to interrupt him while in his "arm thinking" position.

What he needed was a second opinion, he decided. Cliff walked over to Aviva's desk and asked her to listen to the recorded conversation. Returning to his own chair, he started a broad outline review of Loony-Life's financial condition for the approval of his editor, Paul.

Nervous excitement fluttered in Aviva's stomach as she slipped on headphones. Cliff's eyes had conveyed the prospect of intrigue, and the whiff of possible corporate fraud made Enron flash through her mind. *The Smartest Guys in the Room* had chronicled the inside account of the executive subterfuge that led to Enron's bankruptcy. When Aviva had started at *Barron's,* she contacted one of its authors Bethany McLean for guidance. Aviva had been inspired by McLean's skeptical *Fortune* magazine article on Enron, published months prior to the company's collapse.

They first met for coffee at Starbucks, where, to Aviva's surprise, despite Enron and the gravity of the financial markets' crisis, she found McLean less cynical and more a believer in the business world than she had expected. Yet McLean stressed it would be a lapse to give Wall Street and the finance industry unlimited leeway to screw up and reset without massive scrutiny.

Long after their conversation, McLean's remarks stayed with Aviva as a prized lesson: "I'm a true believer in business, albeit skeptical at times. The market is a great wealth creator, but it needs to be policed. I've learned that just because everyone has signed off on a corporate action, that doesn't make it legal or ethical." These were the comments Aviva took most to heart.

Almost as an afterthought, perhaps reflecting on her own tip-off from Jim Chanos about Enron, McLean suggested Aviva get to know the people putting money at risk on their own research and ideas. Although merely an offhand remark, it was a suggestion Aviva intended to pursue.

Aviva held one hand to her earphones and the other on a pen as she listened to Holly's brazen accusations. Her foremost thought was of Bethany McLean's advice to "have faith in the facts." She just needed to understand what the facts were.

She pulled off the headphones, walked over to Cliff, and whispered, "Wow, have you ever heard of anything like this? A CEO funneling money back to a company account to pump up profits?"

"Not that I can recall, but it can't be unprecedented." He made a note to search for past occurrences.

"How are we supposed to verify her story?" Aviva asked.

Cliff sighed. "Right now, we'll assume her statements are accurate, but we must maintain a healthy degree of skepticism. The burden of proof is on *us* to try to ensure the veracity of any possible accounting fraud." He spoke sternly, but even as he uttered those cautious words, his inner desire to expose a bad actor started to burn.

"Definitely understand," Aviva said. "Did you catch where she said, 'What *they* are doing is wrong'? It sounds like the CEO is not the only one she thinks is in on the scheme."

Cliff nodded approvingly. "Good point. She probably has more details than she disclosed. I would guess the CFO is also involved. I'll follow up with her about that another time."

Ever the detective, Aviva was eager to get underway with the case. "Where do we start?"

"I've written up an outline for Paul to approve." Cliff motioned to a full page of handwritten notes. "He'll make the other editors aware we're working on an open-ended investigation. Let's first chart out every reported insider sale, work through the math, and set up a timeline. We'll need legal to corroborate the bank transfers as best they can. And we'll also need our China contacts to see if there's any way to obtain monthly sales estimates at Loony-Life's retail stores." She raced to write down the details as Cliff paused. "But most importantly, we need to understand the scam and its endgame. Most scams serve to enrich the perpetrators. Right now, money generated by selling stock is purportedly transferred back into the company—the payoff at this point isn't clear. Although, obviously, the increase in his 25% stake in the company would be worth far more than the $15 mil he may have funneled back in." He shrugged. "Perhaps that inflated stock has been pledged as collateral? We need to know this."

"Hmm, good point. Let's do some digging. Anything we can learn about their rising inventory?" Aviva looked up from her note-taking, still awaiting a satisfying answer that could explain Loony-Life's disproportionate inventory build.

Cliff pondered for a second as he drew a big circle around the word "inventory" on his pad. "Yes, it could be a red flag. Listen, if they would fraudulently inflate profits abroad, their domestic business and accounting are certainly suspect as well. We'll need to set up a spreadsheet of all their balance sheet items with changes year over year, adjusted for each store. Also, the online sales will need to be factored into their inventory carry, so check into their warehouse square footage. I'll read through their conference call transcripts." Cliff asked Aviva to set up spreadsheets while his mind raced through other possible avenues to pursue. He rubbed his forehead as he glanced around the newsroom.

Aviva finished jotting her notes. "I'll start working on it."

"Also, very quietly and casually, talk to a couple of the smarter hedge fund managers you know who follow retail." Cliff instinctively spoke more softly. "Inquiries coming from you shouldn't raise any suspicion, so please see if anyone has an investment thesis on Loony-Life, long or short. But try to broaden it to an industry dialogue."

Aviva felt a rush of adrenaline as Cliff's tone lowered toward intrigue. "Will do. I have a couple of people in mind I can speak with after the close today." She walked back to her desk, pondering the questions that would get her the information she needed.

Chapter 10

THE TRADING DESK

"Yo, Bud, whatcha got there for breakfast?" Mitch glared at the desk trainee. "Looks like a cinnamon roll."

This simple question perplexed Bud. In the loose atmosphere on the trading desk, no subject was off-limits—from *Atlas Shrugged* to escapades in Las Vegas. Conversations could go anywhere. Questions for him often led to a humbling lesson on his lack of knowledge. Bracing himself, Bud silently reviewed the lingo they'd recently berated him for getting backward: You *hit* the bid and *take* the offer, not the other way around. "Yeah, that's what it is," he responded warily.

Over time, stories of past traders and trainees grew more and more exaggerated until they became parodies. Mitch walked over. "We had a trainee once, and every morning this guy would break out a cinnamon roll and a Red Bull. By nine thirty, he'd be fast asleep with his feet up on Sneaks's desk, right as there'd be crazy action at the opening bell." Mitch grinned, but he added seriously, "He didn't make it too long."

"Whoa, let me finish the story," Sneaks jumped in. "Not only feet up but crumbs everywhere on my desk. Goldie should have fired him, but when he quit, he gets a few of us together for a meeting and tells us that he's tried to be *frivolous* with his money, but he wasn't making enough to make ends meet." He smacked his hands together.

Mitch added, dumbfounded, "Seriously, the dude said 'frivolous' instead of 'frugal,' and he was supposedly the smartest one in his family. What a character." He laughed, shaking his head.

"Did anyone correct his use of 'frivolous'?" Bud asked meekly.

Mitch chuckled. "Only the Ivy Leaguers—Brandon and Goldie—correct people's grammar, and they weren't there. Just another trainee disaster we'll be laughing about indefinitely."

Brandon turned to stare incredulously at Mitch. "Come on! You were an English major—you could have helped the guy out with some vocab."

A familiar squeaking sound rose above the din as Mitch squeezed a handgrip with his Popeye-esque forearms. His workspace included an array of small workout toys, including a ThighMaster he'd received as a gag gift. He smirked and shook his head. "Believe me, I would have loved to hit him with, 'That word you used—I do not think it means what you think it means.' But it was too funny imagining he'll use that word wrong for the rest of his life."

"That dude really loved Mitch, too," Sneaks said. "Except when the kid called him a 'funny guy' and Mitch gave him the full Joe Pesci routine. 'Funny how? Like a clown? I amuse you?' Right in his face: 'What the fuck is so funny about me?' The kid was shitting in his pants—probably the real reason he quit."

"That's a little warning for you, Bud," Brandon said. "The trainees who have a shot at making it know how to take a joke, but also know when the joking stops and the business starts. Some people think it's okay to goof around all day because it gets loose in here and we're dressed real casual, but they forget we're dead serious about our business."

Bud shifted uncomfortably in his chair. "Hopefully, I can

buck the trend of your bad trainee hires. Not looking forward to being the butt of jokes indefinitely if I don't make it."

"If you can stay awake at the opening, you're ahead of your predecessor," Sneaks said. "But you'll be the butt of plenty of jokes whether you make it here or not—it's just part of the game."

"Well, nobody was a bigger character than Mike Cohn with all his practical jokes," Goldie said authoritatively. "He had some classic 'Mikey Special' phone checks."

"Phone check? What's a phone check?" Eli chimed in curiously, surprised he was unaware.

"Yeah, nothing important, I'll show you some other day." Goldie waved his hand dismissively. "Mikey was way before your time."

The early morning chatter continued around the most discussed topic on the desk: NCAA and pro sports. Half of the traders seemed to maintain full preparedness to take the reins as Yankees general manager. Every move the team made was debated ad nauseam.

As the lone Mets fan on the desk, Brandon quickly moved on to other topics. "Bud, let's focus on some business. Did you read the Facebook follow-up in *Barron's* this weekend?"

More than most aspects of his job, Brandon liked to mentor. The ability to pass along his knowledge to the next generation felt, at times, like a gift. He was happy to take Bud under his wing and share his war stories and perspective with an intent listener. Although the winning percentage of trainees on the desk was remarkably low, the traders never stopped giving young and enthusiastic newbies a chance. They recognized that trading wasn't something learned in school and honored the tradition of mentoring the skill.

"Yes. It read quite negatively," Bud replied, like an army private addressing a superior.

"Okay, good," Brandon said. "Unfortunately, we can't borrow Facebook to short it, but it should go lower at some point. You're going to get your fill of Facebook chatter today, but I want you to keep your eye on another situation. We won't be trading it, but watch IBM. Goldman has negative comments out this morning: They say their European business looks especially weak this quarter, and they may miss revenue estimates."

"So, what do you think the stock will do?" Bud asked, then attempted to answer himself. "I'm guessing it gets whacked."

"That's a good guess, but I have no clue; that's why we won't be trading it. IBM's trading action doesn't make as much sense as some other stocks. They buy back so many of their own shares that the buybacks cover up the softening business. They always manage to make earnings numbers even if the revenue is weak."

"How does that even work?" Bud grabbed a pen.

Brandon nodded; although the bar was set low, he appreciated the trainee's curiosity and motivation. "Well, imagine a meeting in the executive suite of a company with a weakening business. And out of the meeting, management decides the solution is to buy back more stock to meet earnings expectations. That's IBM. Their goal is to divide their net income over fewer shares, which improves the earnings per share."

"Why doesn't the company just disclose the bad news and buy the stock cheaper?" Bud furrowed his brow.

Brandon displayed mock surprise at the insightful question. "Well, that makes perfect sense. But now you need to understand that corporate America sometimes operates counterintuitively. They're always buying high when business is good, and conserving cash on the balance sheet when things get tough and stocks tank. But in this case, if IBM buys back enough stock, they can make the bad news go away. Now the headline reads, 'IBM Beats Earnings Expectations,' and the revenue weakness gets lost in the shuffle." Brandon shrugged. "Look, this has worked out for so long, they've possibly lost logic in their decision-making."

Bud looked up from his notebook. "Sounds like too much effort spent trying to keep Wall Street happy."

"Exactly." Brandon opened his arms. "Doing things that please the Street can be nice in the short term but could be detrimental in the long run. So, the point is, Goldman could be perfectly right about IBM's business, but wrong for now about the stock headed lower."

"Okay, understood. Now, when you say Goldman, you mean Goldman Sachs, right?" Bud asked.

Brandon sensed the collective eye roll around the desk. He shook his head and laughed it off. "Dude." As Eli handed Bud a copy of Goldman's research, Brandon tried to sound as serious as possible. "Don't *ever* ask that again."

Sneaks yelled out to Bud, "Yo, rookie, can you go grab our coffee delivery?"

"On my way." Bud hurried off.

Sneaks turned to Brandon, his salty persona showing reliable pessimism. "To be honest, I don't think he understood a fuckin' thing you just explained to him."

"I think he got it," said Brandon uncertainly. "The concept is quite straightforward. They're not going to teach the art of making earnings estimates in his accounting course. Doesn't take a genius, though."

"Oh, well maybe Bud *did* get it then." Sneaks laughed. "Fuckin' osteopathy school dropout."

"Yeah, I hear you, but let's give the kid a chance. Medicine isn't for everyone—better to figure that out early. Hopefully, with his background, he could give us an edge in biotech. Either he'll prove his value or go down in flames. We'll see."

"Hey, thanks, Bud," Sneaks said loudly as Bud walked up from behind Brandon with their coffees. He added quietly, "I'm thinking flames."

Goldie's morning meeting was intended to help the traders focus on ideas but also to help Bud understand the traders' thought process.

Goldie rose out of his chair. "Good morning, gents. Running a little late, so I'll make this quick. We've had a weekend to digest the Facebook IPO debacle, and I'll tell you this: It still doesn't sit well. The level of Nasdaq's incompetence was stunning. There's some talk about lawsuits, but my guess is, we'll never see a penny from Nasdaq for the quarter mil out. But what makes us a great trading desk is the ability to take a loss like big boys and move on. So, let's not look back because there's nothing to learn from what happened—we're just going to move forward." This monologue elicited a low grumble from the traders. Goldie continued, "Now that that's out of your system, how are we going to kick ass going forward? To start, no revenge trading. Steve got away with that on Friday but only at risk of cardiac arrest when Zynga was halted."

"No worries—my doc doubled me up on the blood pressure meds," Steve said without a trace of humor.

Goldie studied him for a moment, then nodded before moving on. "Okay. So, right now, the smart move is the same trade. Facebook will probably break down, taking the sympathy shit stocks even lower. I already discussed this with Brandon earlier." He motioned for Brandon to take over the meeting.

Brandon jumped up and cleared his throat. "For starters, Cliff Ludwig, from *Barron's*, nailed that Facebook was valued too high at its IPO and published a follow-up this weekend trashing the stock. Basically, he said there's no fundamental reason to even pay $38, and the stock should go to $30—no argument from me. If Facebook breaks $38, it's over. If Morgan steps away from supporting the deal, there's no getting the genie back in the bottle: Everyone's going to run for the exit." He motioned toward the front door and banged his fists together in a crude representation of a logjam. "All the Facebook sympathy stocks we shorted on Friday are still headed lower, so let's stick with those and look to add to short positions on any strength. Their destiny is much lower; it's just a matter of how long it takes to get there. I'm also watching Loony-Life. There was some interesting put buying on Friday at the bell. I don't see any news out this morning, which is good. Goldie and I discussed the stock, and we'll be building a short position while I finish researching the company." He sat back down. "That's all I have, Goldie. You want to finish?"

"Sure. I'll just pass along my initial thoughts on Loony-Life. As I discussed with Brandon, in my experience, every electronics retailer eventually goes bankrupt. Whether it's Circuit City, Comp USA, Ultimate Electronics, The Wiz, or... what was that one downtown?" Goldie snapped his fingers, trying to jog his memory. "J&R Music World—the list goes on and on. It's as shitty a business as you can get: low margins, intense competition, Amazon and Walmart breathing down your neck. So, I'm not afraid to be short this stock. We're going to keep doing our homework on this one." He gave a quick clap. "That's it. Keep it smart today."

Sneaks still had something to say. Simmering anger had gnawed at him all weekend, and he needed to vent. He stood up tentatively, rubbing his tattooed arm as he strained to speak calmly. "I'm going to put Facebook behind me, but I'm not doing business with Nasdaq if I can avoid it. I'm routing all my business away to other exchanges *indefinitely*." He jabbed his pointer finger in the air as he added, "And if I ever run into Greifeld, I'm going to get right in his face and let him know what a fuckin' joke of an exchange he's running." As most of the traders nodded in agreement, he slowly sat back down.

"Perfectly reasonable, Sneaks. Plenty of other places to route orders. You never have to do business with them again," Dominick said in an effort to placate.

Steve had his attention completely focused on trading. "There's still 45 minutes before the opening bell, and Facebook already looks weak. I'm adding to my Zynga short."

"Well, it's still a question of whether Morgan holds Facebook in at $38, but Zynga probably goes lower anyway," Dominick said.

Steve looked down the desk. "Eli, what are they saying at Morgan about supporting Facebook at $38?"

Eli, who had already made his usual morning calls to his various sales traders, shook his head. "No word. Morgan is radio silent about Facebook. They have such a mess on their hands that the last thing they're gonna do is give color to the Street. Don't spread this around, it's not officially confirmed, but what I've heard is that when UBS didn't get their buy orders filled at the opening on Friday, they re-sent the orders and got double-filled. Now they're stuck wearing those shares—millions!"

"Well, it looks like Morgan's got nothing going on. It just broke syndicate bid without a fight." Steve swung a combo of punches through the air. "This thing is going to open already broken. It's getting crushed—that was a quick 75 cents down. UBS clearing the decks?"

"This guy on CNBC just said that Morgan *has* to support Facebook at $38. Someone, please give the man a quote because, um, apparently they *don't*," Mitch noted wryly.

"It's *over*, Johnny," Goldie said in a perfect imitation of Colonel Trautman's voice from *First Blood*. None of the other traders retorted, as was the custom, with John Rambo's famous next line ("Nothing is over, nothing! You don't just turn it off!") because they all knew it was over for Facebook. Nothing could save it now.

On the second day of trading, Facebook opened at $36.50, the high of the day, then plunged to a low of $33 before closing at $34 per share, more than 10% under its IPO price. In the days to come, UBS stunned the Street as they announced a $350 million loss from selling their overbought shares.

After the close, Brandon strolled over to Bud. "I've got one more lesson for you. Everyone who dumped Facebook's stock today bought it higher on Friday. You have to admire that people on Wall Street know how to take a loss." He spoke slowly for emphasis as Bud took notes. "*Never* underestimate a trader's willingness to sell, book a loss, and live to trade another day."

Bud glanced back at the day's notes, which started with, "Never eat cinnamon rolls at work."

Chapter 11

THE CALL

Shortly after the closing bell, Brandon's phone rang with a call from Aviva Goddard. "Hey, Aviva, that was a great job *Barron's* did on Facebook. I saw you were mentioned as a contributor to Cliff Ludwig's article last week."

"Yes, I was," she said proudly. "It's been an exciting few days for us. We've gotten much praise—well, Cliff has, actually. But it was great to be part of it because we totally nailed this one."

"Definitely. Awesome work. What a plunge in Facebook to $33—just nuts. It's been crazy trading these sympathy stocks moving around the deal. We've been super busy here." Brandon rifled through a stack of paperwork. "I should have sent you my negative article on GSV Capital—it got clobbered."

"Hmm, yeah, I know they own some Facebook." She paused to look up the stock. "Whoa, I just looked at the chart—that's a terrific call."

"Thanks. It's a classic proxy stock decimation. It only works one hundred percent of the time." Brandon tried unsuccessfully to repeat Goldie's line without sounding smug.

After many interviews with hedge fund managers, Aviva was accustomed to far more arrogance. However, she didn't know Brandon well enough to tell whether it was part of his usual disposition. They had spoken a handful of times after meeting at a book signing. "Oh, only one hundred percent of the time. I'll keep that in mind," she said with a slight laugh. "What I'm calling about, though—I would like to know if you have any thoughts on electronics retailers. I know you follow the group, which we've spoken about."

Brandon followed multiple sectors, but he researched retailers closely since they were relatively easy to analyze. "Yes, I do. Actually, today I shorted some Loony-Life."

Aviva was taken aback by the coincidence but kept her tone nonchalant. "Interesting. What's the thesis for your short position?"

"Hang on a sec. Just need a quick breather after all that trading action." Brandon slowed down to sound more professional. "Okay, here's what I know: For starters, some notable put buying late on Friday got the stock on my radar. That seemed to hit the shares, though they came back today. In general, it's the kind of company I'm inclined to short. Margins and competition are always an issue not reflected in the valuation. Also, the company's accounting may be suspect. Do you remember a couple of years ago when David Einhorn asked a question on one of their earnings conference calls?"

"David Einhorn from Greenlight Capital? No, I don't recall." Aviva noted the reference as she typed away.

Brandon quickly recited his vivid memory of the incident. "Well, on the earnings call, Einhorn asked a skeptical question that knocked the stock down 20% before anyone knew what happened. Of course, it doesn't take much for Wall Street players to shoot first and ask questions later. But it's highly unusual for a hedge fund manager who isn't a top holder to gain permission to ask a question on an earnings call to begin with, and Greenlight wasn't even a holder."

Brandon had closely followed David Einhorn's perennially

successful career, in part because he had a vague recollection of him as a classmate at Cornell. They'd lived near one another, and Brandon would often visit the open bar at Einhorn's fraternity house.

Four years earlier in 2008, Einhorn had authored a book, *Fooling Some of the People All of the Time*, which detailed his epic six-year battle against a company he believed was using fraudulent accounting. When the Cornell Club hosted a well-attended book signing and discussion, Brandon was fairly certain he was the only one in attendance who had actually read the book. This had given him an edge to corner Einhorn for an in-depth conversation about his book and the then-precarious state of the stock market.

Brandon continued, "So Einhorn asked an accounting question, and, you know, people figured it's a safe bet that there's some questionable accounting and he's short the stock—that's why they crushed it. As you know, when he questioned Lehman's accounting a couple years earlier, the company ended up in bankruptcy—not many better ways to get Street cred. But I digress." Brandon chuckled. "So, on Loony-Life's call, Einhorn asked how they account for the depreciation of new store openings and which expenses they were capitalizing. There may have been more, but I'd have to go back to the call transcript."

"Very interesting." Aviva also made a note to read the transcript and interview Einhorn about the incident, but asked anyway, "What do you think his concerns were about capitalizing expenses?"

Brandon went on to explain how a shady company can improve its financial results by improperly capitalizing expenses, thereby spreading costs over many years instead of taking the full expense up front.

Aviva acknowledged that the story sounded intriguing,

while Brandon heard the clattering of her keyboard in the background. He continued slowly, "So now, years later, nothing's come of that. Einhorn never disclosed he had a short position, and the stock has trended higher. But it still leads me to wonder about their accounting and whether something's not kosher. But even so, they're an electronics retailer, a notoriously problematic business with a long history of failure. Why is this company's formula any better? Extra, extra low prices?"

"Yeah, I don't see their edge either." Aviva immediately regretted her statement. Her goal was to extract information and say as little as possible; she didn't want to tip Brandon off as to whether her angle was positive or negative. After a long pause, she wrapped up quickly. "This has been helpful. Thanks, Brandon."

"No problem. I'm still doing due diligence on Loony-Life. If I find anything else interesting, I'll let you know. Oh, hey, while I've got you on the line, you went to Columbia, right?"

"Yes. Both undergrad and grad school." Aviva relaxed with the shift in conversation.

"I bought tickets to the Simone Dinnerstein piano recital at the Miller Theatre. Have you seen her perform?"

"No, not yet. But I know her—we both live in Park Slope. I'd love to see her perform, especially at the Miller, my old stomping ground."

"Well, my wife can't make it in on a weeknight, and my colleagues are totally uninterested, so I've got an extra ticket. Care to join me?" For an instant, Brandon questioned his assumption that Lily would understand an evening out with a young female companion, even if she happened to be a journalist. The benefit of building a rapport with financial journalists always felt paramount.

"Thanks for the invite. Email the date to me; I'll check my schedule and let you know. Talk to you soon, and thanks again for your input. It's very helpful."

"Any time. I'll email you the info. If the date works, we can grab a quick dinner first," he said casually. "I never get out for lunch."

Knowing *Barron's* was snooping around electronics retailers, and perhaps also Loony-Life, gave Brandon a jolt to work briskly and research the company. He contemplated passing the idea of shorting Loony-Life to Jim Chanos, but first, he needed to get a better handle on their accounting. The bar had been raised on the level of ideas and research he would have to generate, since Chanos did some of the most thorough accounting analysis in the industry.

He stood up to talk across his desk to Goldie, the only other trader still in the office. "Did you catch any of that conversation?"

Goldie wasn't going to admit he'd overheard until prompted. "How could I miss it? *Barron's*?"

"Yup. That was Aviva Goddard, coincidentally inquiring about electronics retailers. Sounded more like a bearish take, and she seemed especially interested in my Loony-Life position." Brandon shrugged and, half-kidding, said, "Look, we were going to add to our short anyway this week. It's not like we know anything is coming out from them. It doesn't change our short thesis."

"Yes, but it does sound like they have a story cooking. That's fine for them. I was dead set on adding to our short anyway. Let's double up the position and buy some puts as well." Goldie sounded confident as he clicked away at his calculator. "I think we would have done that anyway—it's the direction we were headed."

The idea of front-running a potential negative *Barron's* article left Brandon slightly uneasy. Adding to a short position after speaking to Aviva seemed a little suspicious. *How's this gonna pass the smell test?*

"Okay, slow down." Brandon didn't like to debate with his quick-witted colleague, but years of friendly deliberations left him up to the challenge. He had to temper Goldie's conviction to aggressively short more stock. "I was thinking to add, but I'm not too keen on doubling up—it seems right to keep it under 10% of our capital anyway. And forget about using options; I just spoke with Aviva. You know that."

Goldie perfectly understood the predicament, but never hesitated to bump up against the ethical line. A decade earlier, the SEC had fined Goldie for a blatant trading violation. He had created trading profits by a method only possible in the old days of manipulating an inactive stock with a huge spread. Basically, he had dramatically narrowed the spread by giving one market maker a small order while asking another to execute against that bid or offer for a far larger amount. With long-standing relationships with the firm in place, the dealers willingly competed. After only a few flips back and forth, while Goldie pocketed some trading cash, the market makers got wise to the scheme and blew the whistle to the SEC for manipulation. A train ride to D.C. later, upon the advice of counsel, Goldie had admitted guilt. To this day, he still bitterly cursed his attorney for that recommendation. Among Wall Street's transgressors, Goldie knew of no other person to actually *admit* guilt rather than make the customary plea: "Pays fine but neither admits nor denies the charges."

"I think you're being too cautious." Goldie shook his head. "We have room to margin the position way higher than 10%." He sounded doubtful that his words would convince Brandon. "We cleaned up on those Facebook sympathy shorts. The firm would be riding high if we could recoup the Facebook loss. This is the chance but I think we need to be more aggressive to do it. Listen, I'll leave you at the helm in command, but I'll just say this: I *love* the short thesis."

Brandon clenched his jaw as his partner put him in a tough position. "I get where you're coming from. Even if the position is a little undersized to start, I can always add if there's more compelling information out there. Let me finish the research. *Barron's* could still drop a positive piece; you never know."

"Now you're just talking yourself into being too cautious." Goldie laughed.

Brandon knew him well enough to suspect Goldie would quietly buy put options in his personal account when he had this much conviction. He figured Goldie would keep any such plans to himself, feeling he stood on shaky moral ground, at a minimum.

"Just saying, there's always a flip side. Let's not do anything *stupid*." Brandon smirked, betraying his suspicions about Goldie. "I have a lot of reading to do. See you later." He grabbed a stack of SEC filings and walked out the door.

On his short walk to Grand Central, Brandon reflected on how Goldie's judgment was unreliable in ethical matters. He wondered what Goldie's keen intellect could accomplish if it were focused on virtuous endeavors instead of devious ones. He knew Goldie as a poker player and gambler who liked to push the envelope but only doubled down when he sensed the odds were well in his favor.

Although Brandon was a conservative risk-taker, Goldie's polar opposite, they worked well together, and he trusted Goldie's unmistakable good sense for risk and reward. Over the years, they had managed to capitalize on innumerable trading opportunities. He considered how Goldie usually got these calls right. His ego prodded him: *Take the opportunity to be the ball—size up*. Yet, as Brandon thought about his Loony-Life position, he still concluded it would be unwise to add puts. He doubted they would ever get questioned, but it was his contact at *Barron's* and his ass on the line if the firm took an option position right before a negative article. Everything was explainable, he thought, but he'd rather not get an inquiry letter from the SEC. The desk lived with the imperative to avoid having to "neither admit nor deny" anything to the SEC.

Chapter 12

SCHLOCK HOUSE

On the train ride back north, drinking a beer and procrastinating before he read through Loony-Life's 10-K, Brandon thought back to his own brush with illegal securities activities.

Eighteen years prior, age 24 and a few years out of college, he'd worked as the head trader at a Long Island boiler room operation called the Harriman Group, whose tactics were modeled after the notorious firm Stratton Oakmont of *The Wolf of Wall Street* infamy. From the outside, the firm maintained a patina of legitimacy, but once on the inside, Brandon quickly discovered that, behind a sea of dress shirts and ties, he was the odd man out. Not for a second did he imagine he belonged in a firm full of white-collar criminals, community college graduates, and used-car-salesmen-turned-stockbrokers.

The irony was not lost on him that a few years earlier, in the depths of a recession, he had sought for the limited number of coveted jobs available at the top Wall Street firms, yet he was working at a schlock firm in the dregs of the industry. Upon learning their corrupt business practices, he became acutely aware that it would be hard to defend himself as principled while working at the firm. Not only did Harriman operate without a shred of ethics, but its standard operating methods were routinely illegal. This prompted him to further his education with evening classes in the Stern School of Business part-time MBA program. He rationalized that the good pay from his morally objectionable day job helped finance a necessary educational pursuit.

He could only smirk as he recalled the way the Harriman brokers aspired to acquire a work of 3D art by Charles Fazzino. In their minds, that was the pinnacle of class. Brandon had always found the clamor for a Fazzino amusing, even though his own upbringing in Bayside, Queens, had left him unsophisticated enough to believe vinyl siding was an improvement over cedar shake shingles, and that signed and numbered lithographs were especially valuable pieces of art. The reaches of Bell and Springfield Boulevards would never be accused of elevating the aesthetic order.

Recollections came back to him of the firm's rigged IPOs and the stereotypical sales manager who led the brokers by intimidation. He mused, with a flicker of humor, over how the muscle-bound man managed to squeeze his oversized body into a tiny Ferrari parked out front.

From Brandon's vantage point as head trader, he'd witnessed activities that left an indelible mark on his psyche. The SEC had failed to detect the firm's unscrupulous dealings, while the brokers continued to brazenly and systematically fleece clients. The firm ultimately collapsed under the weight of broken deals, capital losses, and regulatory scrutiny—at least four years too late, Brandon figured.

Long after Harriman went under, Brandon received an unannounced visit from an FBI agent and a postal inspector. The co-op doorman, who would always call in visitors, had been silenced by the two government employees. Upon their startling introduction at his apartment's front door, he reflexively blurted, "What took you so long to find me?" He would later wonder if that question made him sound guilty. He was eager to share his recollection of the improprieties he saw in his time at the firm. As Brandon methodically explained the securities violations embedded in Harriman's business model and how clients were bilked, the two visitors sat stone-faced, flummoxed by common industry lingo and standard operating procedures. They stubbornly emphasized that their only concern was to learn how one particular client had made an exorbitant amount of money. Unable to recall the client, Brandon never heard from them again. In the wake of their visit, he made peace with an earlier decision not to personally report the firm's security violations to regulatory bodies—a lack of courage that had always gnawed at him.

Although the moral stench from his stint at a bucket shop had faded, what lingered was the cynicism from having seen the practices of lax regulatory authorities, pliant compliance officers, slimy executives of the two-bit corporations whose stocks the firm peddled, and the shameless tactics they all had used to line their pockets at the expense of retail investors.

As he focused back on his second read-through of Loony-Life's latest 10-K filing, he scanned the document with a skeptical eye, looking for red flags. Brandon thought their inventory turns looked low and made a note to look at Best Buy's numbers.

There was an additional nugget of information to warrant a red flag: He noticed the CEO and COO shared a surname and discovered they were cousins. This alone wouldn't warrant suspicion, yet he thought family members were more likely to conspire on accounting schemes, as he'd encountered several times in the past. A few shady companies Harriman brought public had been led by related executives, both blood relatives and couples.

This red flag added to a mosaic of concerns that had the makings of a compelling short thesis. With this, Brandon decided to quickly type out and share his idea with Jim Chanos via email. He had to go with his gut—it had all the ingredients of a winning short. He sensed time was of the essence because of the options trading, yet he refused to consider whether his conversation with Aviva played any role in hastening his decision.

Moments later, a reply from Chanos sat in his inbox. He stared at it warily before opening it. He read the unembellished note with a slight wince. "We're very familiar with Loony-Life and have done extensive due diligence on the company. Thanks for sharing your idea. –JC"

Brandon couldn't tell whether Chanos's reply was a dig at the superficiality of his thesis or a signal that he was already short the stock. Perspiration formed on his brow. He felt embarrassingly out of his league and questioned whether he'd made a mistake in sending Chanos the idea at all. He closed his eyes and put his head in his hands, second-guessing the wisdom of starting his email with the line, "Whenever I see the word 'Chaos' in a headline, I often first think it says 'Chanos.'" He soaked in self-loathing for impulsively including that flippant line. *Idiot. Dumbass. Loser.*

Chapter 13

SCHEMES AND A HEIST

On Tuesday morning, Aviva crossed the newsroom and made a beeline for Cliff. She had thoroughly read David Einhorn's questions during the old conference call and came ready to discuss.

To her disappointment, Cliff was already up to speed. "I recalled the incident clearly while reading through their conference call transcripts, but it had slipped my mind," he said. "I never looked into their accounting myself at the time—that now seems like an oversight. In fact, since Loony-Life went public four years ago, *Barron's* has never done a feature article on the company. It speaks to the deluge of work we have and the hundreds of other companies out there to focus on. But that's still not a good excuse." Cliff frowned and shook his head.

Aviva quickly shook off his negativity. "Well, it doesn't seem like anything came of it. Sure, the company has been right under our noses with their ubiquitous advertising, but I wouldn't say you missed the scoop not looking at it for the last few years. This story is just beginning, and we're on top of it."

He responded sternly, "Look, one of our jobs is to find these companies with questionable accounting and report that to our readers. We're here to do the hard job, exposing companies at the zenith of respect, not after the fact when everyone knows their problems and their executive malfeasance. There were enough red flags here to warrant our attention even before our inside source." Cliff paused. "I've heard about some active put buying recently and short players getting more vocal. There's something brewing here, and I think we've got to move on this."

"I've heard the same, and I agree."

"I'll tell you, I feel pressed to get the story out," Cliff said. "Let's try to peel this onion and get an article out by this weekend. Don't talk to anyone else on the Street about the company. We have four days to keep our heads down and see if we can get this done."

Chagrined, Aviva scratched the idea of attempting to contact David Einhorn. "We can go over the financials anytime you want. I've completed the spreadsheet work, including all the reported insider sales since they came public four years ago." She turned to head back to her desk, but Cliff lifted a hand to halt her.

"Oh, you know what I forgot to tell you?" Aviva raised an eyebrow, and Cliff paused for effect with a sly smile. "The offshore accounts set up by Ethan Atlas are domiciled in Panama. That country is one of the biggest sources of crooked shell corporations for tax cheaters, money launderers, and other miscreants. Probably only a fraction of the business that runs through their banking system is legitimate." He paused again, then added, "That's an *enormous* red flag."

Aviva could only marvel at the discovery. When she started at *Barron's*, she hadn't known Panama for much other than its jungles and shipping route. She'd quickly familiarized herself with their banking system and how it facilitated white-collar criminals. Still, she knew her own understanding of money laundering ranked as nothing compared to Cliff's.

He had spoken proudly of his work on several stories in which he had unearthed, investigated, and reported on various schemes where money was laundered through banks and the stock market. What he found reached worldwide: North Korean arms smugglers, Mexican drug cartel money, international religious charitable funds, and dirty Russian money in the Magnitsky affair.

Cliff had been dismayed by the details of Sergei Magnitsky's death. The 37-year-old lawyer had been investigating a $230M Russian tax heist from Hermitage Capital when he was accused of wrongdoing. Magnitsky was arrested by Russian authorities, tortured, and left untreated to die in prison. Cliff had set out to diligently trace the money trail from the heist and question how the cash traveled so easily. He found illicit money, laundered through Credit Suisse via shell corporations, that found its way around the globe, including into New York City real estate. If not Panama or Cyprus, he observed that the money found its way into Swiss bank accounts. He discovered that the consultants who created the shell corporations for the Russians linked right back to his other money laundering probes of North Korean arms smugglers and a Mexican drug cartel.

That kind of story always stuck with Cliff; it was the kind that made Aviva grasp just how much he knew when he called Ethan Atlas's account "a red flag." *We're onto something big here, and we both know it,* she thought.

Once their attorneys authenticated the bank records from Holly and gave Cliff the green light to report the story as he saw fit, he and Aviva proceeded. Although Cliff thought the method of a CEO sending personal money into the company unusual, he assumed the end would justify the means for Atlas if he planned to pocket the money from future stock sales, attempted to sell the company, or borrowed aggressively against his shares. At a minimum, Atlas had been able to sell stock at much higher prices; Cliff figured the fictitious profits had raised the stock price by over 50%.

While Cliff sat at his desk, he caught a peek at Facebook's stock on its third day trading as a public company. As he watched it trade even lower at $32.25, his sense of journalistic gravitas swelled. He relished working on the article about Loony-Life, which he thought would be another market-moving article.

Barron's has a "no surprises" policy. This means any time an article is written about a company—positive or negative—they must inform the company before it is published and offer management a chance to comment on the record. This is also standard practice at the *Wall Street Journal* and other business publications.

To adhere to this policy, Cliff and Aviva organized a meeting with their editor, Paul, to formulate a list of questions to send to Loony-Life. Cliff paced around the conference room while he waited for the meeting to begin. He had an uneasy feeling he might have missed something as he looked over his checklist. Aviva sensed his stress and put extra effort into examining her notes.

Paul entered the conference room prepared for business. He'd read through their early drafts and eagerly waited for updated details.

Aviva looked over to Cliff, who said, "First, I want to go over Loony-Life's accounting. At this point, we have serious questions about their multiyear per-store inventory buildup—it looks bloated. I would expect some margin pressure from clearance sales, but it's not reflected in the numbers or guidance. Not one question about this from analysts on any of their conference calls." He paused to look at Paul, who took notes. "Also, the amount of depreciation they report on a quarterly basis relative to their capital expenditures looks far below the industry average, and well below Best Buy's. This has had the effect of inflating earnings and may be related to an issue David Einhorn questioned a few years ago. Lastly, the company's income tax rate also looks below the industry average, and about 400 basis points below Best Buy's."

Paul looked up. "Does that sufficiently sum up the areas of their accounting that you intend to question?"

Aviva referenced her detailed notes and responded, "Yes, I have inventory build, depreciation, income tax rate, and the bank transfers. Still digging, but that covers everything we expect to highlight for now."

"Of course, we'll also query them on our suspicions about the wire transfers to China coinciding with stock sales by Ethan Atlas." Cliff flipped through his notes. "I think we're ready to go with these inquiries."

Paul pondered the questions. The editors at *Barron's* oversaw queries sent to 10–15 companies per week. Fewer than half of these companies with an opportunity to respond to negative issues provided a comment. An issue as serious as presumed accounting fraud, however, almost always prompted a forceful company defense. Only once in Paul's career had a company's response assuaged concerns about an issue enough to quash a negative article. "Obviously, we'll give Loony-Life ample opportunity to comment before publication. If we get these questions out to them by this afternoon, we'll still have a window open to report your story by this weekend's issue."

Cliff rubbed his forehead. "We'll dispatch our inquiries to the company today. I intend to stay on track with the article for

Friday's deadline." He wanted to get the crux of the narrative in print, although he knew the onion had more layers yet to be peeled. "There are a few more things we're working on but probably won't cover in this article."

Paul looked from Cliff to Aviva. "If you use the information on the bank transfers, I expect you to cite a source familiar with the matter. I've discussed this with the attorneys, and we're comfortable in this case with citing a single source. We understand the additional risks, but we're comfortable with the veracity of the source and the documentation you've obtained, which we'll share with the company if they make a request for it—except, of course, the name of the individual. Cliff, tell me more about how you intend to present your information."

Cliff spoke confidently as he laid out his case against Loony-Life. He explained the effects of the stock's high P/E, which left the shares especially vulnerable to a pullback. He then detailed the company's aggressive accounting and how those methods inflated earnings and led to poor cash flow, and delved into the suspected phony earnings from China. Cliff paused to see if Paul was keeping up with how fast he was racing through issues.

At Paul's nod, Cliff shrewdly expounded on why he thought the stock was worth less than $20 per share compared to its current $50. He assumed break-even earnings in China without the transfers, which equated to Loony-Life only earning $1.85 per share. Since most of their earnings growth last year appeared to come from China, he figured a slow-growth electronics retailer ought to have perhaps a 12 P/E, which took the stock to about $22. But, he said, with their aggressive and potentially fraudulent accounting in the mix, the stock could trade down to the teens.

Paul appeared impressed with the magnitude of the issues and made a priority note to feature the article on the cover.

"This story could drop like a bombshell. Let's see what feed-back we get from Loony-Life and how they spin these issues. Will you present a theory for the basis of the wire transfers to China? Or only that they inflated the revenue and earnings?"

"I'd like to explain that Ethan Atlas may be a scam artist," Cliff answered. "But I'll let readers figure that out. I think it'll be evident that the reason for the transfers was to inflate earn-ings. We've cataloged the CEO's stock sales and transfers over the past year. The effect of about $15 million in transfers on earnings will be clear. People will draw their own conclusions on why Mr. Atlas made the transfers."

"What about their domestic business? How do you intend to angle that?" Paul asked.

Aviva jumped in to explain the charts she'd set up to com-pare Loony-Life's metrics with those of its competitors, which also pointed to some red flags in Loony-Life's accounting.

Determined to publish the article in the upcoming week-end's issue, Cliff emphasized why he thought it was inap-propriate to delay an important story that would inform and protect their readers. Finding the others agreed with his goal, he expected to work day and night until Friday.

As Cliff pondered inquiries to submit to Loony-Life's PR department, he faced a dilemma: He wanted to be fair with his deadline so they would have time to respond, but not enough time to mount a public rebuttal ahead of his scoop. He gave them 48 hours to address the allegations.

The poor excuses and deflections he'd received from corpo-rate executives over the years had Cliff wondering what Loony-Life's management would cook up in their defense. Yet their silence over the next two days was a greater mystery.

By Thursday's deadline, Cliff had become impatient with Loony-Life's lack of response and was ready to call the company. Reporters from *Barron's* often arranged calls with CEOs through PR personnel but also received calls directly from CEOs to rebut impending negative commentary. Cliff had been on alert for a call from Ethan Atlas all day. But on Thursday afternoon, it was Paul, not Cliff, who received an email from Loony-Life's PR department. Their terse statement read, "Loony-Life's accounting abides by GAAP standards and is compliant with all federal and state tax codes. Furthermore, our accounting has been professionally and thoroughly audited by Peabody, Marwick & Company since 2002."

Paul studied the response and scratched his head. He pondered for a moment, then printed the email and walked over to Cliff.

"Cliff, we received what reads like a boilerplate response from Loony-Life's PR department. It's not what I expected. Take a look." Paul handed him the printout. "Make a decision whether you want to go ahead with your article or arrange a call with management first. You know, it's possible they still contact us directly, but time is running short for this week's issue."

Cliff had consulted with the paper's legal staff during the week. They green-lighted the article after altering some of the phrasing. Confident with the legal backing, he said resolutely, "Let's publish. Legal's covered it, and we've fulfilled our responsibility to disclose the impending article. I think the obligation of disclosure will move to their management." He shrugged. "It would be hard to justify sitting on this story."

Historically, innumerable SEC investigations had commenced in the wake of the financial press reporting on possible corporate wrongdoing. Many times in Cliff's career at *Barron's*, he and his colleagues had been the first to expose outright corporate fraud. Reporting now on Loony-Life reminded him of the spotlight *Barron's* shone on Bernard L. Madoff Investment Securities 11 years ago.

In 2001, he'd watched Erin Arvedlund, a *Barron's* colleague, publish a dramatic article on Bernie Madoff's money management operation. Arvedlund had questioned Madoff's strategy, his "too good to be true" returns, and his practice of forsaking standard performance fees. Arvedlund's exposé had prompted the SEC to audit Madoff's firm, but they had failed to uncover any wrongdoing in their six examinations. Looking back, Cliff remembered how appalled he'd been. Had the SEC merely checked Madoff's purported positions using the firm's DTC number, the subterfuge would have been uncovered. Only the 2008 financial crisis, which led to a flood of redemptions, had prompted Madoff to confess to his $65 billion Ponzi scheme as it imploded.

As he considered Loony-Life's accounting, Cliff concluded that his evidence and source were solid enough to warrant an SEC investigation. Yet he was aware of the unpredictability of an SEC probe. He harbored doubts about the SEC from previous cases, especially from their handling of Madoff. Many SEC employees were much like himself when he started at *Barron's* two decades ago. With a law degree but few math skills, he had worked diligently to improve his accounting ability. The experience left him to fear that even the SEC would not recognize when numbers were used to disguise, rather than illuminate. Nothing would surprise him less than if a corporation's team of accounting and legal big shots managed to bamboozle a young SEC staffer who'd majored in political science. Cliff cringed at the SEC's reverse natural selection—many of their best were lured away to Wall Street or private practice to defend companies and corporate executives.

Over the years, he'd learned to accept his role as a journalist, to hold wrongdoers accountable by alerting stakeholders, customers, and regulators of potential issues. Ultimately, he knew only the SEC could conduct a thorough investigation with its subpoena power, first authorized in 2009 as a result of the agency's failure to detect Madoff's Ponzi scheme. Though he found the SEC capricious at times, he always hoped they would follow through on red flags. He prayed his impending article would put Loony-Life on the SEC's radar.

Chapter 14

THE CHINA SYNDROME?

At the crack of dawn, Brandon heard a familiar thump outside his bedroom window, marking the beginning of his Saturday morning ritual. In boxer shorts and flip-flops, he tiptoed out of his old farmhouse, past an aging Prius, to the bottom of the driveway, where a freshly delivered *Barron's* lay at his feet. Through a thicket of brush and brambles, he could see his fully camouflaged neighbor, Jimmy, packing an ATV. *Wild turkey season*, Brandon remembered and sighed. He scooped up the paper and slipped off the protective plastic. His heart leaped. Standing agape, he stared at the front cover rendering of a cracked television screen with the article's title, "Loony-Life's China Syndrome: Why Its Stock Could Fall Over 50%."

Chills ran down his spine. *Jackpot*. He charged back up the driveway, the wheels turning in his head. At that moment, Brandon was oddly relieved that he hadn't added puts to his short position. Making money was good, but he figured making too much money with options would be bad if it raised suspicion at the SEC.

On the porch, he grabbed a wool blanket and dropped into a chair, tossed aside the paper's middle section, then folded *Barron's* in half to peruse the lead story. The first thing he sought out was the reporter's name, and he was psyched to see

Cliff Ludwig and Aviva Goddard listed in the byline.

Scanning through the narrative, he realized the accounting issues were far more serious than he'd imagined. *Barron's* raised skepticism about the aggressive nature of the company's domestic bookkeeping, but the wire transfers from the CEO's account to China were flat-out damning. The more he read, the lower he thought the stock would trade.

Brandon vacantly stared into the forest and fantasized, *If the SEC had a SWAT team, they'd be circling Loony-Life's headquarters right this minute.* He envisioned how the debacle would logically play out on Wall Street, imagining the downgrades, panic selling, anticipated SEC investigations, and comparisons to past frauds. He cooled his excitement by humming "The Gambler." *You never count your money when you're sittin' at the table / There'll be time enough for countin' when the dealing's done.*

The porch floor creaked as Brandon rocked in the chair. With China's involvement, Brandon realized Chanos might be connected to the article in some way. After all, he had mentioned doing extensive due diligence on the company. Not only was the questioning of aggressive accounting methods typical of Chanos's work, but he was in the midst of an ongoing verbal campaign warning against overdevelopment and credit excesses in China. Perhaps Chanos had uncovered issues in Loony-Life's China business and was a source for Cliff Ludwig. *Either way*, Brandon thought, *I should be redeemed with Chanos for this idea; it's right here on the cover of* Barron's.

Brandon often pondered Wall Street's bulls and bears. His experience at Harriman had turned him cynical early on and made him gravitate toward bearish reasoning. Even his Saturday morning ritual of reading Alan Abelson's witty, sardonic column in *Barron's* (which expressed dignified irreverence toward stocks) helped him focus on risk, with the ancillary benefit of expanding his vocabulary.

Brandon thought labels of "bull" and "bear" were often mis-construed on Wall Street. In addition to defining where some-one thought stocks were headed at a certain point in time, the labels represented an ideology that became an ingrained way of thinking—like Republican or Democrat.

Debates between bulls and bears were as constructive as political debates: Generally, there was little to no chance of convincing those of the opposing viewpoint to abandon their position and move to the other side.

To Brandon, maintaining a bearish mindset about stocks meant he had an overly developed sense of cynicism and con-cerned himself with investment risks and downsides. He also understood the flaws in human nature that led to corporate malfeasance. As a result, it took far less to persuade him to embrace a negative story like Loony-Life than it would for the bullish, who lived optimistically, seemingly carefree of risk, fo-cused instead on the reward of the upside. Sometimes he en-vied them. Begrudgingly, he knew the bulls held the historical advantage of a generally rising stock market.

Brandon couldn't wait for his family to awaken. He wanted to show the Loony-Life article to Lily and tell her how fortu-nate he was to be positioned short. They planned to take their kids, Dylan and Ella, fishing later that day, and he felt a rare surge of optimism. He was a terrible fisherman, but six-year-old Ella loved to fish and had gathered the worms herself from an old pile of mulch in the yard.

Ella loved animals and had named every frog in their pond. She would spend hours catching them and introducing each one to Brandon while he read in a nearby chair. In their brief en-counters, Ella always tried to befriend the fish she caught, while her older brother was thrilled to be the captain of the small mo-torboat. They all looked forward to Lily's picnic lunches.

Back to humming Kenny Rogers, Brandon stood, wrapped the blanket around his shoulders, and tucked *Barron's* under his arm. As the sun inched over the treetops, he ambled to the old maple to fill a bird feeder. He flung a pile of seeds on the ground for the usual flock of roaming wild turkeys unwittingly in need of refuge.

Chapter 15

CHAPTER 7 OR CHAPTER 11 —EITHER WOULD DO

On Monday morning, Brandon found himself suppressing a smile when he walked onto the trading desk. Rarely had he felt this good about himself at work. He'd surely cover the Facebook loss for the firm, and he wanted to celebrate with Goldie for urging him to size up the position. Perhaps for the first time, he had to make an effort to adhere to the unspoken protocol at Glacial Capital: Take your losses without whining and your gains without gloating.

The instant Goldie saw Brandon, he uttered, "Pay that man his money," in John Malkovich's faux Russian accent.

"Where's Loony-Life trading?" Brandon asked nonchalantly before turing on his computer.

"It's getting smoked—in the $37s, down about 22%," Sneaks replied.

"What did you guys think of the article? I'm not sure if I'm biased because I'm short, but I thought it read *terribly* for the company." Brandon looked around for corroboration.

"Looks like a complete shitshow." Sneaks sipped his coffee. "Down 22% looks like just a start. How much debt do they have? This shit could be Chapter 11 before we know it."

"I'm hoping for Chapter 7—straight liquidation." Mitch jumped up, waving his arms like an umpire emphatically calling "safe" at home plate. "Hold off on any large-screen TV purchase."

Brandon searched through Bloomberg and scrutinized Loony-Life's balance sheet. "Hmm, looks like over a hundred mil in net debt—about what I figured. They've been feasting in the debt market."

"Listen, *Barron's* didn't have to convince me it's a shitty company," Goldie said. "But the article was brutal, like run-on-the-bank bad. I don't see why it wouldn't go to the $20s." In a British accent, he added, "This one may even go to 11."

"Yeah, I agree," Brandon added. "I thought it would be lower already, but it's early. I'll probably watch it from here. I'm not anxious to add more short down this much, but there's no way I'm covering a share."

Once every few years came an opportunity to hit a grand slam, a situation set up so perfectly with an unassailable rationale that it didn't feel greedy to swing for the fences and let a big winner ride. This felt like such an occasion.

Through Brandon's bearish inclination, he'd developed a rapport with other bears. Few epitomized his cynicism better than his long-time industry friend Herb Greenberg, a financial journalist and CNBC correspondent. Greenberg was the definition of a scold, who would unfailingly point out the risks of investing, find the flaws in a company's earnings report and accounting, and approach most stocks with a biased caution.

Years earlier, when Greenberg worked for the *San Francisco Chronicle*, he'd sought the viewpoint of short sellers to add an edgy angle to his six-day-a-week business column. Whether the shorts were right or wrong, he came to appreciate the value of their information and the important role their skepticism played on Wall Street. Here, he had found his calling: to give voice to the underdog and question the Wall Street club.

Brandon called him that morning to get his point of view. "Hey, Herb, *Barron's* has an interesting article on Loony-Life. Did you read it?"

"What a story!" blurted Greenberg. "You see why Ludwig is one of the best in the business. But I'm sort of kicking myself. This is a short idea I've been pitched before, and I glanced at it, but never got around to taking a good look. I had no idea how deep the issues go at Loony-Life."

"It is an amazing write-up. Sounds like you think Ludwig made a good case then." Brandon waited for a reply, wide-eyed and agape.

"It definitely looks well researched. Bank transfers to China—journalists usually can't use the word 'fraud,' but this sounds like fraud. It's a scoop I wish I had. There seem to be a bunch of other red flags also. Some of them may go back years." Greenberg continued with suppressed excitement, "Certainly looks like all sorts of shenanigans are going on to inflate earnings."

Brandon pumped his fist and imagined how low the stock could go. "Those China revenues—the SEC is going to be all over them after this article."

"They ought to be. I wish I had the formula to know when the SEC investigates. So, who knows?" Greenberg said wryly, "Of course, Loony-Life hasn't disclosed a thing—yet."

"Well, still a big story. Sounds like this could snowball."

"Assuming the details are accurate, I wouldn't doubt it one bit."

"Thanks for your thoughts. Have a good week."

Brandon was enthused to get confirmation from Greenberg, who had seen and reported on all the accounting gimmicks companies used. He was cognizant, however, that finding accounting discrepancies didn't always amount to anything.

Sometimes Wall Street didn't care much when companies whitewashed over years of accounting duplicity. But the accounting machinations of the true frauds would eventually come crashing down, along with their stocks. Brandon was wary of categorizing Loony-Life as a fraud, but the prospect energized him.

Brandon snapped his fingers to get Goldie's attention. He tried to speak calmly but was too pumped up. "I just spoke to Herb Greenberg. He also thinks these accounting issues are a *really* big deal and may go back years."

At once, Goldie replied, "I think you should get more aggressive with the position. How about adding if it goes over $38, maybe take the position from 30K to 45K."

"Maybe I'll just take it to 40K." Brandon exhaled deeply. "I feel really good about adding to the short. But that's plenty of stock if the shit hits the fan. There's probably going to be a lot of selling off the opening. With the suspect accounting, institutions will probably have a fiduciary duty to clear the books of the name."

During the trading open, Brandon took the rare posture of leaning back in his chair instead of hunching over his keyboard. Content to relax and take in the trading action, he was enjoying the supreme satisfaction of sitting on a huge profit when the stock opened at $37 and quickly dropped to $35.

As planned, when the stock soon rallied over $38, he added 10K to his short. Seconds later, with barely time to assess his lower average, the stock was halted for trading.

"Ho! The stock just got halted." Mitch pushed his palms against his temples. "That's it? A half-hour of trading, only to halt it? The SEC is probably all over them already."

"Well, the halt is for news pending, so let's see what they have to say," Dominick added. "Probably sending out the PR team to defend."

Brandon piped up to ask for corroboration that the rally before the halt looked like nothing more than a dead cat bounce. Without receiving much insight back, he said, "Well, hopefully it's halted indefinitely for an SEC investigation and reopens on the pink sheets."

"That would call for lobbies," Steve said, grinning.

Sneaks was quick to explain Steve's remark to Bud. "During the financial crisis in 2008, Steve would short as much Bank of America and Citigroup as he could in the morning, especially when this one bank analyst, Meredith Whitney, was bearish. By lunchtime, he'd usually be up a pile of cash and send me to pick up lobster rolls for the desk. That's how I learned to trade, watching over his shoulder." In a tone of self-discovery, he added, "It's no wonder I keep shorting bank stocks."

"Just looking for a little payback. Man, I miss those days— I'd gladly foot that bill again." Steve smiled and shook his head in frustration at today's tougher trading environment. "Back then, all you had to do was fade any shred of optimism until rock bottom."

"Until Mark Haines called the bottom," Goldie noted.

"I miss that guy," Brandon added, nervously searching for news on Loony-Life. "He was the best host CNBC ever had."

"Without a doubt," Goldie replied.

"I miss Chuck Prince—that dancing fool." Mitch turned to Bud. "Right on the eve of the financial crisis, as the CEO of Citigroup, he pronounced that 'as long as the music is playing, you've gotta get up and dance.'" He chuckled. "Meanwhile, the music had already stopped as he danced Citigroup over the cliff like Wile E. Coyote."

"Hey, looks like a press release just hit the tape," Dominick announced.

As his heart raced, Brandon peered at Loony-Life's press release on a Bloomberg terminal and read slowly:

Over the weekend, Loony-Life was the subject of an inflammatory article in Barron's *that impugned the company's accounting and the actions of our CEO, Ethan Atlas. We view the reporters' critical assessment as baseless and contrary to the facts.*

Last year, in 2011, Ethan Atlas set up an offshore trust to facilitate computer equipment donations to schools in various provinces of the People's Republic of China. The computer equipment was acquired from Loony-Life at cost, through our Chinese subsidiary, and subsequently donated. Although these purchases increased the company's revenue in China, it did not increase the profitability since they were purchased at cost. Our business in China has strengthened through-out the year, and we are optimistic about future pros-pects for growth and profitability.

Due to an administrative error in our investor rela-tions department, this information was not forwarded to Barron's *in a timely manner prior to Friday's pub-lishing deadline.*

Additionally:

- *Loony-Life's inventory fluctuates seasonally due to the effects of stocking and destocking of vari-ous items. As our balance sheet has improved and our store base has grown, the company has stocked more items, resulting in higher aggre-gate inventory levels.*
- *Loony-Life's corporate tax rate and the rate of depreciation fall comfortably within industry norms.*
- *Loony-Life's accounting has been thoroughly audited by Peabody, Marwick & Company since 2002 and conforms to all Generally Accepted*

Accounting Principles (GAAP).
We appreciate the long-term support of our loyal
shareholders, and we hope for their continued support
as our business expands.

Brandon stood up, incredulous. "Well, that sounds like a bunch of bullshit—and I'm not just saying that because I'm short 40 thousand shares. Fuckin' A."

"I agree," Goldie began with a slightly upbeat tone, which radiated from his undeclared triumph of having closed out of his personal put option trade before the halt. "But they're going down swinging here. Donations of computer equipment in China? Who the fuck does that? What about the Bronx or West Virginia? That sounds dubious."

"It reeks of bullshit." Sneaks scowled.

Brandon waved an arm toward Sneaks. "Thank you."

Steve peered over at Brandon. "But this muddies the water enough that I have no idea where the stock will trade."

"I have no idea how the market will react either." Brandon clenched his teeth. "But it still sounds shady. Not so sure if the SEC investigates now, though it clearly needs to happen to make the short work in the big picture." He reread the press release and took a deep breath. "But I still trust Greenberg and *Barron's* that their accounting is aggressive, even if the company claims the China business is legit." He took a long pause before mumbling, "'Improved balance sheet,' my ass."

"Oh, CNBC is finally 'breaking' the news." Sneaks rolled his eyes.

When CNBC's sharp-witted veteran reporter David Faber began to comment on the press release, Brandon jumped up, turned the volume higher, and pleaded to the screen, "Come on, Faber, get this right. Please explain that this sounds ridiculous." With their shared Queens upbringing, Brandon found

Faber's Street smarts especially keen.

The desk listened quietly to Faber's commentary. After he concluded his remarks, Goldie said, "Well, he did sound somewhat dubious about their defense. Let's see where the stock settles out. Looks indicated to open between $43–$45."

"Faber looked good there—he definitely sounded skeptical. Guess I didn't need to short another 10K, but I think it'll be okay." Brandon felt his pulse quicken and took a long breath. "My average is still good. That press release seemed very perfunctory—I doubt anyone buys into it. Where there's smoke, there's fire," he added, trying to convince himself as much as his colleagues.

Aware that the eyes of the desk were studying his every move, he evaluated his need to react as the stock reopened at $45, almost seven points higher than where it had closed. Disbelief was the only response. "What the fuck?" he barked when it quickly rallied to $48, only down $2 on the day. "This just got uncomfortable." He nervously ran his fingers through his hair. "It doesn't make any sense for this to go higher. That China story still sounds like bullshit. Goldie, I'm hanging in with the position."

"That's fine." Goldie looked over at Dominick for approval. "But I'm not feeling quite as bearish with this stock action."

Eli banged his phone down. "Brandon, CS defending Loony-Life, raising their price target to $70."

"Raising their price target?" Brandon slapped his desk. "What the fuck is the rationale there? That makes *zero* sense." He waved his arm at Eli. "How in hell are they still drinking the Kool-Aid?"

"They're saying that the bull case looks even better than they thought." Eli continued as though it should be totally obvious, "Once they strip out that CEO's charitable purchases, it makes profit margins in Asia even higher—they're raising estimates for their Chinese business."

Brandon stood and leaned across the desk, getting as close to Eli's face as possible. "That has just a kernel of rationality. I get what they're saying, but that's fucking bullshit! Tell Winston his analyst is buying into *bullshit*—he's going to just ignore the aggressive accounting?"

"Brandon, these guys know what they're doing," Eli said as if speaking to a child. "This analyst has been covering the stock since they took it public."

Brandon wagged his finger at Eli. "Shut the fuck up! That analyst knows what the company tells him to know. End of story." Brandon pulled a phone to his ear, mocking the analyst listening to the company's executives. "What's that? The *Barron's* piece is nonsense? You say everything's going great? Margins even better?! Perfect!" He slammed the phone back down. "*Fuckin'* stock just went up on the day." He looked around, bewildered. "Sorry, Steve, I messed up lobbies for lunch by not covering at $35. Now I've got a mess on my hands."

"That's all right," Steve said. "I would have done the same thing. Gotta press the winners."

"Nothing about the way the stock is trading looks right," Goldie noted. He exchanged a wary glance with Dominick. "Looks dangerous here. This looks short-squeeze eligible." Goldie stared at Brandon, as if to nudge him to cover the short position.

"I mean, could this be a rogue algo?" Brandon asked feebly, feeling a swell of discomfort descend through his gastrointestinal system. It was common lore on the desk that trading algorithms gone haywire accounted for some inexplicable stock moves.

"Ivan the K tweeted that it's 'Beeks out with the crop report—shorts and longs trading places.'" Sneaks shrugged with his palms up.

"Okay, no mood for jokes here—the guy never stops with that movie. I just bought 5K to cover my ass... not too much damage. I'm feeding right into this little buying frenzy. *Asshole.*" Brandon sat hunched with his hands on his head as he stared, disbelieving, at his computer.

He and Goldie would always joke about *Trading Places* when traders were forced to sell exactly when they least understood why the stock was moving against them. "Why's everyone selling?" Goldie would often quote, parodying the scene. "There's something wrong here. *Mortimer*, they're not *buying*, they're selling! Wilson, get in there and sell!" For Brandon, this qualified as one of those times. *Except this time*, he thought angrily, *the joke is on me.*

Brandon endured watching Loony-Life swing higher throughout the day, closing at $54, where he covered another five thousand shares. After the close, he digested the events, wringing his hands in frustration.

"Goldie, any suggestions here?" Brandon looked at the ceiling. After years of working alongside him through numerous stock battles, he trusted Goldie's opinion. Goldie was adept at arguing any side, although he usually went out of his way to be a contrarian. Brandon, his face flushed, continued, "Here's what I'm thinking: I don't see how it goes much higher, but I'm back short 30K. I'm comfortable with that position, and I think there's still a real possibility the SEC will investigate. Look, don't forget that even Greenberg thinks these accounting issues are a big deal. And there's chatter that some of the smartest people were already short the stock."

"That's why the stock goes higher—too many shorts," Goldie countered without a trace of doubt. "I agree with everything you're saying, but I don't like the position anymore. I know you're a big fan of Greenberg, and he may be a *hundred* percent correct, but that's the long run."

Brandon walked around the desk and sat next to Goldie. He didn't want to give up on the trade, and he wanted Goldie's blessing. The idea that he would run and cover the position at a loss, especially after failing to book a huge profit, felt desperate and illogical. "Listen, I recognize this position could work against me for a few more points higher. That's risking $75K, maybe $100K, for this to work big to the downside. This could be another Enron or Lernout & Hauspie—stocks that went to *zero*."

Goldie shifted in his chair. "Again, I agree, but this may not happen in the timeframe we're comfortable riding out, so it's hard to like the position. Since you mentioned Lernout & Hauspie, you do recall that the stock went from something like $20 to $60 in six months in an epic short squeeze? The shorts got *destroyed*." He leaned forward with his eyebrows raised and a know-it-all smirk.

Brandon gritted his teeth and strained not to roll his eyes. "I remember, I remember. But I also recall the stock went to zero in the following six months, and the shorts who hung in made a score. Listen, you just said last week that you *loved* the short idea. We went over the whole thesis." Eyes narrowed, he leaned back and folded his arms.

"You're right. The thesis is still intact—I'm not saying it's thesis creep—but the price action is telling me to step aside, at least for now. This could make some crazy Lernout move higher, and we're not prepared for that sort of capital commitment."

"*That* I agree with." Brandon gave a tight-lipped nod. "Okay, I won't let the stock get away. I'll stop it out in a few points, *if* necessary."

"Fine." Goldie paused. "By the way, Eli is upset with you."

"As if I don't have enough shit to deal with. What's his problem?"

Goldie chuckled. "He didn't like that you told him to shut the fuck up."

"Please tell me you're kidding?" Goldie shook his head. Brandon stood up and gestured in mock outrage. "That was in the heat of battle, and he did say something really dumb. He's always throwing around the 'fucking *malakas*' and '*poutánas*,' and yet that hurt his feelings?"

"You know what a drama queen he can be. We all hear how he argues with every new girlfriend and always thinks it's them." Goldie tapped his temple. "Listen, next time, say it in Greek, and he probably won't take it so seriously."

As Brandon laughed, some tension loosened, with a long day behind him and nothing more to be done. He grabbed Loony-Life's press release, the *Barron's* article, and the company's Form 10-K to reread on the train back to Cold Spring. But the only person he could turn to now for clarity was Aviva Goddard.

Chapter 16

THE SUSPICION

In a small conference room off the newsroom floor, Cliff, Aviva, and Paul sat mute as they read Loony-Life's press release.

Paul broke the silence. "I cannot accept this at face value. An administrative error? That doesn't sound right. They responded to our inquiry—how could they forget the charitable donation information?" Paul furrowed his brow as he glanced at Cliff. "Is this even possible? Donations in China? This seems like something that should have been in an SEC filing. What's their obligation to disclose this?"

Cliff had investigated money laundering under the auspices of charitable giving in the past, but couldn't grasp whether it applied in this case. He stared at the press release, slowly shaking his head. "Maybe they made some deal with Chinese authorities to donate computers as a quid pro quo for permission to open retail outlets—that's the only thing that makes sense. But I agree, nondisclosure of such a material item is problematic. I went through every one of their SEC filings and read every conference call transcript; this is the first-ever public disclosure that I'm aware of."

"I'm not prepared to accept the veracity of the donations claim," Paul said. "Any way we can check with the IRS?" Cliff looked at Aviva, then shrugged. "Okay, let me know when you get in touch with your source. We need some additional inside color on this situation, if possible. What about the other claims? It seemed clear from your research that the depreciation and income taxes are well below normal. How can they claim to be 'comfortably within industry norms'?"

Cliff felt a knot in the pit of his stomach. "It's clear they want to spin this as they see fit. I'm sure the company wants to convince the SEC and investors that their accounting is fine." He peeked down at his phone. "The stock just went positive on the day, so Wall Street seems to be buying into their defense." Cliff wanted to shrug off the market's reaction, but it was hard to ignore.

Aviva interjected, "I know this is out of left field, but is it possible Holly set us up to run a false story? It seems strange to me that the company provided so little information last week."

"Why would you think it's a setup?" Paul folded his arms.

"I don't necessarily think it's a setup—I just think it's *possible*." Aviva paused for a second. "She's his personal assistant. It's hard to imagine she wouldn't know about this charitable giving. So, once they refute part of our narrative, it calls the whole story into question. Maybe that was their goal."

"Anything's possible." Paul shrugged. "But why call into question a story we weren't even investigating to begin with? Let's say they wanted us to run an article only to refute it—what's the purpose?"

Cliff shook his head as he blurted an answer. "While everyone looks at China—which may be perfectly legitimate—people disregard their domestic business, which may have issues."

"That's kind of what I was thinking. Or perhaps someone else is already probing, and this throws them off stride," Aviva said.

"Perhaps. Still, I don't know. An article would only add to the scrutiny, so I'm not convinced that makes sense." Cliff wiped his glasses on his shirt as he spoke. "The truth is, at this point, nothing matters unless the SEC gets in there to investigate. Wall Street wants to believe the company, but we know how little that means right now."

The door swung open and a young office assistant walked into the conference room with a large envelope from the corporate offices of Loony-Life. Paul quickly opened it and scanned through the documents.

After a few moments, he read aloud, "Enclosed herein is the information to verify the charitable giving of Ethan Atlas, along with the documentation of the electronic equipment purchased and donated." Paul grimaced as he continued, "We hereby request a retraction of the core elements of your false and defamatory article on Loony-Life, or your publication's management may expect to hear from our attorneys regarding a libel suit."

Cliff slapped the tabletop, and the clank from his wedding band rang loudly through the room. The sound triggered a reminder of his wife and kids. In both work and family life, he felt as if he played a crucial role in upholding the moral order. With an inflated sense of his own rectitude, he preached the importance of acting ethically and taking personal responsibility, especially to his two sons. Cliff had to stop and wonder: Was he a hypocrite if he didn't own up to a mistake? His visceral answer came flowing out.

"A retraction? That's horseshit—I'm not retracting my article." He jumped up and began to pace. "If we retract the China part of the article, it will discredit the rest. Our competitors would have a field day running the retraction of the Loony-Life story, and the nuance will be lost. Now I'm starting to believe I was set up."

"Okay, calm down; we're not retracting your article. They can square off against legal." Paul spoke haltingly as his mind worked fast. "Look, they cannot dictate how we handle this after failing to respond properly to our request for information. I think there's still a serious issue with the lack of disclosure. But let's backtrack about being set up. It doesn't make sense for your source to disclose information only to have it discredited; it's not like you were planning to write a negative article anyway. Companies fight to have stories like this quashed, not in print. You spoke several times with your source and judged her to be reliable. I very much doubt it was a setup. I think she just got the account wrong, and obviously there was no way we could have second-sourced the information." Paul paused and shook his head. "Unfortunately, now we have to tackle how much of the story we got wrong."

As Cliff searched for an answer, he sat back down, second-guessing his decisions and quietly pondering whether his zeal to pursue a great scoop led him to rush the article. He questioned whether his intense competitive spirit had worked against him in his eagerness to be the first to uncover the wrongdoing. He wanted to be the one to take down Ethan Atlas. But now his stomach churned at the thought of the lost credibility and frayed trust of his readers. Slumped over with downcast eyes, Cliff said, "Paul, I need to apologize. This is not how I wanted to follow up my Facebook story. Maybe I rushed the article."

"Cliff," Aviva said, "we had all the research done. I don't think sitting on the information would have helped—it wasn't rushed." She mustered all her confidence and added, "This story isn't over, not by a long shot."

"It was my responsibility. I should have called Ethan Atlas directly." Cliff looked Aviva in the eye. "That's what I keep thinking. I wanted the article published, and I didn't want a delay. I should have spoken to him first."

"I agree with Aviva," Paul said. "There's no need to

apologize. Your article was timely, and we gave them ample opportunity to respond. We'll figure out how to handle this in the best way possible. What's your gut reaction on their domestic business?"

Cliff sat straighter as his fight rekindled. "I completely stand by the accounting issues. I will keep beating that drum."

"Okay, good." Paul desperately wanted to get his top investigative journalist back on the case. "I have an idea. Loony-Life has gone out of its way to open up about this China business, although it was never disclosed in any filing. How about requesting access to their auditor? Let's send in our forensic accountant to scrub their audit. I wonder how they'll respond to that."

"That sounds like a good idea. Has that ever been granted before?" Aviva frowned slightly.

"I haven't a clue," Paul responded, thinking there was probably zero chance. "But it'll put them on notice that we're on the offensive and still focused on their accounting."

"I'll give it a try." Cliff added, "But first, I have to get back in touch with my source."

At the end of the day, Aviva glared at her phone when she saw Brandon calling. "Hi, Brandon, how are you?"

"Eh, okay. I'm sure you're following the Loony-Life saga."

"There's not much I can discuss with you about that right now, sorry."

"Perfectly understandable," Brandon replied. "I just want to know one thing: The China charitable donations sound completely fabricated—it's nowhere in their SEC disclosures. I think Ludwig's take on the transfers sounds much more reasonable. What's the discussion there?"

Aviva paused for a moment. "Right now, I'd say it seems possible that what the company said is true. There's a lot more to it, but that's all I can say."

Brandon threw a hand over his eyes and sank back in his chair, utterly dejected. "That's not at all what I expected you to say. I'm flabbergasted. You must have a lot to deal with, so thanks for talking."

"Yeah, no problem. See you next week for the concert," Aviva said.

"Wait, just one more quick one," Brandon cut in before she could hang up. "What about the administrative error in responding to *Barron's*? It seemed odd to wait until ten o'clock to halt the stock, no?"

"That's actually two separate issues, but all I can say is the timing did seem strange. They messengered a packet of documents to us sometime before eleven A.M."

Brandon's eyes widened. "Ah, interesting. I'll leave it at that." He hung up and thought, *If the CEO's donations were legitimate, I'm just grasping at straws.*

Chapter 17
THE 1% PROBABILITY

Any player on Wall Street understands an irrefutable oddity: The higher a stock goes, the more traders want to buy it; the lower it goes, the less it's sought after. The reason is momentum, which is arguably the most significant force in the stock market. Traders are eager to buy when there is upward momentum, when odds favor a move higher. Conversely, they are reluctant to buy when there is downward momentum, for fear the stock will fall further.

Brandon walked into the office on edge, this oddity on his mind. He had barely slept. Aside from the unsettling call with Aviva, yesterday's strong momentum had him concerned. He figured traders would be interested in buying the stock for no other reason than the previous day's reversal higher. *Strength begets strength*, he fretted. What he didn't expect were the rumors swirling around the buying in shares of Loony-Life.

Brandon sat down without exchanging any morning pleasantries. He locked his eyes onto his computer while his colleagues carried on a fierce debate.

"I would definitely rather Martha Stewart over Jane Fonda," Sneaks said adamantly. "Martha's been in prison. That's *hot*."

"Not me." Mitch shook his head. "I don't care how old Fonda is—she looks amazing in *The Newsroom*. And those thighs!"

"I used to work out to those thighs—she's awesome. I go with Fonda," Eli added, as Mitch grabbed his ThighMaster for a few sets.

"I think you'd have to say that age-weighted, Jane Fonda clearly wins for 74," Goldie said as if analyzing a stock. "But they're both very attractive for their age."

"Um, can we backtrack for a sec?" Bud looked around the desk. "Martha Stewart was in prison?" In unison, the desk broke down laughing.

"Yeah," Dominick responded, still chuckling. "You were probably still in junior high, but she was convicted for insider trading."

"Completely ridiculous," Sneaks began. "She owned a bio-tech stock that she sold after speaking with the CEO, who was her friend, before bad news came out. Considering what goes on in the market every day with inside info and options trading, it was basically nothing."

"Six months in the slammer." Mitch shook his head. "Crazy."

"She actually went to jail for lying to investigators about the stock sale," Goldie added.

"They got her on the cover-up? Even fuckin' worse." Sneaks scrunched his face in disgust.

"I see Loony-Life is gapped up," Brandon said begrudgingly, finding a moment to comment. "*Awesome.*"

"I'm hearing Carl Icahn's been buying Loony-Life stock and is trying to get Dell to take them over. My guy at Jefferies hit me with that," said Eli, touting his information gathering on the most widely followed hedge fund manager on Wall Street.

To Brandon, Eli seemed all too pleased to relay the positive call. Without a pause, he dismissed the exclusivity and logic of Eli's info. "Yeah, I see that pump-and-dump Icahn chatter on Twitter. The stock's up a lot on the rumor, but it's total nonsense. They're just trying to screw the shorts. Icahn bought

Dell to thwart Michael Dell's deal to take the company private—or at least get him to pay higher. They're not taking over anything. I've heard a dozen rumors over the years that Dell would buy RadioShack. Never happened." He stared coldly at Eli. "So let's not perpetuate bullshit."

Eli defended himself with a Patrick Bateman line, along with his eerie tone. "I'm mulling over business problems, examining opportunities, exchanging rumors, spreading gossip."

Near exasperation, Brandon took a deep breath and turned to Goldie. "Obviously, I should have covered more yesterday, but I don't want to cover on this stupid rumor with the stock gapped up. If I weren't already knee-deep short this shit, I'd be aggressively shorting on this cock-and-bull story."

Eli coughed, then murmured loudly, "Just because you're getting cocked doesn't mean the story's bull."

"And you wonder why I tell you to shut the fuck up," Brandon snapped. "You say some stupid shit."

Eli scowled at Brandon, grabbed a pack of cigarettes, and stomped off.

To defuse the drama, Goldie jumped up and gestured to Brandon to leave it to him, rolling his eyes with a glance toward a departing Eli. Goldie segued to address Loony-Life. "Look, this kind of move higher just shows how many shorts are already in the stock. But you know, I'm not even sure which came first, the rumor to explain the stock action or the rumor moving the stock." He continued in a preachy tone, "Seems like the stock was already strong, and someone came up with the Icahn story as an explanation. So, I agree it would be ridiculous to cover on this rumor, but I don't think the rumor moved the stock much. I think it was already gapped up beforehand—which makes staying short even more dangerous."

Brandon shrugged. "Let me just say, I think the stock is totally mispriced here. Probably buying that triggered through a line in some technician's chart." He raised his voice and added, "Monkeys will chase anything moving higher, especially if they smell a short squeeze—you know that, Goldie. How can the price have truth with that inefficiency?"

Brandon knew he was hitting a soft spot. Goldie was on a personal crusade to chastise anyone who used the term "price is truth" to signify that a stock's price represented some unassailable correctness. Pundits on CNBC who cleverly used the term to legitimize where a stock traded found themselves in the crosshairs of his intellectual diatribes. Goldie would hammer in the illogic of the phase by detailing how George Soros thought reflexivity created inefficiency in price through the self-reinforcing effect of market sentiment.

Goldie absorbed Brandon's words. "You know, I agree, no argument about what's driving the price—momentum monkeys buying for all the wrong reasons—but this is about risk management, not some exercise in rationality about the fundamentals."

"I hear you. I'll probably have to take some lumps today and reduce the position if it doesn't pull back." Feeling besieged by the market, Brandon turned to Bud to vent his frustration. "Ninety-nine percent of rumors on Wall Street are total BS. Total BS! But *one hundred* percent of them are used to pump up a stock. In 2008, the SEC made a big stink about cracking down on rumors, but they only cracked down on negative rumors to make sure short sellers couldn't manipulate stocks lower. Now every rumor is positive, and the SEC doesn't care a whit that longs are manipulating stocks higher." He flailed his arms wildly. "It's fucking ridiculous."

"Definitely. Definitely is." Bud scribbled furiously in his notebook.

Brandon was still conflicted on the extent of Loony-Life's issues. If their China business was legitimate, as Aviva had

intimated, then there possibly wasn't much of a negative catalyst in the short run. Mostly, he thought the stock was propped
up by a force he couldn't interpret. *Is it short-covering?
Perhaps a sophisticated investor bought shares during the
morning selling. Could Icahn have bought? Could this be the
1% of the time a rumor is accurate?*

A confusion of thoughts churned in Brandon's head as he
stared blankly at his screens, lamenting his lost trading discipline and poor decision-making. As a trader, he prided himself
on synthesizing the mosaic of information that led to stocks
fluctuating, yet he no longer had an edge on Loony-Life's trading action.

He failed to register the conversation around him as he assessed the bullish and bearish arguments. Absentmindedly, he
bit down on his lower lip to the point of complete numbness.

"Brandon, did you catch that?" Dominick waited for a response, then shouted, "Shuster!"

Brandon shot a look over at him. "What? I wasn't paying
attention. What'd I miss?"

"I said Herb Greenberg is out with a story on Loony-Life.
It's on his blog. He tweeted that he'll be on CNBC later today
to discuss it."

"Ah, thank you, I'm checking it out right now."

Brandon read through Greenberg's in-depth article on
Loony-Life's aggressive accounting. He felt a wave of comfort
as he realized the article had far greater specificity on how the
company manipulated its accounting to inflate earnings. Many
issues had previously been cited by *Barron's*, but Greenberg
delved deeper and hit harder.

"I'll give the CEO the benefit of the doubt," Greenberg
wrote, seemingly tongue-in-cheek, as he lambasted Ethan
Atlas for the revenue-generating donations in China. If the accounting gimmicks were factored in, Greenberg concluded in

the same fashion as *Barron's*, the stock ought to trade closer to $20 per share.

"Greenberg's got them dead to rights. He's got a great template to decipher all the shenanigans they're using," Brandon said, relieved about how rock-solid the short case sounded. He took a deep breath as a half-hearted smile crossed his face—now he knew for sure he was on the right side of the trade.

"Yup, just read it. Reads terribly for the company." Goldie peered skeptically at Brandon and added, "Now the question is, will anyone give a shit?"

Imagining the worst, Brandon slowly shook his head. "It's gonna be a bleak feeling if I'm the lone guy on the Street who cares. Only idiots would chase this thing higher. Unfortunately, there's no shortage of those."

Chapter 18

THE TERMINATOR

In general, traders have two instincts when a position is working against them: fight or flight. Brandon was naturally humble and self-doubting, so his instinct was usually flight—to close the position, step back, and reevaluate. More confident traders would fight for their side of the trade, insisting it was the market that had it wrong.

As the day wore on, Brandon succumbed to the reality that Greenberg's article had failed to dent Loony-Life's stock. The worst-case scenario he'd dreaded while he lay sleepless last night had come to pass: unstoppable momentum. As the stock crossed over $60, his self-doubt and instinct to flee overwhelmed him. He folded and covered his short. With the position closed, he was relieved for a moment, even though he'd booked a total loss of over $450K, which devoured over half a year's profits. The moment of relief vanished like a droplet on a hot pan.

Feelings of self-loathing and worthlessness washed over him as he sat staring at his screens with unseeing eyes. His fear of failure had always caused him to trade conservatively and take tolerable losses. *How could I have let the trade slip away? How will I face Lily at home tonight and break to her the biggest loss of my career, and so soon after boasting how well I was positioned?*

The loss to the firm's capital and the trader bonuses began to sink in. Brandon couldn't tell if he heard whispers of discontent from his colleagues or if he projected his own disappointment onto them. He hoped his low spirits would be eased by the firm's mantra, "We're all big boys willing to accept the risks."

Unexpectedly, but not at all surprisingly, Mitch walked over to cheer him up. "Look, sometimes the market grabs you by the balls and won't let go." Mitch paused. "And I don't mean in the good way." This elicited a slight smile from Brandon. "It's painful, but there's not a damn thing you can do about it. All cool; it happens." He slapped Brandon on the shoulder.

Mitch's brotherly reassurance was welcome. Still, Brandon couldn't quell his anxiety. Eyeing the Tums across the desk, he pictured further consequences. The decision to book a significant loss was painful, but even with no position, the next big move the stock made was also important for his mental health. If Loony-Life continued higher, his relief would intensify with discipline rewarded. If the stock swung abruptly back down, it would take an additional psychological toll as he agonized over closing the position at an unnecessary large loss.

Fortunately for Brandon, the next big move came quickly as the stock's ascent continued.

"Boom." Eli banged his fist on the desk. "Icahn disclosed a stake in Loony-Life. The stock just traded up to $70! Man, that CS call yesterday was *mo-ney*—just hit their price target. And who said this morning's rumor was bullshit?" He turned and shuffled through research stacked on a windowsill. "Try to pass along some good info, but he still crushes the firm."

Mitch called down the length of the desk, "Yo, Eli, easy on the auto-fellatio—you're gonna hurt yourself."

Brandon shifted in his chair. "You know the BS part was

about Icahn getting Dell to buy them out."

"Either way, you fucked up, bro." Eli pointed across the desk at Brandon. "I can't push the buttons for you."

Without missing a beat, Sneaks coughed loudly, which sounded vaguely like "dickhead."

Mitch walked over to Eli's stack of papers. "Come on, you know how much dumb shit comes out of this research you print up?"

Ignoring Eli's slight, Brandon said, "Whatever. I'm just glad I covered the stock. This could have been a disaster. A bigger one, I mean. The filing is right there on the tape: He's got a 12.98% stake—that's huge." He breathed deeply in relief. "Oh man, and he's requested a seat on the board. What the heck? This is who he swoops in to defend? Of all the companies..." Sensing Bud watching him, he turned to him and said, "I'm sure there's a lesson here for you, but I can't teach what I don't get. Only that this is how to break the 'live to trade another day' rule."

For an instant, Bud tensed, unsure how serious his mentor was about continuing to trade. He glanced at his notebook, pondering the depth of the lessons he learned while sitting next to Brandon. "Got it," he said.

"Well, now we know who's been buying. It never looked right on the short side." Goldie looked pleased with his assessment of the situation. He turned to Eli. "Get your guy at Jefferies on the phone and tell him what a great call he made, and we're gonna give him a bunch of business tomorrow. Do it right now!"

The urgency in Goldie's tone prompted the desk to scrutinize Eli while he did as instructed. He began by praising his contact. "Dude, that was an awesome call this morning. You're the best. Look, I'm gonna send—" In a flash, Goldie reached over and pulled the phone receiver about a foot away from

Eli's ear. Eli was still holding tight as Goldie released it. With a thud, Eli slammed the phone back into his head. He yelped in pain and said weakly, "Dude, I'll call you back."

Goldie winked at Brandon while the desk attempted to stifle guffaws. With a hand over his ear, Eli faced Goldie. "What the fuck? Why'd you pull the phone away?"

Years earlier, when Goldie had brought Eli into the firm, he'd taken on the obligation to quell his attitude. This was his pain-inducing hint. "That was a 'Mikey Special' phone check, *bro*." Goldie shrugged. "Remember you asked about it?"

"That was a business call. You don't *fuck* with my business." Eli flipped over his keyboard and stormed off the desk, muttering to himself about working with children, his one scarlet ear conspicuous from across the office.

"Wait," Sneaks yelled. "You accidentally just bought something." Eli stutter-stepped and half turned around before continuing out the door, slamming it shut. Sneaks unleashed an evil cackle.

Brandon casually leaned across the desk to fist-bump Goldie, who said, "Man, that was one of the more savage checks, but he deserved that for being such a massive prick. I don't care who he knows on the Street." The entire desk chimed in to concur with Goldie. Brandon quietly felt the strength of their support, and his burden eased slightly.

After he heard Icahn would appear for an interview on Bloomberg TV, Brandon hopped over to the television to watch. Mitch stood beside him.

"I need to understand what this man is thinking," Brandon told Mitch. "He just ignores *Barron's* and Greenberg? There has to be some method to this madness."

Without a pause, Mitch said, "The method is simple: He grabs the shorts by the short hairs and doesn't let go until they cry uncle—Uncle Carl."

Brandon gazed curiously at him for a few moments. "You could actually be right, you know. I guess it's not worth over-thinking, but I have to hear how he explains this."

They looked up to watch Icahn's long-winded explanation of how he saw an opportunity to buy Loony-Life after he recognized it was unfairly impugned by the media and short sellers. Brandon was captivated as he listened. "My firm has done a great deal of due diligence on the company, and I've spoken with their CEO, who I found credible." Icahn concluded by saying the stock was significantly undervalued based on growth in their China business, strong domestic revenue, and prospects for future worldwide expansion.

When the interview ended, Brandon looked around. "Come on, that bull thesis did sound a bit unsophisticated. I didn't catch one number in his analysis except when he said it could be a hundred-dollar stock." He rolled his eyes and tossed up an arm. "But what the heck do I know?"

"No, you're right," Goldie said. "His thesis does sound thin. Retail stocks haven't exactly been his forte, either. If you recall, he had a huge stake in Blockbuster and was on the board when it went bankrupt."

"Well, you know what's amazing?" Brandon said with a slow shake of his head. "Greenberg lays out a comprehensive, sophisticated argument that this company has accounting issues—and nobody cares. Icahn takes a stake, discusses not one number, and everyone's running to buy the stock." He let out a big sigh and sat back down. There was no way to stop things from going loony. He knew the stock market was like the Terminator: It couldn't be reasoned with. Despite his frustration, he accepted that stocks often behaved irrationally for long periods—an inefficiency he knew to be an opportunity creator. And even after a day that reeked of failure, Brandon summoned a moment of confidence to believe he also had one thing in common with the Terminator. *I'll be back*, he thought, nailing the Schwarzenegger impersonation in his head.

Brandon noticed Goldie watching him intently with an eyebrow raised. He was on alert for resentment or disappointment in the eyes of his colleagues, but he knew this look of Goldie's, and it was neither. *Oh, man. He thinks I ought to re-short the stock.* He anguished at the thought, his mind racing again. Brandon knew it was probably the exact right idea, but he lacked the mental fortitude to do it. He wished to be an ice-cold, dispassionate trader—one that could jump right back in and short the stock—but he was too shaken.

He riffled through paperwork to feign distraction and ignore Goldie's gaze. Brandon was all too familiar with the process of mental recovery he'd have to endure before he could start trading effectively again. First, he'd need to briefly assess his skills to reaffirm he was unqualified to work in any meaningful capacity outside of the stock market. After some deep soul-searching and yet another reread of *Reminiscences of a Stock Operator*, Brandon would then commence "survival mode" by seeking out the smartest and most conservative trading ideas to chip away at the loss and regain his confidence. It was a long process, though he suspected this time around, he could add another step to his method: boosting his efforts to work in research for Chanos. Perhaps a career change was what he truly needed after all.

A dream momentarily sidetracked him about how different it would feel if he had covered the short at $35. *Woulda been a hero.* This exercise quickly became irritating, and he vowed not to dwell on what could have been. Instead, he methodically replayed Loony-Life's trading timeline with the new information that Icahn was in the market amassing a big stake. To have accumulated such a significant position so quickly, Icahn must have been buying stock on Monday morning after he spoke with the CEO but before the news was released during the stock halt. Brandon again had the gnawing feeling of being on the wrong side of Loony-Life's move higher on Monday—now from the outside looking in.

Desperate for answers, Brandon called Herb Greenberg, unsure where else to turn for a rationale behind Icahn's buying. He gathered himself to sound upbeat. "Hey, Herb, Icahn must not read your research, or he would have sold today. What's he thinking?" The tone of his question implied some irrationality.

"That's funny, but you know, the man marches to his own beat," Greenberg said. "After the *Barron's* article, I dropped everything to dive in."

"You found even more red flags than *Barron's*."

"It sure seems like a lot of shady stuff going on. I'll tell you this, though: After I released my article this morning, I got calls from a couple of hedge fund managers. They only wanted one thing from me. Just one thing." Greenberg paused dramatically. "They wanted to know whether I thought the SEC would investigate the company. That's all they cared about."

"Figures. What did you tell them?"

"I told them I never know when the SEC decides to open an investigation, but I believe their books certainly warrant closer inspection."

"That sounds like a dissatisfying answer. Just curious, do you know whether they were interested in buying the stock or shorting it?"

"As strange as it sounds, I'm pretty sure they were both buyers," Greenberg said. "They heard the rumor that Icahn was buying, and they wanted to jump on a possible short squeeze, but didn't want to get burned long if the SEC announced an investigation."

Brandon dropped his head. "That's unbelievable. But I

ought to know better, that's just par for the course on Wall Street. They go right to the source of a great cautious analysis, and all they want to do is get long on a rumor for a squeeze? Herb, you know that's BS." Brandon resigned himself to being irritated. Few things irked him more than losing money overthinking a company's fundamentals when being on the right side of a trade required merely riding along with the momentum of the herd.

Greenberg quickly added, "The real BS is that if they bought in, they made a ton of money with the stock up huge. Look, I've been around Wall Street long enough to know anything can happen in the short term. So, I'm just going to step away. I never argue with a crazy person, and likewise, I never try to make sense of an irrational market." He paused for an instant to change his tone. "Did you catch my Loony-Life segment on CNBC earlier? Like I said, my 'Hostile React-o-Meter' is spinning out of control. Outta control, I tell ya! And you know what that means..." Over the years, Greenberg had deduced that the more hostile the reaction to his negative stories, the more zealot-like behavior investors displayed. He always asserted it to be a reliable contra-indicator.

"Saw it. Was a good tip, thanks. We know price action drives sentiment. So, of course, nothing like a rally to get people all bulled up, and everybody talks a great game when things are working. But I agree about stepping away. That's the only way not to drive yourself mad." Brandon paused. "By the way, your article was really compelling. You did a great job."

"Thank you. You know, I've always thought sunshine was the best disinfectant, so we'll see what happens and if the Street cares at some point. Look, I gotta run."

"One quick question!" Brandon pleaded as he struggled to come to grips with the sequence of trading events. "If Icahn bought the stock after speaking to the CEO but before it was halted on Monday morning, do you think that's considered insider trading?"

"That's a darn good question." Without a pause, Greenberg added, "Gotta go."

Brandon frowned. *There's another dissatisfying answer,* he thought as he hung up. He wanted to hate Icahn for playing the game too well. Any excuse would do to help redirect the loathing away from himself.

He looked up to see Goldie still mulling over something. He wondered if they were thinking the same thing: *How on Earth am I going to recoup the Loony-Life loss if I'm too gutless to fade the stock up $10 on this news? It's the perfect contrarian play after this parabolic move.* Brandon shuffled toward the door with his head down, still rationalizing his inaction: *Perhaps "buy the rumor, sell the news" is too obvious.*

Part II

Chapter 19

INSIDE LOONY-LIFE

Loony-Life's corporate headquarters was a purely utilitarian facility located in Queens, a nondescript pile of yellowish bricks indistinguishable from its neighbors. The only employee amenity was a gym in the basement with a dozen flat-screen televisions.

Ethan Atlas often worked out there. He appeared perpetually well-tanned, spoke with a confident Brooklyn accent, and wore an indiscernible hairpiece sprinkled with gray.

People considered Ethan a natural salesman, a trait that made his first electronics store a success decades earlier. Even after a brief exchange, customers were impressed by his knowledge and fully trusted him.

For many years, Ethan remained reluctant to take his company public to avoid scrutiny and regulatory burdens. Ultimately, he was convinced of the benefits of access to the capital markets and soon found that his gift as a salesman took him a long way on Wall Street.

Throughout his four years as CEO of a public company, five epiphanies regarding Wall Street occurred to Ethan.

The first epiphany came right after Loony-Life's IPO in late 2007, and it was this: Analyst research on the company was usually highly optimistic. The reports forecasted rosy earnings, revenue, and same-store sales growth far into the future. Ethan also found that analysts were quick to read into his level of confidence and body language. Some would even relay these cues to investors as a helpful outlook for Loony-Life's near-term business.

His second epiphany came in 2008, after the FBI arrested Bernie Madoff: Investors who were making money asked few questions. Stories had emerged about the lack of basic due diligence Madoff's clients had done on his firm. When investments proved profitable, investors were grateful just to be connected to a money-making operation and didn't want to burden the CEO with requests for additional disclosures. He also noted the pattern of investors who had no clue they were being defrauded until they wanted their money back.

The lesson from the second epiphany was reinforced as Loony-Life's sales fell during the financial crisis and accompanying deep recession in 2009. The barrage of ensuing investor concerns went on for months. But as soon as the stock strengthened, even before business turned up, investors quieted down. The queries slowed to a trickle. This made Ethan mindful that a strong stock price alone could be a panacea for most stockholder complaints. The game on Wall Street would always be to keep investors happy by finding ways to keep the stock price high.

Ethan's third epiphany came well over a year after Loony-Life became a public company. He learned that he could attract investors who thirsted for growth above all else. Many growth investors prioritized store expansion and per-share earnings growth, but were less interested in Loony-Life's actual cash generation. This meant a switch from Ethan's private-company days, when the annual cash flow held paramount. He noted how these investors dreamed about future expansion possibilities, so he cultivated that lust for growth in his sales pitch. "Investors live on hope" became a constant refrain in the executive suite.

When the fourth epiphany struck, Ethan realized how inefficient stock valuations could be. Loony-Life's fundamentals didn't change nearly as much as Wall Street's perception of them did. Analysts and investors routinely turned a blind eye to commonplace accounting maneuvers that allowed his CFO to easily generate improved quarterly earnings per share. He never tired of seeing investor excitement over aggressive accounting assumptions that made his company look far better on paper than in reality.

With conviction in his voice and a solid earnings per share report, he learned to manipulate Wall Street from quarter to quarter.

Ethan's fifth epiphany was the darkest. Sparked by an idea from his COO, he discovered the company could juice earnings even further by using one simple trick: counting empty warehoused boxes as product for sale to inflate Loony-Life's reported inventory.

While executing this scheme to bolster earnings, at no point did Ethan think of himself as a crook. When he first considered augmenting inventory levels, the idea was to deliver better-than-expected quarterly numbers for Wall Street, but only as a temporary, short-term tool. He always thought his management prowess would achieve the lofty expectations he guided investors to for the following period.

But once the plan launched, it quickly snowballed into something much larger than he ever imagined. The growing scale of the ruse forced him to hatch plans to undo the inventory charade.

In time, he trusted that a sixth epiphany would become clear, then perhaps a seventh. Ethan Atlas's epiphanies had never yet failed to aid him in navigating Wall Street.

Gliding through an afternoon workout in the corporate gym, Ethan abruptly halted his treadmill as Carl Icahn appeared on an overhead TV screen. After years of fine-tuning his ability to sway investors, Ethan felt emboldened by the famed hedge fund manager espousing his company's current and future success.

Captivated by the interview, he watched with sweat dripping down his chin, immediately relating to the brash confidence of Icahn's Queens accent, which he thought would resonate well with viewers. Ethan hoped he'd gained an ally by letting the stock trade for half an hour on Monday morning before he sent out the press release refuting the claims made by *Barron's*. Instinctively, he knew of no better way to make friends, especially on Wall Street, than to put money in someone's pocket. When he heard Icahn talk up Loony-Life's expansion potential and online sales growth, he was almost inclined to believe the possibilities were limitless.

Ethan beamed as Bloomberg reporter Trish Reagan agreed with Icahn that Cliff Ludwig had done a disservice to readers by improperly fact-checking the charitable donations in China. Both were incredulous that *Barron's* had published the article using an unnamed source without directly contacting the CEO.

In a disused conference room five flights up, Holly's face was ashen as she stood alone talking to Cliff on her cell phone. She nervously tugged the ends of her straight, chestnut hair. Only later would they both hear about Icahn's Bloomberg interview.

"Holly," Cliff began sternly, "we received a detailed package

of documentation that seems to legitimize the charitable donations of computer equipment Atlas made to schools in China.
Is there anything I'm missing here?"

Holly still had secrets to keep, but she was glad to find
someone she could trust and wanted to tell him as much as
she could. Mouth parched, she said softly, "First, let me say
I'm sorry this didn't go as planned—believe me. I've looked
through all the documents, and I guess they look real. He's discussed giving computers to schools in China, but that account
isn't set up for charitable giving, so I didn't connect the two."

Cliff weighed her words carefully and attempted to contain
his frustration. He couldn't help remembering Aviva's idea
that he was intentionally given unreliable information as a
setup. "So, you were aware that Atlas had discussed donating
computers in China? That would have been a helpful piece of
information to relay."

"I really didn't think it was important to mention." Holly
sounded abashed but continued to plead her case. "He's sending his cash into the company—that's what I thought was
important. I've never heard about the orders for computer
equipment as a donation." She paused, mulling over what
she'd just said. "It seems strange to me that I haven't."

Cliff peered at his notes and continued to prod. "So even
though you knew of the computer donations, a fact that you
should have mentioned, you weren't informed about equipment purchases in China with his money? Is this information
you'd expect to be privy to?"

"I thought I would have known about something like that.
How could I not have known? Keeping quiet about charitable
giving isn't something he'd..." Holly's voice trailed off as she
stared out the conference room window to a perfect view of the
Empire State Building in the distance.

The sincerity in her voice gave Cliff the same feeling of

trustworthiness he'd sensed from the beginning. "Okay, got it. I'll have to deal with this. As far as I'm concerned, the fact that this went undisclosed in their SEC filings is still problematic. Listen, I'm going to call Ethan's office and try to set up a phone interview. I'd like to speak with him directly to discuss a few matters—hopefully he doesn't object. But please keep in mind, if you hear anything else relevant, it's still okay to contact me."

Cliff looked over at Aviva listening intently, and heard her words from earlier echo in his mind: *This isn't over.*

Holly racked her brain for anything suspicious she could pass along to redeem herself. She steadied her quaking knees by thinking about the courage of other whistleblowers. She knew something was wrong at Loony-Life, and she wanted to set a good example for her son by taking action even under difficult circumstances.

"I'm not sure if this proves much," she said. "But a while ago, Ethan remarked to me about the irony that before the company went public, he'd take out millions of dollars, and now as a public company, he's putting millions back in. He said he thought that was fair because being public made him worth a quarter billion dollars."

"Hmm, that's interesting." Cliff tried to sound encouraging. "But, yeah, that doesn't prove much. Thanks."

Holly returned to her desk inside the CEO's suite of offices. Ethan sauntered in, freshly showered, a half-hour later. He never hesitated to brag about his success in bending things to his will. "We have a new backer on Wall Street—it's amazing. You have to watch Carl Icahn's interview on Bloomberg TV. He was masterful. I've successfully managed to turn the *Barron's* article on its head. Our stock's trading up another $10 after the market closed." He pumped his fist.

Before Holly could respond, an office assistant interrupted

to pass along Cliff Ludwig's request to schedule a phone conversation.

Feeling at the height of bravado, Ethan said, "He's a day late and a dollar short. Even on Bloomberg TV, they're saying he should have called me sooner. He probably wants to apologize for his misreporting after seeing that interview. Set up the conversation for tomorrow morning."

In a moment of placid satisfaction, Ethan sat at his desk and watched the company's stock trade still higher after Icahn's interview. Although Loony-Life was not the company Wall Street thought it was, he knew he had to project confidence and buy time to fix his accounting troubles.

Eyes closed, he quietly basked in the value of his personal stock, now worth over $300 million. He fantasized about selling every share to spend the rest of his life cruising around the world on a yacht. A twinge about investors who would buy his overvalued stock was quickly swept from his mind. He shrugged to absolve himself from responsibility with one thought: *Caveat emptor.*

Yet Carl Icahn's rant motivated him to keep fighting for his company's potential, even if it cost him tens of millions of dollars in his own stock to fix. *All I need is time to undo the inventory accounting*, he thought. Ethan partly blamed Wall Street for his mess—he'd gotten caught up in their demands for growth and performance, which had hooked him on the accounting scam his COO had devised.

Ethan slowly infused his money back into the company in an attempt to rectify the whopping accounting hole they'd created, and he accepted this as a small penalty. Thus far, his $15 million in sham donations to China, booked as pure profit for Loony-Life, had allowed them to discard empty boxes purported to hold $10 million in inventory.

He would come out of this unscathed, he thought with

confidence. The *Barron's* article had only served to do good things for him, despite the efforts of the "unnamed source" they'd spoken to. Here, Ethan's thoughts were still troubled. Who could have talked to Ludwig? Who could have helped *Barron's* uncover the scheme? He would discover the whistleblower's identity, Ethan vowed, imagining all the ways he could discredit the person and make their life miserable.

Ethan summoned his cousin Stan Atlas, Loony-Life's COO but also the de facto CFO. Stan was short, bespectacled, and mostly bald, and he often exhibited a sincere dimpled grin. He was an accounting guru who could run circles around most anyone on Wall Street. He viewed accounting as an art form and himself as Picasso. The spreadsheet was his canvas, and the income statements and balance sheets he crafted were modern masterpieces. "Engineers would never make it in accounting," Stan once scoffed. "The numbers are too imprecise and open to interpretation." Deception through numbers was the game he most enjoyed playing, the sport where he found the best challenge. Stan paired his accounting acumen with the ability to smooth-talk his way out of any problem, making him an invaluable and trusted partner in Ethan's gamesmanship with Wall Street.

"Stan, did you see our stock after the close? Over 70 bucks! We have a tremendous new supporter in the market, and we need him. Feels like attacks from all sides—first *Barron's*, and today Herb Greenberg." Ethan continued slowly, watching Stan's reaction, "We need to dig in and fight back to make sure your numbers hold up to scrutiny."

Stan enjoyed the game itself and didn't care as much about the stock price, but he respected it as a scoreboard for his accounting prowess. He smiled. "Well, giving Icahn a seat on the board is a no-brainer. He's our new spokesman!"

"I almost choked when he parroted my line about

international expansion," Ethan said. Unable to believe their good fortune, both laughed heartily. They instinctively knew landing a prominent investor would attract a myriad of other stock buyers.

"But don't worry about my numbers—just worry about the PR," Stan said. "Remember when David Einhorn questioned my accounting? How fast did I put those issues to rest? And we never heard from him again after we hired a new CFO," he added smugly. After David Einhorn exposed potential accounting issues, Loony-Life hired a former equity analyst as their CFO, whom they compensated handsomely to talk Wall Street's language and smooth relations. "Any plan to respond to Herb Greenberg like we did for the *Barron's* article?"

"I think Icahn will give us cover for a while—Greenberg's just out fishing," Ethan said. "He's doing a lot of speculating about the way things are run around here, but I think it'll blow over. Apple will have an updated iPad out this fall, and I got a 'definitely' on a mini iPad from my contacts in China. Both will be huge sellers this Christmas. It'll get our business right back on track. I'll be speaking with Cliff Ludwig tomorrow—I expect him to set the record straight about my charitable giving in China."

Stan was bemused by the way Ethan said, "my charitable giving in China." It sounded too much like he really believed the money he sent to China went to charity instead of reversing their fraudulent inventory accounting. "Yeah, let's get the charitable giving story out there so this media cloud can blow over. Just be careful when you discuss our inventory. Like I've said, we'll need at least another 24 months to get the numbers under control, and that's if our business picks up."

Ethan sat and pondered his situation: How fast could he fill a $45 million hole in his balance sheet while not digging it deeper? His plan to replenish cash to the company coffers set too slow a pace, he thought; a year was required to fill back $10 million. He would have to step up the company's computer trade-in program, which gave a discount on a new computer for a redeemed older one.

Chapter 20

THE GRILLING

The following morning, anticipating some groveling and an apology, Ethan took a deep breath and prepared a haughty voice before he answered Cliff Ludwig's call. "Ethan Atlas speaking."

"Thank you for agreeing to speak with me." Cliff's voice was firm.

"I would also have gladly spoken with you last week; maybe we could have saved ourselves a little trouble," Ethan said cordially, sprawling comfortably in his leather chair.

"I agree. After Loony-Life failed to respond adequately to the queries we sent from *Barron's*, I should have personally followed up with you. But can you explain what sort of administrative error caused your company's failure to respond with the proper information?"

Ethan smirked as he realized an apology wasn't coming. At once, he flipped the call to speakerphone to convey a more assertive presence. "Unfortunately, I had been ill-advised by our general counsel that my charitable donations in China were not necessary to disclose. As you've seen, we've resolved that disclosure issue in an 8-K filing with the SEC." He cleared his throat loudly. "At the time, our investor relations department was confused by your query and made the improper decision not to elevate the issue to the executive suite. They were unaware of the donations, as they are a personal matter."

"It seems like something you would be proud to disclose. You've made generous donations to schoolchildren in China," said Cliff, his words tinged with skepticism.

"Like many philanthropists, I have chosen to keep my donations private," Ethan responded calmly.

"Respectfully, last year you were pictured with an oversized check of your donation to the Boys & Girls Club." Cliff paused. When Ethan did not reply, he continued to press. "Do you expect to continue aggressively selling stock and donating computer equipment in China or perhaps in the United States?"

Ethan knew the computers exchanged for discounts at his stores could not be refurbished and passed off as high-quality donated computers in the United States the way they easily passed muster in China's rural communities. "Look, I'm selling stock to fund my charitable giving, like Bill Gates selling Microsoft." He paused to allow his comparison to sink in. "And like Gates, I prefer to donate to help more impoverished countries outside of the United States. For one, the people of China have been very good to me and my company. I've had wonderful cultural experiences there with my family. It's been my honor to help provide children with computers. That, you can publish." Ethan eased back in his chair, satisfied and relaxed.

Cliff knew he needed to move past Atlas's canned answers to something more substantive. "Is there any quid pro quo for your donated computers? Has this helped ease the way with the Chinese government for your company to open retail stores?"

Ethan was fully prepared for such questions. "There has been absolutely no quid pro quo for my charitable donations. Neither my company nor I have received any benefit in return, only the satisfaction of helping schools better educate their students. Don't get me wrong, it's hard to open and operate in

China, but we've done it well."

"Understood." Cliff spoke with a confident grin. "Can you please explain what your company does with the computers that are exchanged for discounts in your domestic stores?"

Ethan's jaw clenched. "Those get shipped to China, scrapped, and recycled."

Cliff pursued quickly. "Does Loony-Life participate in any of the recycling programs through Apple, Hewlett-Packard, or Dell?"

Ethan knew full well that Loony-Life paid a company in China to refurbish the computers under the auspices of recycling them. A bit flustered from the unexpected grilling, he collected himself and responded, "No, we've chosen to send the computers to the recycler directly."

Like a vise tightening, Cliff continued with the poise of a district attorney. "In a footnote in last year's 10-K, Loony-Life recorded an expense of $1.5 million on its recycling program. Why does your company choose to incur an expense when Apple, HP, and Dell offer free recycling?" Aviva had scoured Loony-Life's footnotes and found this nugget of information.

"Look, I appreciate the dialogue, but you're inquiring about a strategic corporate decision, which I'd prefer not to comment on. We did over two billion in sales last year, so your question regards a nominal amount anyway."

Cliff knew he'd hit a nerve and took the opportunity to drill in. "Your competitors choose to use the free computer recycling programs that I mentioned. It seems like an unusual decision on your part."

Years of obfuscation and deceit had left Ethan cool and collected, even when pressed for a difficult answer. "Again, I'm not going to comment on our strategic decision-making. I'm answering your questions as a courtesy, but you're not being very courteous."

Cliff let him off the hook to seek another nerve center. "Please allow me to change direction. You were forthcoming in your disclosure of documents to *Barron's* regarding your donations in China. Would you be as forthcoming by allowing us access to your auditor for a forensic analysis of their work?"

Ethan paused for a moment and smiled, thinking about Stan's method of distracting their auditor's young assistants, whose job was to verify Loony-Life's inventory. Their auditor allocated a fixed amount of time for the assignment and closed the audit whether the work was completed or not. The attractive young female associates Stan tasked with flirting and small talk were more than enough to sidetrack the auditors. Due to the scripted distractions, only a fraction of their work was ever completed. "I chose additional transparency regarding my charitable giving because it was important for us to respond to your erroneous reporting. Access to our auditors is completely unorthodox and therefore unacceptable."

Cliff had known it was a long shot and continued unperturbed to new ground. "Okay, but I'd still like to better understand your inventory situation. Your inventory has grown well ahead of your store growth, yet your profit margins have remained steady. Historically, for electronics retailers, there has been an inverse relationship between inventory and profit margins—when inventories swell, margins decline. How have you managed to alter that well-established relationship?"

Ethan worked his mastery of self-assured bluster, which had been an asset throughout his business career. "Listen, we're leading industry trends—we're increasing sales per square foot and gross profit per square foot. You should be asking our competitors why they can't keep up with our growth and profitability rather than questioning how we get it done."

"With all due respect, most of your growth last year came from expansion into China. With inventory growth outpacing sales and store growth, your inventory turnover is on the decline. In a competitive industry like consumer electronics, that portends markdowns and margin pressure. Yet it's nowhere in your numbers."

Eagerly, Cliff awaited Ethan's reply.

As Stan had instructed, Ethan was careful while discussing Loony-Life's inventory. "Cliff, I see you want to continue to grouse about how you'd like our business to be performing, rather than celebrate the fact that our business continues to be strong. We've gotten huge volume rebates from OEMs on our current inventory." Ethan hollered into the speaker, "I have no interest in continuing to debate what I consider to be an obvious point—the dramatic economies of scale. You clearly do not understand the business. I'm sorry—I am ending the interview." He hung up with no hesitation.

Cliff's mind raced as he glanced down at his unasked questions. A few deep breaths calmed his visceral reaction to the phone call's abrupt conclusion. He strained to hold back a snap judgment, but reflexively, he wanted to believe that the CEO's hostility was a red flag signaling he'd probed close to damning information.

He racked through his mental trove of past conversations with various CEOs, some innovative industry leaders, others pathological liars who thought they could talk their way out of anything. Like rummaging through a heap of laundry for a matching sock, he pondered who Ethan Atlas reminded him of. Unable to place him quickly, Cliff made a journalistic effort to put his suspicions aside and keep an open mind.

After the call, Ethan sat for a moment, then called Stan to his office. With intense concentration, Stan listened to the recorded conversation. Unsettled, Ethan watched his glum expression.

"Two out of the three things I've always worried about may be conspiring against us right now," Stan whispered, "a tenacious reporter and a source from within our company. But I'll tell you, as long as the SEC doesn't formally investigate, we're fine. I'm not happy about how he picked up on the recycling expense—nobody's questioned that before—but Ludwig sounds like he's still just fishing. He's got nothing on us."

Ethan immediately shrugged off his concerns. "Listen, I can't worry about those things right now. I'll keep the wolves at bay. Don't forget, we have *Icahn* on our side. Just keep me posted on the progress of our computer exchange program; that's got to kick into high gear. In the meantime, I'll double up my stock sales. Let's clean this thing up before any of it can matter." Ethan had always believed he could accomplish anything he set his mind to, even the unrealistic.

Stan winced slightly at Ethan's confidence. He was an accounting whiz, not a magician, but he didn't know how to explain that without sounding pessimistic. He fought his anger and the urge to unload on Ethan, whose plan had put them in imminent jeopardy. Attempting to fix the inventory problem was more likely to expose the scheme than if they just let it play out. He wanted to explain the folly of a crook who tried to return money to a bank he'd already robbed. Instead, he bit his tongue. "That's if business strengthens, Ethan. This is going to take a while—it's a deep hole. You know this was dug over years, so it'll take years to climb out of it. We've got to keep refurbishing costs down, too. I know he's just fishing, but Ludwig could make a big deal about that expense. I still can't believe he asked for access to our auditor—what an asshole."

"Fuck Ludwig!" Ethan shouted. "As long as our auditor stays in the dark about the boxes..." His voice trailed off, waiting for reassurance from Stan.

"Don't worry about a thing." Stan waved dismissively. "I've

got our audit partner so bamboozled that even if Ludwig spent a week with him, we'd be fine. Marwick actually thinks we're *over*-reserved on our inventory—they're fucking clueless. If they ever did get suspicious, I'd just throw some expensive consulting biz their way. You know, I think we're fine with Ludwig. You did a good job. If anybody, it's Greenberg I'm worried about. He's a total mouthpiece for the shorts, but he's got a big platform."

"Greenberg sent an email again yesterday with a bunch of questions—I ignored it." Ethan puffed out his chest before softening to a new strategy. "Look, take him out and make him feel good about our books. I know we try not to put our critics on a pedestal, but I don't think we should let this one slide. Do you think you could pull this off?" The question was rhetorical. Ethan had complete confidence in Stan's ability to fix problems. Stan bragged about his mythic powers to wine and dine their audit partner into accepting anything.

Stan smiled broadly at Ethan's question as innumerable ideas ran through his mind. "I'd love to work my magic on Greenberg—charm to disarm." A sly look crossed his face as he scratched his bald head. "He's going to be a tough nut to crack. I've heard he's like a fuckin' Boy Scout. But I'm sure I can make him good and comfortable with our books. Everyone on Wall Street wants to hear the same shit—our numbers are conservative and business is strong."

Ethan saluted to send Stan off on his task. As Stan turned to leave, Ethan asked, "So, what about the third thing that worries you?"

Stan cringed and sat back down. "We do not want to find ourselves targeted by any crazed short sellers. I'll take on a journalist like Greenberg any day—I'll run circles around 'em— but we don't want to be dogged by some Sith Lord with huge money on the line and a financial incentive to spend day and night trying to destroy us. Those assholes always claim to be doing some good deed, but, of course, it's just for the bucks."

Taken aback, Ethan straightened up in his chair, staring at Stan. In Stan's eyes, where in the past there'd been nothing but confidence, Ethan now spotted a shadow of fear. Stan nodded to affirm that he was dead serious as he got up and shuffled out the door.

At the sight of Stan, Holly tensed slightly and shifted her arm to cover a notepad where she'd jotted down the only words she had managed to overhear: "Fuck Ludwig."

Chapter 21

BOOZE, BROADS, AND BULLSHIT

Stan Atlas had several qualities that helped Loony-Life pull off their deceit: an in-depth knowledge of accounting, a mastery of exploiting human weakness, and a thorough enjoyment of the Wall Street game.

Apart from his many abilities, he simply held different ethics and goals than the average man. When he first learned accounting, he regularly conjured up ways he could use numbers to hoodwink others.

As Stan mastered accounting, he also took to studying human behavior to gain a psychological edge over his rivals and counterparts. He relished the opportunity to go toe-to-toe with Herb Greenberg to convince him that Loony-Life's accounting was clean.

Stan had a well-tested strategy in store for his dinner with Greenberg. For starters, he only agreed to meet Greenberg on his terms, at a restaurant of his own choosing. He expected Greenberg would feel compelled to be more pleasant on an adversary's turf.

They met at Bryant & Cooper Steakhouse in Roslyn, a step up from Queens in Nassau County. Stan often took his auditors to strip clubs to distract and dull their senses. For this occasion, he would manage without girls and lap dances, but alcohol would be a must, so he planned dinner on a Friday night to avoid an excuse of work the next day.

When Greenberg walked into the restaurant, he eyed the decor—subdued browns, framed horses, all in step with their advertised goal from their opening in 1986, "to bring the top-tier New York City steakhouse experience to Long Island." Stan greeted him warmly, like they were old friends catching up rather than two people meeting for the first time. Greenberg instantly felt at ease with the affable, unassuming man.

Stan introduced Greenberg to the maître d', who escorted them to a quiet corner. Earlier, Stan had slipped the maître d' a C-note and asked for two things: his sexiest waitress to spend extra time at the table and to delay serving bread.

With a glance at his watch, Stan took note of the time. His goal was to spend at least half an hour bullshitting before Loony-Life entered the conversation. His first order of business was getting Greenberg to like him. He thought it was harder to believe someone you liked could commit fraud.

"I've followed your career for years," Stan began. "I could not have more admiration for what you do. The frauds you've brought to light, the overvalued stocks—you've been the voice of reason. Tell me, how is your family doing with your move to New York?"

"What can I say? My wife misses San Diego." Greenberg already seemed comfortable sharing details.

"You can't blame her for that. You're a devoted husband, so it sounds like you may end up back out West." Stan was eager to dish out compliments, although he felt no actual admiration for men devoted to women—in his opinion, wives caused far more trouble than they were worth.

"I'll never rule out going back to California, especially for my wife." Greenberg narrowed his eyes behind his glasses, wary about the conversation's direction.

Their buxom waitress came over to ask what they would be drinking tonight. Her eyes widened. "Hey, I recognize you from CNBC! But you're much more handsome in person." She touched his shoulder. "You're practically a celebrity—you must have a lot of fans."

Greenberg blushed and denied that he had any celebrity appeal. "Trust me, my only admirers are hedge fund managers—unfortunately, all men." They all laughed. Stan chimed in about how successful Greenberg's career had been.

Greenberg played along obligingly but had a vague notion that Stan must have set up the conversation with the waitress. He wasn't about to embarrass her with a quiz about anything she'd ever seen on CNBC, but he also wasn't about to get duped after 38 years as a business journalist.

For his part, Stan noticed that Greenberg didn't swoon over the waitress. He was miffed, yet respected that Greenberg couldn't easily be exploited by a weakness for women. He couldn't fathom having so little reaction to a voluptuous woman and had rarely encountered such restraint in other men. He thought it odd that Greenberg must not only love his wife but actually *like* her. But Stan fully embraced the extra challenge, like Vizzini vying to best Westley in a battle of wits.

The waitress chatted a bit longer, then asked for drink orders. "I'll have a martini. Herb, join me for a drink?" To Stan's satisfaction, Greenberg ordered a beer. Intent on interruptions, he added, "Come back and tell us about the steaks." When she sashayed back with a martini and a draft Heineken in a frosted beer glass, Stan quickly toasted "to new friends."

The waitress nudged Herb and winked. "Ready to order, handsome?" Right behind her stood a tall, tanned waiter who recommended boneless sirloin—"from our own butcher shop."

"Medium rare?" Stan asked, figuring they'd both go for that.

"Please, go ahead. I had my eye on something different."

After they ordered, Stan continued his quest to humanize himself while he looked for a commonality. Greenberg appeared more complex than his usual prey, but he found his opening when he discovered Greenberg liked to talk about food and health. Stan felt relieved he didn't need to resort to conversation about grandkids. "What's your favorite San Diego dish?"

"San Diego has amazing Mexican food, as you'd expect. A burrito with some tasty guacamole works for me. You wouldn't believe the avocados."

"Come on, you gotta learn to live a little. Never too late," encouraged Stan. "If you'd ordered the sirloin, that would have been a good start."

Greenberg maintained a comfortable patience to question Stan. He tried to keep his focus as he thought about a friend's admonition: Never walk into an alley you've been invited into. He couldn't let himself be ambushed by the good rapport.

"Okay, let's discuss some business," he said abruptly. As he'd taken a liking to Stan, Greenberg already sensed he'd be more cordial and less confrontational than he'd imagined hours ago.

"I'm here to give you as much information as possible within regulations. What would you like to know?" Stan smiled broadly and opened his arms.

With Stan's hint about restrictions on disclosures from Reg FD, Greenberg knew not to expect complete candor. He still intended to dig as deeply as possible. "Thanks. Let's start with your inventory. It's been up significantly. What's the explanation there?"

Stan was more than prepared for questions about their inventory levels. He knew Greenberg was an excellent journalist but not highly knowledgeable about accounting, so he didn't expect to be challenged on his assertions.

"Listen, the more product, the better. I'm stretching out our accounts payable to inventory ratio. I have the inventory, but I haven't even paid for it yet. Not to mention, we've got price protection from the manufacturer—if it has to go on sale, the manufacturer takes the hit, not us. In fact, our auditor thinks we're *over*-reserved on our inventory," he said truthfully. "I'd be glad to send you the letter where they've concluded that." Stan sipped his martini. "I know you're looking for a story here, but I gotta be honest with you, you're barking up the wrong tree."

"Really? What would be the right tree?" Greenberg promptly regretted asking the question, mindful that the conversation could quickly wander.

As part of Stan's deception, he'd planned to confide something to Greenberg in a show of trust and good faith. He took his opportunity. "Look, I'll tell you something," he said softly. "I've pored over Best Buy's financials, and they're a mess."

Greenberg was suspicious of Stan's attempt to turn his attention away from Loony-Life, but his journalistic instinct took over. "How so?"

"Half their profits come from extended service warranties. Two problems with that: First, it's a dying business—customers just don't want it anymore. Second, their warranty reserves are way too low. They've been moving the warranty dollars to the bottom line far too aggressively. Take a look at our books; our warranty reserves are higher as a percentage of the liability."

"Okay, I'll take a closer look at Best Buy. Thanks for the info. I guess I'm not surprised you've examined their financials."

"It's a hobby of mine." Stan chuckled. "I like to know exactly what my competitors are up to." Stan interlaced his fingers and placed his elbows on the table. "And that one's going to be a good angle for some reporter to focus on."

Again, the waitress stopped by to ask about drinks. Stan

studied his adversary's steady eye contact with her as he sipped his martini. "We'll take another round," Stan told the waitress. His mind wandered along with his eyes as he stole his own peek at her cleavage.

Greenberg vigorously buttered a piece of bread, frustrated with the friendly conversation and how little substance he'd gotten from Stan. He looked up and said, "You know I need to ask you about this China business. Help me understand—why has this been such a secret? Where'd Ethan Atlas get this idea from, and how could this not have been disclosed? The SEC must be asking about that."

"For starters, the SEC hasn't contacted Loony-Life in any capacity. In fact, I would gladly welcome them—we have nothing to hide. I will admit, it was probably a mistake not to disclose Ethan's charitable giving, but we've acknowledged the mistake and detailed the situation in an SEC filing. The case is closed."

Mildly surprised to hear the SEC hadn't even informally contacted Loony-Life, a recurring thought crossed Greenberg's mind: *I need to do the SEC's job for them.* "Well, not so fast. I gotta hear more about how this decision was made to donate computers in China. I'm not familiar with any American donating to China outside of a natural disaster, yet Ethan Atlas is making millions of dollars in computer donations? This doesn't smell right." Greenberg shook his head.

"What Ethan does with his money is his business. I'd rather he spent more on employee morale, frankly." He winked at Greenberg. "But I think he intended to be generous in a private way. You can't fault him for that."

"Wait a second. *Wait a second.* The problem isn't the donations; it's the fact that these donations were run through the company's income statement without a single disclosure." Greenberg finally sensed an advantage and pressed harder.

"Just saying it sounds ridiculous. How could this happen?"

The waiter arrived with their food, placing a still-sizzling sirloin with a large, cracked-open baked potato in front of Stan, who paused to sip the last of his martini and calmly gather his thoughts. Stan realized he had to reach deeper into his bag of tricks than he'd expected. He changed his confident, jovial tone to a conciliatory one. "Herb, you're asking the exact right question—that's what makes you a great journalist. If I were in your shoes, I'd ask the same. And you're right, even though it was just a pass-through, the lack of disclosure was a mistake. Ethan has been up-front in saying that. But he trusted and re-lied on the judgment of our general counsel. I've already rec-ommended to Ethan and to the board that we dismiss him for offering the opinion not to disclose—it was too big a mistake."

Stan watched Greenberg as the admission sank in. He con-tinued, "My policy is, when there's nothing to hide, just dis-close as much as possible. But Ethan is more private about his affairs. Ultimately, it was a poor decision but an honest over-sight." Stan elaborated on the board of directors and took the opportunity to discuss Carl Icahn's shrewdness and how he would be given a seat on the board.

Only somewhat appeased, Greenberg continued to press, even as he savored the first bite of his dinner. "Look, I know all about Icahn, but I'm looking for the tie-in back to the company with these China donations. Surely there must be a benefit." When Stan didn't respond, Greenberg threw up his arms. "You're going to tell me there's no benefit for the company? Zero?"

Stan leaned in. "I know it's your job to take a cynical view of everything in the corporate world. In truth, that's probably the right way to look at things with all the bullshit that goes on—but not with Loony-Life."

"Perfect corporate citizen, right?" Greenberg sipped his beer.

Stan dismissed him. "Nobody's perfect. To be completely honest, we'll stretch out an accounts payable here and make an aggressive assumption there, but Best Buy does the same shit and even worse."

Greenberg was pleased to get some punches in but found himself unable to break Stan's wall—he had a plausible answer for every question. He'd been misled in the past by smooth-talking management and sensed he was being deceived today as well. His only recourse was to allow Stan to think he had sincerely bought into everything in the hope that he would let his guard down. "I hope it's okay if I look deeper into your Best Buy story. It seems like there's more meat on the bone there."

"Absolutely." With that, Stan began to enjoy his dinner. He cut into his steak with gusto, confident that he, like Vizzini switching the iocane-poisoned goblets, had successfully out-witted his opponent. He added casually, "There are a few other details you'll want to take note of. I'll email you."

Greenberg sipped his beer, then asked with a note of genuine curiosity, as innocently as he could, "Let me ask you, why do you think the short interest in your stock is so high? Why the skepticism of your business?"

"Electronics is a tough industry. There's a lot of price competition," Stan said. "But I think we're misunderstood— therefore the skepticism."

Greenberg prodded, "So many electronics retailers have failed, and you're competing on thin margins with your *loony* prices. You've told me the warranty business is on the decline. How do you maintain the consistent profitability your share-holders have come to expect?"

"Look, I don't worry about the shareholders; I worry about the numbers. Investors may think they own the company, but they don't. They own a ticket, like to a Broadway show. Most are just trading paper—they don't care. They're observers who can leave any time they want. Ethan owns the company."

Greenberg nodded, suspiciously absorbing Stan's view. He wasn't about to argue the notion but found it unduly hostile to shareholders. After a moment, Stan concluded, "But what's important is that shareholders know we have years of success under our belt, and that we use every tool in our power to make the business work."

"Come on! You're basically telling me right there you're using every trick in the book."

"Don't put words in my mouth, Herbie. I said we use every tool in our *power* to make the business work." Stan grinned, in part to deflect the feeling that Greenberg had landed an unexpected blow.

"That's true, you did—but it doesn't sound like words that come from the management of a thriving company. Your stock reflects a thriving company." Greenberg folded his arms.

"You see it in the numbers—our business is strong. It's a tough business, and it takes work, but we're thriving. Do you have any idea the total addressable market in China?"

"Yeah, sure, a billion people. Good one." Greenberg laughed and wiped his mouth with a napkin. Not for a second would he gesture that Stan's notion was persuasive. "And I'm not saying you're not doing well; I'm trying to understand how you get it done." Greenberg slowly finished eating and mentally loaded one last bullet. He had uncovered a change of wording in Loony-Life's latest SEC filing. To avoid letting on that he thought it could be significant, he asked as casually as possible, "Oh, one more thing. Earlier, we were discussing your inventory volume rebates. So, in your filings this year, there was a word changed from last year."

Half chuckling, Stan said, "Come on. Now you're gonna bust my balls over one word?" He reached out to gently slap Greenberg's arm.

"Well, yeah, but hear me out. This is not an insignificant change." Greenberg's emphasis made it clear he'd done his homework and wanted an answer. Stan gestured an invitation to continue. "So, last year, in your 10-K, it was stated that Loony-Life's 'purchase rebates were booked when *received.*'" He stared directly at Stan to judge his reaction. "Then, this year, it was changed to, 'purchase rebates were booked when *earned.*'" Greenberg gave a quizzical look.

Stan instantly knew all the details of the alteration, yet he matched Greenberg's perplexed expression as he thought, *Fucking detective.* He hated that he had no choice but to play dumb. "Wha—what are you referring to, rebates received or earned?"

"Yeah, the wording changed from last year. You know, if the rebates are booked when earned instead of when they're received, it would seem that revenue could be shifted to boost profits in an earlier period. Any thought as to why the wording changed?" Greenberg sat back and enjoyed watching Stan grope for an answer.

As part of the accounting on Loony-Life's fictitious inventory, Stan booked nonexistent volume rebates to pad earnings. Since the company never actually received them, he'd changed the wording to "earned." He slowly nodded. "Yeah, that's interesting. Our CFO must have made that change. I'm sure I know what's going on, though. It's not at all about booking rebates early, it's about booking them right on time." He watched Greenberg's skeptical expression closely. "I'll tell you, our suppliers have been significantly delaying rebate payments. We're just trying to book them in the same period the merchandise was sold. That's what makes sense to us *and* our auditor." A broad smile spread over Stan's face.

Greenberg's expression loosened with a wry smile as he thought, *Gotcha.* He didn't buy Stan's explanation at all. That moment of feigned uncertainty was all he needed to see. But he didn't want to belabor the point, so he lied, "Ah, that makes sense." He quickly pivoted. "So don't forget to send me that info on Best Buy."

They ended the evening amicably. As was Stan's tradition for a last psychological ploy, he picked up the check and re-marked that Greenberg could get the next one.

As he walked away, Stan thought that his tried-and-true plan, which he fondly referred to as "booze, broads, and bullshit," had been a success.

Heading to his car, Greenberg reflected on how he'd en-joyed the dinner and conversation, but his suspicions weren't assuaged. Stan had been strangely convincing, but in his gut, something seemed off. He sensed an unsettling vagueness in Stan's answers.

As Greenberg drove off, he recollected old stories where he had been wrongly skeptical of companies. *Starbucks's store count wasn't saturated when they opened up across the street from one another. Coca-Cola hasn't yet managed viable competition to Monster Beverage. Pre-paid legal expenses actually worked as a business, as did Amazon...*

Instead of focusing on his wins, he thought about when his instincts had failed him—when his past experiences hadn't given him the proper perspective to foretell the future. He accepted that sometimes an idiosyncratic business model succeeded, or a company emerged unscathed from a cloud of accounting suspicion. He'd been wrongly skeptical of many companies in the past, and that made him question whether his present suspicions about issues at Loony-Life were warranted. Still, Greenberg wouldn't be deterred from warning investors to avoid the stock. At the same time, he felt a pang of regret for not ordering the sirloin.

Chapter 22

BUYING TIME

Stan sauntered into Ethan's office the following Monday. They tried to avoid discussing sensitive issues on the phone and hadn't spoken all weekend, so Ethan was curious how Stan had handled dinner with Herb Greenberg.

"Did you get that prick off our back?" Ethan blurted.

Stan sank calmly into a chair, his face poker-player inscrutable. "Well, I'll tell you, the stories are true—he really *is* like a Boy Scout. I took him to the best steakhouse on Long Island and he ordered the *sole*. I thought the poor bastard was going to order milk with it." Stan bellowed a hearty laugh, quickly joined by Ethan. "Look, if he was our audit partner, we'd be fucked—he's very cynical and thorough. But I think we had a truly productive conversation. I had to use my full repertoire of skills." Stan smiled proudly. "But I doubt he'll be giving us any more trouble. I also turned him on to issues at Best Buy, which should throw him off our scent." He flicked his hand as if to shoo away a pestering fly.

Ethan had never doubted that Stan could allay Greenberg's concerns. He quietly marveled at his cousin's ability to outfox their auditor and how he nonchalantly put every inquiry to rest. "Yeah, let him chase that bone around. Sounds perfect."

Perhaps still harboring some self-doubt about how well he

had fully thwarted Greenberg's skepticism, Stan, despite his bravado, quickly changed the subject to avoid elaborating. "Enough wasting time on critics. We need to put our heads together and get the business cranking. The comp sales from last year are pretty aggressive and analysts have been *raising* numbers." Through his glasses, he peered sternly at Ethan to express displeasure. Ethan's confidence when speaking to analysts led them to assume business was stronger than it actually was, making it harder for Stan to finagle numbers. "So, get the marketing engine running. Our prices this summer may need to be the *looniest* of all." Stan chuckled to break the tension as he raised his arms to the sky. His goal was always to keep business as strong as possible to minimize the need for additional accounting gimmickry.

"I'll talk to marketing, but we may have to go with the Black Friday in July shtick." Ethan disliked discussing accounting details. He slowly made a full revolution in his swivel chair before he spoke again. "But listen, let me ask you: Would it be possible for us to take a one-time inventory charge and clear up most of our issue? You know, I'm getting a lot of pushback about the money I'm sending to China. Even Carl Icahn mentioned that maybe I could avoid making the donations, just for cosmetics. I'm thinking we take one $30 million charge, and more than half our problem goes away."

Stan started shaking his head even before Ethan finished. "That's the one thing we can't do. I know all these companies do these fuckin' one-time charges, and Wall Street lets them get away with it, but we can't."

Ethan stood up and leaned forward on his desk to press his case. "Do you realize any amount you write off will save me from going into my own pocket? We're a billion-dollar company; even a $20 million charge would help me. It would help us!"

"It's not even a consideration." Stan spoke calmly but firmly to put this idea to rest straightaway. He was beginning to worry the pressure of the scheme was weighing on Ethan. "First, Marwick thinks we have room to write off some inventory but not a big new charge. Second, I told Greenberg that we have price protection, meaning we won't take *any* hit from selling our products cheaper—you know, that we could blow out inventory without any charge. Third, we have too huge a gap between actual and bullshit inventory. Already a third of it is sitting in empty boxes in Red Bank. It'll send up red flags all over the place. If Marwick rechecks the audit, they could find the gaps in their work." Stan glared at Ethan, tempted to ask, *Are we clear?*

Like he read Stan's mind, Ethan sighed and said, "I see. I see. But if you can think of anything other than me plugging this hole with tens of millions of my own money, it would really help."

"Listen, Ethan, you don't have to put money back into the company. In fact, it would be far wiser if you didn't—we have better alternatives. We'll ride this thing out as long as possible, maybe indefinitely."

"Maybe indefinitely?" Ethan slammed his hand down. "No. I want this thing fixed—*permanently.*"

"I can do that," Stan responded quickly. "That's what I'm trying to explain; we have good alternatives. So, I think the best way to reverse the inventory build, without you putting in money, is to overstate the cost of goods sold—it'll put a hatchet to our profit margin, but that'll be Wall Street's problem."

"No, no way. That would make it *my* problem. We need to keep cranking out the profits." Ethan weighed the investor scrutiny if the stock tumbled precipitously on earnings issues. "Okay, for now, let's keep working our plan. I'd love for sales to pick up, though." His mercurial demeanor turned. "We'll be fine. You're right, gotta pick up the marketing—that's the way to go. Black Friday in July it is. I'll get a memo out to the employees." He stood and slid his phone into his pocket. "I'm headed for a run. I'll come up with some other sales ideas."

Ethan had refined his natural marketing prowess to create sales strategies while running on a treadmill. As he jogged, he could compartmentalize his thoughts and focus without distraction. Ideas about a motivational memo to employees took shape: *We're being attacked since we aim to be number one. When one aspires to be the leader in an industry, everyone tries to bring you down. Donating computers is part of my mission to help people worldwide access technology. Let's throw pie in the face of all the naysayers on Wall Street and the media who keep insisting Loony-Life can't churn out profit growth!*

More ideas swirled while he glided on a treadmill in the corporate gym. As Herb Greenberg's segment started on CNBC, Ethan paused his music to listen. With a hasty slap on the emergency stop, he stood agape as Greenberg railed about Loony-Life's accounting, the logic of Ethan's computer donations, and his exasperation with the SEC for not looking into these issues.

Ethan scowled at the TV, furious when Greenberg said, "I spoke directly with management and was unconvinced by their evasive answers."

Ethan couldn't fathom how Stan had failed to quell Greenberg's attacks. He trusted Stan entirely. He'd even confided a marital indiscretion to him, and Stan had been brilliant at covering for him with his wife. Yet, for the first time, he had an inkling of doubt. He murmured, "Fuckin' son of a bitch," not even sure if he was referring to Stan or Greenberg. "We will never engage with critics again."

He felt the pressure to escape from the mounting

scrutiny—to work quickly to clean up the inventory and ac-counting in case the SEC investigated. They desperately need-ed to buy time to fix things and prove the naysayers wrong. At once, his sixth epiphany hit him hard: Under the glare of the financial media, unwinding the sham accounting would be more challenging than creating the ruse to begin with.

Chapter 23

DINNER BEFORE DINNERSTEIN

Aviva and Brandon had only met in person once before, at a book signing event for one of her colleagues at *Barron's*. An instant professional connection had sparked.

In the center of Dos Caminos, a bustling Mexican restaurant in Midtown, Brandon was one margarita down as he waited at the bar. Since they first met, he and Aviva had spoken numerous times on the phone and through email about various companies and market events. When she walked in, wearing a sleeveless black dress, they chose a table in a quiet corner, both feeling an immediate sense of kinship.

Although he was still distressed over his Loony-Life loss, Brandon intended to keep the conversation light and upbeat. He started with the most banal of questions. "So, how'd you get into journalism?"

Aviva spoke of her time at the Columbia School of Journalism, including her notable professors, Sylvia Nasar and James Stewart.

Upon hearing Stewart's name, Brandon's eyes lit up. "Jim Stewart is a legend. *Den of Thieves* was literally the first Wall Street book I ever read—well, perhaps the first was *Liar's Poker*—but I found it fascinating."

"Jim's an amazing storyteller and truly inspirational." Aviva looked upward, then back at Brandon. "His course taught me how to craft a story. He teaches the importance of a central character and how to get that character to confide in you. But you'd be surprised to learn that Jim thinks the best stories are in corporate filings and financial statements."

"I'm impressed he taught his students to examine filings. I have to say, I've been following your writing at *Barron's*, and it looks like you've put that knowledge to good use."

Aviva smiled. "I've learned so much at *Barron's*—it's been quite an experience. The newsroom is eye-opening. I've partnered with Cliff Ludwig on a few of his pieces, and he's taught me a lot."

"Ludwig's articles are great," Brandon said. "He pulls no punches." Even though he knew little about journalism, he couldn't resist passing along a tidbit of advice. "You'll need the perspective that comes from *Den of Thieves*, you know, to be properly cynical about the Milkens and Boeskys out there. Wall Street seems to attract people who put money-making ahead of ethics. Too many ways to abuse the system..."

His voice trailed off as Aviva gestured dismissively. "Oh, don't worry about me. Even if I hadn't experienced it at *Barron's*, I've read everything written by Bethany McLean and Gretchen Morgenson, so I'm well briefed on the murky underbelly of Wall Street." Brandon nodded as Aviva continued, "You can't read Bethany's book on Enron without questioning corporate hype and seeing Wall Street firms as unscrupulous, fee-grubbing enablers." She tilted her head and flashed a toothy smile to soften her harsh words.

With mild astonishment, Brandon shook his head. "I can see I'm preaching to the choir here." Her mention of Enron brought back decade-old memories he was eager to share. "Enron was one for the ages. I heard Chanos's short call on the stock, at about $60, *in person*. Although his thesis was amazing, I didn't pull the trigger to short any and it went down so fast I thought I'd missed it." He rubbed his forehead. "I'm still not sure what I was thinking. I was too inexperienced to go against the Wall Street machine—I couldn't get over their soaring revenues and universal analyst praise. I also avoid companies I don't understand, and I never could get my arms around Enron. Still, it feels totally inexcusable that I didn't short any." Smiling broadly, he mused, "But in the end, I did take the last puff of the cigar on the short side."

When Aviva gave him an inquiring look, he continued excitedly, eager to relive that victory. "Days before bankruptcy, Enron was still investment grade—which sounds unimaginable. So, if their credit rating gets downgraded to junk, it's well-established that it triggers a huge cash payment, many billions they don't have. *This* I understood. So, with the stock at three bucks and sinking, there's market tension. Everyone's wondering, can it be saved somehow, or will S&P strike a deathblow with a debt downgrade?" Brandon paused. "Sorry, I know this story is like the Titanic. You already know what happens."

"Iceberg ahead!" she joked. "Or should I say, downgrade?"

"Exactly," Brandon affirmed with a chuckle. "So anyway, in the middle of the day—boom—S&P downgrades *six notches*, deep into junk. Deathblow. The stock gaps lower and is halted for an imbalance on the NYSE, but it's still trading everywhere else. So, on our trading desk, we're still able to short a huge amount of shares off-exchange on the third market. The last puff." He put his hands together. "The stock opens back up on the NYSE and quickly trades below a dollar. It closed, I think, around 60 cents."

As he narrated, Aviva attacked her dinner with delighted vengeance, sipping on a glass of sauvignon blanc. "That sounds unbelievable. The off-exchange trading seems puzzling."

Brandon took a deep breath and considered how to explain

it. "True, the venerable New York Stock Exchange had some systemic flaws. Their market structure was especially inefficient and fragmented long after Nasdaq got it right. We were still shorting Enron up top at the offer, around two dollars"—he held one hand high as he dropped his other hand, palm up, on the table—"while the stock was gapped way lower on the NYSE, like at a dollar. Basically, we could sell as many as we wanted, on the uptick, no less. It was crazy."

"I knew the rating agencies had botched the job, but the NYSE trading structure sounds like it was entirely unfair." She spoke in the tone of someone who wanted to right every wrong, even one from over ten years ago. "Uh, say, would you like to try my quesadilla? You haven't touched your food."

"Yeah, I'll get to it. Sorry, I get carried away with the stories." He grabbed a chip and scooped up some salsa. "But, yes, the NYSE had some deep flaws in their quest to maintain market share as the times were a-changin'. It's hard to explain. Of course, there's always some company with a racket going. Speaking of which..." Brandon trailed off again with a pointed look at Aviva, who groaned.

"Loony-Life," she said with a sigh. "We're in a meat grinder there."

"I wish I was only in a meat grinder with that stock. I got chewed up, spit out, and fed to the sharks for breakfast—straight from hero to zero." He checked himself and took a sip of his second margarita. Despite feeling somewhat betrayed by *Barron's*, letting on to this fact had not been his intention. "I'm no longer involved, so the damage is over."

"I saw the stock went on a crazy ride," Aviva added smoothly, not wanting to admit the guilt she felt for how the story had gone off the rails.

He grimaced slightly. Although his angst had been steadily fading, her words brought the loss back into sharp relief and the "crazy ride" he'd taken flashed through his head. Brandon coughed to mask his anxiety. "Yeah, it was crazy." As he drained the last of his drink, he recounted his trading of Loony-Life to Aviva, who looked on with sympathy.

There were still too many unanswered questions for Brandon not to fish for information. How *Barron's* could have gotten the donation story wrong was baffling, but he didn't want to risk sounding confrontational. "Where do you guys stand now?"

"We're still digging. We have a lot of unanswered questions." She leaned forward, circling a finger around her wine glass. "Tell me what you think about this: Loony-Life has a computer trade-in program, and those computers get shipped to China. Last year, their 10-K filing reported they'd spent $1.5 million recycling electronics. All their competitors use free electronics recycling from the major PC vendors. Seems strange, no?"

"Whoa," he said, blown away. "That's gotta be it. They're using the trade-ins. Those are the computers he's donating, not new ones." His mind raced with an urge to get back on the desk in the morning and re-short the stock. He took a deep breath to refocus on the conversation. "Sorry, I tend to make snap judgments—that's from trading stocks—but either way, that sounds highly incriminating." He peered wide-eyed at Aviva, waiting for agreement.

Instead, Aviva put a hand forward to encourage Brandon to take the information more thoughtfully. "Well, we're not so sure; there could be some strategic rationale. And especially after we didn't get the story one hundred percent right the first time, we can't draw unsupported conclusions in print. However, it is something we suspect is a possibility. Not much we can do with our suspicions right now, but I think at some point we may be able to figure out an avenue. Do you have any thoughts?" She swept a rogue curl off her face and tucked it behind her ear, uncovering the doubt in her eyes.

"Well, you're far more circumspect than I am," Brandon said, racking his brain. "All I can think of are serial numbers, or maybe something else to track the computers."

Aviva's eyes lit up. "That's what I thought, too. I want to know where those things go. Cliff is a little skeptical that finding out where the computers end up would implicate the CEO in a scheme, but the company said they're being scrapped and recycled." She pondered for a moment. "Have you ever heard of Roddy Boyd?"

"That sounds like a name I would remember. I'm not familiar with him."

"He's a journalist who recently started a non-profit to investigate financial misdeeds. Bethany McLean is on the board." Imagining if she too could hold executives accountable, Aviva added wistfully, "Just sounds cool to have a dedicated entity to try to ensure corporate accountability. At *Barron's*, I can barely get any funds to explore what's going on with Loony-Life in China."

She leaned back in her chair, put down her wine glass, and dabbed her lips with a napkin.

Brandon's mind wandered to the difficulties of gathering information from China. As quickly as he'd considered re-shorting Loony-Life's stock, the fleeting notion had gone. He'd need more information, and with greater detail and certainty, before he could reengage in a short position. "China is too opaque for me. Jim Chanos may be the only one I know with an edge there." Even as he casually said "Jim Chanos," he realized how perfect passing along to him the recycling tidbit would be. After two margaritas, he had to focus harder on the possible implications of telling Aviva about his open line to Chanos.

Chanos thrived on small, potentially incriminating details in SEC filings. Although he had never mentioned being short Loony-Life, Brandon suspected he was involved. Perhaps this was an opportunity to engage in a dialogue on the issue.

With his eyes refocusing from the ceiling, he said, "Let me ask you; I know Chanos distantly, but he knows who I am." Just a little bit, he indicated by squinting and pinching a tiny gap between his thumb and forefinger. "Can I mention the China recycling expense to him to see if he has any insight on the situation?" He still wasn't positive he'd mention it, but he needed a green light.

"I think that's fair game. I found the recycling charge in their SEC filings, so it's public information. We're kind of in a quandary ourselves. We've exposed some issues at the company, but for now we're still looking for a breakthrough in order to do more reporting." Aviva smiled and grabbed her wine glass. "If he has any insight, let me know—I'd certainly love to chat with him."

"Definitely will. I guess I'd like to find a good reason to short the stock again, so any insight could help," Brandon said. "Obviously, another catalyst would be an SEC investigation, but who knows if that will happen. I would say, just from a trading standpoint, the SEC should investigate the way Icahn scooped up stock on the Monday after your article. He said he spoke with the CEO—he must have known an announcement was coming. Seems like he had some inside info. I'm probably the only one who cares, though."

"Well, it's not like Icahn spoke with the CEO, who told him he was about to make a hostile takeover bid for another company, then ran out and bought a bunch of stock and options on the target company," Aviva said frankly.

"Well, I can't argue with that. It probably wasn't a big deal, just part of the game. It still irks me." Brandon resigned himself to feeling tormented by Icahn's actions.

Every year around this time, he had a notion to quit drinking and train to run the New York City Marathon. It had been on his mind lately, since the intense exercise would be the perfect remedy to clear his stressed mind. As he ordered his third drink, he sensed his marathon aspirations, and the charity for which he'd like to raise money, would be put off for yet another year.

"Are there any other stock ideas you're working on?" Aviva asked.

Relieved by the change of conversation, Brandon chuckled. "I like the way you always think like a reporter."

"It's almost as if I went into journalism for a reason." Aviva winked.

"I wish I had more going on, but unfortunately for now I'm laying low, waiting for a perfect idea to set up. Still licking my wounds from Loony-Life." He winced at the memory and quickly said, "I've still been watching Facebook closely. Trading into the $25s today was such a beat-down—just shows how overhyped the IPO was. You had the story nailed so perfectly."

"Thank you." Aviva blushed slightly. "Cliff never bought into the hype. And I interviewed Dan Niles, who had a helpful angle." Aviva was tempted to mention his off-the-record trading call that he would short Facebook, but instead merely said, "He reinforced the valuation concerns we had."

"I don't doubt it," Brandon added sincerely. "He used to be one of the top tech analysts."

"Ah, I forgot he came from the sell side. He seems to have transitioned well to managing money for a hedge fund."

"Well, he has an edge: Back in the nineties, his research made him the axe in the semiconductor sector. I still remember some of his midday calls that made the whole group plummet.

Back then, I think it was even more rare for analysts to make negative calls, so his caution was widely followed."

Aviva looked suspicious. "Even more rare?"

"Yeah, I know, sounds impossible." Brandon laughed. "But remember, this was pre-Reg FD, which wasn't initiated until 2000. Analysts were sucking up more to management for information, and they usually had to stay positive to get it."

"That's the fair disclosure regulation, right?" Brandon nodded as she continued, "It must have considerably changed the disclosure dynamic."

"It sure did. So, this is funny: Before Reg FD, it was like the Wild West. Favored analysts would get inside info from CFOs about how business was going—with whispers if their numbers were too high or too low. Stocks would make huge moves when analysts leaked this stuff out. The clients at these analysts' firms would get the first call and regularly clean up from that sort of information."

"Sounds too easy." Aviva shook her head.

"It was, and all totally legal. Now, you can imagine how important the relationship between analysts and corporate management was back then. If you were negative about their company, management wouldn't even take your call. Of course, it was a two-way street. Corporate management also wanted to curry favor with analysts to get their stocks more highly recommended. That's yet another thing to admire about Steve Jobs: He couldn't care less what analysts thought about Apple. He was head-down, focusing on great products and avoiding Wall Street's BS—including no buybacks and always completely sandbagging guidance." Brandon had a sullen, faraway look; Steve Jobs's passing seven months earlier still felt fresh. He subconsciously slipped his hand into his pocket and clasped his iPhone. With a quiet sigh, he said, "But I digress."

"Jobs was brilliant," Aviva said. "He will be missed. Even

how he dealt with Wall Street was impressive. Cliff thinks Apple's a buy, even now. Part of his thesis is that they may initiate a big stock buyback."

"Possibly. Jobs had a depression-era mentality about hoarding cash."

"Didn't they once need a bailout from Microsoft?" Aviva asked rhetorically as Brandon nodded. She added, "That would probably do it."

"Good point. But Ludwig's right, probably time to loosen the purse strings. There've been calls for a buyback. Pundits have always loved giving advice to Apple about how to run their business."

"I guess we'll see." Aviva changed gears. "Not to continually bring up a certain electronics company, but Loony-Life is taking a much different track by loading up on debt. And their CFO is a former analyst—I'm inclined to think that's another red flag."

Brandon sat up straight. "Oh, it probably is. The analysts see a former colleague getting paid handsomely as CFO in a job they may like, so, just more incentive to curry favor with the company." He continued, "It's the same strategy on Wall Street anyway—the idea that analysts would rather be friends than adversaries with management has carried over. Even if they're no longer privately getting material nonpublic information, analysts deem constructive communication with management to be important."

"Now you sound like Cliff. He's always preached about how analysts are compromised. Where they ought to be working for investors, instead they're cozying up to corporate management while their firms look for investment banking business. But your story brings some additional perspective to the issue," said Aviva sincerely.

Brandon paused to absorb that she compared him to Cliff

Ludwig, whom he admired. "Obviously, Reg FD made complete sense to level the playing field, but the big players made so much money from those early calls from analysts that, of course, they fought tooth and nail against it. Oh, the howling." He rolled his eyes and shook his head incredulously.

Aviva finished the last of her wine and checked her watch while Brandon droned on. "You wouldn't believe the fight over Reg FD from all the entrenched players on Wall Street who didn't want to play by the new rules. It was like when bar owners and smokers complained about Mayor Bloomberg outlawing smoking indoors. But Arthur Levitt, the SEC Chairman under Clinton, pushed Reg FD through. In my opinion, he was the last SEC Chairman to confront Wall Street rather than kowtow to them."

"Very interesting. Um, though I must have missed the punchline there." Aviva squinted slightly and enjoyed his lighthearted smile.

"Ouch. In my head, I was thinking that story was funny because the things that used to happen before Reg FD were kind of a joke, but clearly not the amusing kind. Sorry 'bout that." They both grinned as they got up to leave.

"Because you're taking me to see Simone Dinnerstein perform, I'll forgive you."

Seated in the Miller Theatre, Brandon and Aviva listened to the magical piano performance of Simone Dinnerstein. Instead of enjoying a relaxing, meditative experience, however, his mind wandered back to Loony-Life. How would he present the information to Chanos? Could he impress him enough to get a job offer? His mind flashed with the pros and cons of re-shorting the stock, as well as thoughts of the money already lost and how much more he could afford to lose. This line of thinking triggered a rumble of stress in the pit of his stomach, and it didn't help that he had downed three drinks with little food.

Unsettled as he heard music without listening to it, Brandon took a deep breath. As he cleared his mind, he acknowledged that the battle of Loony-Life had been lost but the war would go on. Dinnerstein's frenetic keystrokes of Bach's Goldberg Variations filled his brain. Aviva seemed fully immersed in the music. The glow on her face was contagious. In that instant of serenity, he half-smiled and closed his eyes to enjoy the music. For the first time in weeks, he felt at peace.

Chapter 24

WHEN OPPORTUNITY KNOCKS...

As Brandon stepped into the office on Monday morning, Bud cut off his path to the trading desk and asked to speak privately. Brandon opened his ear to the desk to probe if anything market-related was being discussed but only heard carping about the Yankees and CNBC.

"This mother-fuckin' guy is still saying 'price is truth,'" he heard Goldie deride, pointing with both hands at a TV. "Anyone know this dude's email? He blocked me on Twitter."

The rest of the desk seemed preoccupied with sports talk, so Brandon figured there was no urgent need to power up his computer. He walked to the conference room and closed the door as Bud sat with folded hands, waiting patiently like an obedient pup. His slight grin reassured Brandon bad news wasn't imminent.

Brandon sat down. "Those guys will never get over A-Rod's contract. I mean, jeez, let it go already."

"Yeah, I know." Bud's deep voice offset his boyish face. "Every time he has a bad game, they—"

"So, what's up?" Brandon eyed him impatiently, thinking about all the morning news and research yet to be read.

Bud seemed unsure where to begin. He gazed out the window a moment, then at his hands, then finally over to Brandon.

"First, I want you to know how much I appreciate your help in teaching me about the business. I can't tell you how much more I know now than when I first walked in the door."

"I've taught a lot of people about the markets," Brandon cut in. "Trust me, it doesn't necessarily help to make it as a trader. In fact, I don't have a formula for success any better than what you can pick up from reading *Reminiscences of a Stock Operator*. But keep trying to learn—there are a million ways to get it done, and everyone on the desk does it differently. And although we're working together on the same team, trading is every man for himself." He paused. "One day, you may even think you've got it *all* figured out. Next day, your confidence will be shot, and you may wonder if you'll make it at all."

"Oh, understood. So..." Bud fidgeted. "I feel bad about the money you lost on the Loony-Life trade."

Brandon wasn't interested in rehashing his trading loss. "It happens. I pigged out and got slaughtered." His eyes drilled a hole through Bud's head. "It shows that no matter what you think you know, the market may have a different opinion."

Bud fiddled with his shirt buttons. "Yeah, well, I have an idea for you to make up some of the loss." He kept a steady eye on Brandon.

Brandon was skeptical, his mind somewhere else, but he acknowledged slowly, "Okay, what's your idea?"

"Well, my best friend's father is the lead researcher for Biophaser," Bud revealed proudly. "They have a drug for hep B in Phase 3 trials, and I got some good intel on how the trials are going."

Brandon perceived the rookie was well-intentioned, and he had often been impressed with Bud's knowledge of biotech. Still, he responded dismissively, "I appreciate the idea, but the last time I thought I knew something, it cost me almost half a mil. Anyway, biotech isn't my thing. Even if I had info on the results, I couldn't interpret the efficacy or even grasp how the market would react." He rocked forward in his chair to indicate the conversation was at an end.

Bud looked Brandon straight in the eye. "You're missing what I'm saying. I have the results and the efficacy. I can give them to you before they're released."

In Brandon's career, he'd never had access to inside information, yet he often wondered where his ethics would fall if he ever learned of any. He rocked back in his chair. "Hmm, that's interesting. The good news is that it's fine to possess inside information—it's only when you act on it in the market that it becomes illegal." Brandon paused while he rubbed the stubble on his chin. He sensed Bud genuinely wanted to help.

"Let me put it like this." Brandon looked out the window to gather his thoughts. "I've been happily married for 15 years. Every day I live with a clear conscience that I've been faithful to my wife. Yet in 15 years, another woman has never thrown herself at me, so I've never had to deal with the ethical dilemma of cheating. The same is true for inside information—I've never had the opportunity to test myself, because I've never had inside info. Naturally, I've given some thought to how I'd handle these situations in the unlikely event they occur." Brandon smiled broadly. "Especially the 'woman throwing herself at me' scenario." They both laughed.

"I completely understand." Bud's face went stern again. "My intention wasn't to put you in any sort of ethical dilemma. I was just looking to help someone that has helped me."

Brandon hadn't decided what course to take, but he realized he'd never let Bud know if he traded on the information. "Got it. You might as well tell me. I'm just curious whether your info is reliable. There's no chance I'll put on a trade, though—it's too risky."

Bud wasn't a person who thoughtfully analyzed the

implications of passing along inside information. He jumped at the chance to show off the info he'd gathered. "What I've heard is that Biophaser's hep B drug is *one hundred percent* effective at eliminating the virus and safer than anything else on the market. It will definitely get FDA approval."

Brandon clapped his hands together and shrugged. "Like I said, biotech isn't my forte, but I'll keep an eye out for the news." As he spoke, he had a fleeting notion of how to utilize the information for his benefit without creating any suspicion. Either way, he never expected to discuss the stock or this idea again with Bud.

Once Brandon and Bud returned to the desk, Goldie presented the morning meeting on markets being ruled by assumptions—how revisions in assumptions changed underlying stock prices. "How does a stock go up or down 20% in one day? Assumptions. Like it or not, *stocks* move, and *money* moves, every day on changes in assumptions. One change in a data point could alter an analyst's entire model. The market doesn't give a fuck about what people were thinking yesterday. You need to understand what people today are thinking about tomorrow. Plain and simple."

To Brandon, this diatribe sounded a bit too much like a lecture on Loony-Life. He didn't want to sound defensive by inferring too much. Still, he considered interjecting how stocks occasionally have a trading dynamic all to themselves regardless of new assumptions, such as when an investor buys a huge new stake.

At that moment, Jim Chanos appeared on CNBC to publicly declare his short position in Loony-Life. In unison, the traders turned their attention to the various TV screens to hear him explain how buyers of Loony-Life's stock must be ignoring the risks of the company's aggressive accounting.

"Oh, that's right in Icahn's face!" Sneaks said.

In his usual uncompromising manner, Chanos outlined his bear case. He posited that if the earnings were stripped of the overlooked accounting trickery, they'd be lucky to earn $2 per share. The stock shouldn't be treated like a growth company, he argued, given their lack of domestic growth, and due to the competitive issues with electronics retailers, a P/E above 15 was too rich. He suggested a steep pullback in the stock from its current price of $65. "You also have to question their dealings in China," Chanos added. "We've never seen anything quite like it." Ultimately, he warned that their binge in the debt market and weak cash flow could possibly lead to a bankruptcy filing.

Brandon sat silently, unsurprised that Chanos was short. As the desk buzzed about the interview, Brandon thought the trade dynamic didn't necessarily change. As the most respected short seller on Wall Street, Chanos added credibility and gravitas to the bear case, yet he had a similar story to Herb Greenberg's, which was not unlike the one reported in *Barron's*. Why should Chanos have an effect the others didn't? Unable to pull the trigger, Brandon watched painfully as the stock dropped several points in pre-market trading.

In a swift counterpunch to Chanos, Carl Icahn discussed his long position in Loony-Life during a midday CNBC interview with Scott Wapner. Much like he did in his Bloomberg interview, Icahn explained, in his off-the-cuff manner, how the stock was unfairly under attack from the media and hedge fund short sellers.

Again, Brandon studied him closely for clues to his unanswered questions. Was Icahn acting as a contrarian on principle? Or did he have a real edge in understanding the accounting? Did he genuinely believe in holding a long-term position?

When challenged with Chanos's bearish take on Loony-Life,

Icahn replied, "Look, I've known Chanos for years. Sure, I respect him, but I've been on the other side of his short ideas throughout my career, and I've made fortunes betting against him." He exhaled a slight chuckle. "You know, I don't mean this in a derogatory way, but I don't see Chanos on the Forbes 400 list." It was a moment of hubris only a billionaire with a five-decade track record of success could have pulled off.

The guys on the trading desk sat stunned as Mitch jumped up toward a TV. "Ho! Icahn throws down the gauntlet. Sounds like he's not buying Chanos's bear case." He cackled. "Break out the popcorn and beer—this should be a good one."

Wapner nimbly countered Icahn, "Chanos, in fairness, has done pretty damn well for himself. Wouldn't you say, Carl?"

Icahn agreed, yet asserted, "I didn't hear anything new from him." With the high short interest, he threatened anyone on the short side. "Look, this stock could have the mother of all short squeezes."

Sneaks spoke as if personally offended. "Icahn's a billionaire—he can say whatever the fuck he wants—but that was still a shitty thing to say about Chanos. I so badly hope he takes a bath on this stock."

Goldie nodded. "He must be sporting quite the pair to accompany being that big a dick." He stared at Brandon. "You still want to just spectate on this one?"

Without a smoking gun, Brandon knew he couldn't stomach the battle. *"Possible bankruptcy" from Chanos or "mother of all short squeezes" from Icahn—I'll pass, thanks.* The middle of a dogfight between two hedge fund titans was the last place he wanted to be. Icahn's mere mention of a short squeeze left him queasy. He kept to himself that his confidence was shaken; he wanted to take only the most careful and calculated risks to regain his footing. "I don't feel like I have an edge to get involved again, to tell you the truth." In a poorly imitated Australian accent, he adapted a line from the movie *Wall Street*: "Ya know, mate, Icahn could buy Chanos six times over. He could take this company private himself just to *burn* Chanos's ass." He added, "So I doubt I'll reengage in the position, not yet at least. But clearly, I'm rooting for Chanos."

Before Chanos declared his short position, Brandon had wavered on whether to write him about Loony-Life; now he quickly finished and sent him an email. He concisely explained Aviva's discovery on the cost of recycling computers in China, hoping Chanos's China connections would enable him to sort through the theory that Ethan Atlas had donated refurbished computers.

Impatient for a reply, Brandon perched on the edge of his seat for the rest of the day. At a minimum, he believed the premise deserved a response from Chanos as a compelling avenue to explore. When a reply arrived later that afternoon, Brandon was suffused with nervous excitement. Unlike Chanos's previous responses, this one included a number and an invitation to call.

Chapter 25

REGRETS, I'VE HAD A FEW

Brandon paced the conference room as he considered how to start his conversation with Chanos. He stopped to stare at a corridor of buildings up Park Avenue to clear his mind. He tried to suppress his wishful thoughts that this might lead to a job interview. After years of letters and dreams, he vacillated between believing the idea was ridiculous and hoping that maybe it wasn't so crazy after all. When the flutters in his stomach finally quieted, Brandon phoned his industry hero.

Brandon held his breath as he dialed. "Hi. This is Brandon Shuster calling for Jim Chanos." An assistant put him on hold.

"Hi, Brandon, this is Jim *Chaos*; I mean *Chanos*." A hearty laugh erupted from Brandon's phone.

He exhaled with nervous relief to find Chanos recalled his old email. "Nice to speak with you. I'm glad you found the chaos thing amusing. I thought the connection was kind of apropos, in a way. But Icahn's take on you today was not too funny."

Chanos let out a lighthearted snort, clearly not offended by Icahn's banter. "Well, let's just say it's a two-way street with Carl. We've both been in the business for a long time. Keep in mind, I have no obligation to disclose my short positions, and I've been on the right side of several of his"—he paused mid-sentence to clear his throat before continuing—"less than blockbuster ideas."

Brandon suppressed a chuckle at the jab directed at one of Icahn's most infamous failures. "I hear that. His track record is certainly not flawless. Personally, I think he's *way* out on a limb with Loony-Life."

"Well, let's discuss that," Chanos began smoothly. "Their accounting is riddled with red flags, the balance sheet is deteriorating, the business is highly competitive, and the stock is trading at an aggressive valuation. To say nothing of the CEO running undisclosed charitable donations through the income statement, which may fall under the category of legal fraud with the intent to deceive. So, yeah, I'd agree that Carl is out on a limb." He paused. "I'm intrigued by your theory on the recycling expense related to the donated computers."

Brandon looked at his fingers shaking, and tried to relax. Too nervous to focus, he overlooked his plan to explain that it was Aviva's detective work. "It does seem possible that the donated computers are sourced from computers redeemed here. I thought your China knowledge could be of assistance..."

"Well, it's an angle we might pursue. I can check with some on-the-ground contacts. Frankly, even without direct evidence, the fact that there was no disclosure at all leads us to believe something untoward is happening in China. I'll tell you, even for those of us who've studied China for years, it's still a black box in many respects. Fortunately, there is a raft of other problematic accounting at Loony-Life, most of which has been outlined in the media. I think Herb Greenberg did an exceptional job of laying out the issues."

Brandon hesitated to interrupt, but he couldn't contain his curiosity. "Why did you decide to go public with your short position, since it was kind of out there already? The thesis, that is." He winced as he stumbled over his words.

"Well, for a few reasons." Chanos's calm tone made Brandon wonder if the man could ever get flustered. "First, I'd mention that *who* is long the stock—in this case, Carl Icahn—played no part in our decision to disclose our short position. The media makes a big deal over that kind of stuff, because they'd rather discuss *who* is long and short rather than *why*. It's typical lazy journalism."

"Yup, agreed."

Chanos continued, "That being said, disclosing our short position serves two purposes for us. I have come to realize that when short selling is anonymous, it's far easier to vilify and attack, so I strive to put a face to the investment thesis. When our short is explained—whether people agree with it or not— at least they understand it, and it adds to the debate. I would note that European hedge funds outside the UK stay cloaked in anonymity, *never* go on the record, and consequently get heavily regulated."

"Wow, I didn't realize that."

"So lastly, I can admit that disclosing our position and being part of the conversation is also a bit of marketing. Anyone who sniffs and claims they don't have to market themselves hasn't been managing money long. I would hasten to add that we have a high degree of confidence in our Loony-Life research."

"That definitely makes sense." Brandon smiled, impressed to receive such a detailed and candid answer.

"Look, Brandon, I wanted to speak with you to thank you for passing along your latest thoughts on Loony-Life—it's an avenue of interest that we'll attempt to uncover." Chanos sounded like he had conveyed the reason for the conversation.

"Sounds good. One more stock idea?" Brandon asked, compelled to discuss stocks while he had the opportunity.

"Sure."

Brandon hadn't prepared for this, but thought he could

wing a discussion on one stock, at least. Focusing on a company finally calmed Brandon's nerves. "*Barron's* has been skeptical of Facebook's valuation, and I have to second their opinion. I don't see how Facebook doesn't go the way of MySpace when people flock to the next hot website. I know it just came public, but the valuation is sky-high, and their prospects seem so uncertain."

There was no pause in Chanos's response for even the pretense of consideration for the idea. "We've looked at it. However, it's not in our wheelhouse at this stage. We don't often short stocks just because they're expensive, and we're generally reluctant to short open-ended growth stories, a category Facebook currently occupies. Our bread-and-butter short ideas are ones where a company tries to hide things going wrong through aggressive accounting or acquisitions. But thanks for the thought."

Brandon's anxiety swelled. *Would it be appropriate to ask Chanos about a job opening*? He couldn't think quickly enough to assess, so he decided to take a swing. "Do you have another minute? I wanted to ask you one more thing."

"Sure, I have a minute."

After feeling chided for his short idea, Brandon was flustered and unsure of how to begin. With a nervous stammer, he explained how he had always been a trader but had done his own research and thought he might be better suited to analysis than trading. After an uneasy prelude, in which he knew he had done a terrible job selling himself, Brandon took a deep breath and found some equanimity. "Does your fund have any current employment opportunities?" He cringed in preparation before Chanos could utter a reply.

Chanos sounded unsurprised by the request. "Well, your detective work on Loony-Life has been good."

Brandon's mouth suddenly parched. He didn't intend to

leave Chanos thinking he had found the recycling expense. At some point, Aviva would surely contact him. "Um, I should tell you, the recycling discovery was made by my friend at *Barron's*, Aviva Goddard. We've been discussing the company since before their article was printed."

"That's good to know. Well, what I'd say is we've done an excellent job of retaining our analysts by treating them well, and currently there are no openings. Our analysts usually stay with us for 10 to 15 years, so there's little turnover. I'd add that in our experience, traders don't transition well into analysts and vice versa. However, we'd always consider if an opening arises."

Brandon leaned his head back and closed his eyes. He felt the brush-off. It was a sharp stab of disappointment. There was no basis to argue the point; stories of analysts who failed in their foray of managing money in the hedge fund world were common. Although he didn't know of any trader who'd attempted to become an analyst, he regarded Chanos too highly to dispute his claim. He opened his eyes and tried to sound as polite as possible. "Thank you, I appreciate it. Please let me know if you find anything interesting in China."

As the conversation ended, time slowed to a crawl. Brandon sat in the conference room, regret filling his mind. *Where was the conversation headed if I hadn't told Chanos about Aviva? Really doesn't matter, does it?* He lamented that his first chat with Chanos ended the way it did and regretted hoping his years of letter-writing might pay off with a job. He remembered being told in college, "It's the things you *don't* do in life you regret the most," but now he seriously questioned that philosophy.

Traders don't transition well into analysts. These words resonated in his head. His worst professional fear—no viable backup plan to being a trader—was now palpable. The skills he had weren't transferable within the industry, and they were utterly useless outside of Wall Street. His vision to advance to the more cerebral challenge of research and analysis had been snuffed in the blink of an eye. He felt physically ill.

The sound of four TV screens tuned to CNBC echoed off the walls of the empty trading room as Brandon walked back to his desk. The weight of a crushed goal started to sink in. Gloomily, he pondered an indefinite life as a trader, a career he both loved and despised. In an eat-what-you-kill profession, the lean periods were difficult, especially when they endured for long stretches. And with the cosmic force of algorithmic trading hurtling toward them, there was also the looming concern that they were a desk of dinosaurs destined for extinction.

In a spiral of self-loathing, Brandon furtively looked over his shoulder as he checked out a Bloomberg terminal to examine Biophaser.

Goldie, at times, liked to bring up hypothetical scenarios of how not to get caught while using inside information. It was in the spirit of "things I'd do if I won the lottery." Brandon slouched as he considered one of Goldie's strategies that carried a minimal risk of detection, but also had the least reward. He pictured himself buying puts in the stock of Biophaser's main competitor, figuring they'd be adversely affected by the approval of a new and better drug. An easy trading win was what he needed most, and Bud's information sounded too good to pass up.

Shortly after five o'clock, Brandon walked out through the Helmsley building's lobby and detoured north onto Park Avenue. Wandering the busy sidewalks, he reflected on the blow his integrity would take if he used Bud's info. His stomach churned as a bitter taste in his mouth persisted. He *needed* a successful trade to get back into sync. The firm and his family counted on him. His intention wasn't to make a fortune, he reasoned. He just needed to put one toe over the line to get back on track.

The junk bond deals of the 1980s crossed his mind. Drexel Burnham had swindled *billions* using the firm's renowned insider trading exploits. At once, the notion that the penny-ante transgression he contemplated would never get flagged seemed obvious.

Not far from Park Avenue, Aviva purchased a new HP laptop at Loony-Life's Midtown store.

Against mild resistance after an editorial review, Aviva and Cliff had secured a small budget to pursue their fact-finding scrutiny of Loony-Life. To accommodate their limited funds, Aviva had reached out to her dad.

The desktop computer she brought for a trade-in discount was carted away. The old computer contained a cellular tracking device expertly installed by her father, Stew Goddard, an electrical engineer. She dropped off the newly purchased laptop on her desk at work, then picked up the other beat-up computer they'd outfitted with a tracker and hurried back out of the building. She lugged it on the subway to the Wall Street station, where Trinity Church loomed with its soaring spire and old cemetery. As she passed the weatherworn headstones, Aviva glanced at Alexander Hamilton's burial site and sighed.

She stepped into a cavernous Loony-Life store and repeated the trade-in purchase swap, hoping the process would yield answers but sensing the information could ultimately prove inconclusive. Her father only expected the trackers to work for three or four months, and she had no idea whether that would be long enough. As futile as it seemed, however, tracking the computers was their only solid lead, and she had to attempt to learn their final destination.

As she walked out of the store, Aviva reminisced about the first time she'd felt like a detective. Growing up in Oregon, large family gatherings for Passover Seders were customary. Her father would create a riddle as a hint to help the kids find the hidden matzo, known as the afikoman. Competing against her siblings and cousins, Aviva always triumphed. The prize appealed to her less than the acclaim for living up to her reputation as the family super-sleuth. Strolling down Broadway, she smirked, remembering how her little sister and cousins followed her around in their vain attempts to jump ahead to spots she would search.

As Aviva headed back to the subway, she reflexively clenched the shopping bag with the second new laptop, gripped by a steely determination to discover what the company was hiding.

Chapter 26

BACK TO THE WELL

Cliff spent the summer of 2012 in a rut. The very thought of Loony-Life continued to vex him, especially when he saw the stock on the "52-Week Highs" list.

His diligence to perform at the highest level in the industry led him to perpetually assess his work. There was nothing more satisfying than helping investors the way Clarence Barron would appreciate most: endeavoring to prevent a wrong by exposing a con artist. Yet he wondered if he'd overreached in his zeal for a big story.

Cliff tried to change his focus. He watched DC with great interest as new legislation called the Magnitsky Act wended its way through Congress. It was devised to punish Russians associated with the tax heist Sergei Magnitsky had been investigating. *Perhaps some justice for Sergei,* Cliff mused as he continued to report on the money trail from the heist that cost Magnitsky his life. Even as he focused elsewhere, frustrations with Loony-Life kept needling him.

With tenacious optimism, Aviva monitored the progress of the tracked computers. She watched the blinking dots on her screen trek slowly across the country, make an extended stay at a California port, then finally launch out to sea. At sea, she could no longer track the progress, but the computers seemed to be on the slow boat to China, literally, which took over a month.

By September, the computers finally arrived at a facility in Guangdong Province in southeast China, more than three months after Aviva's initial drop-off. Within two days, the signals from both computer trackers ceased. She confirmed with her dad that the batteries were likely dead.

Dejected by the failed plan, Aviva needed a day to brace herself before giving Cliff the bad news.

"Cliff," she admitted the following morning, "it looks like our attempts at computer tracking have come to an inglorious end. The batteries in the trackers died."

Cliff seemed blasé in the face of news he was prepared to hear. He slowly shook his head and reflected: *One way or another, I figured the effort was for naught.* To Aviva's bewilderment, he didn't belabor the defeat. "Well, that's unfortunate. Thanks for letting me know."

Aviva summoned her indomitable spirit and tried to rally Cliff to persist. "You know this is not over. It would have been great if it worked, but there are other avenues to pursue. I'm not giving up."

Cliff no longer wanted to discuss it. Instead, he pivoted to his Facebook victory, which had brightened his summer. While the stock had traded as low as the mid $17s, by September it was back well over $20. After the quick 20% rally, he saw an opportunity and aimed to revisit the story. "Look," he told Aviva, "there's one question I get more than any other: Is Facebook a buy? I've been dissecting their numbers, and I don't think the stock is worth over $15. So, the answer is still a definitive 'No.' I could use your help—there's still a good story here."

Aviva was surprised that Cliff blew off Loony-Life in favor of writing another bearish article on Facebook only four months after the IPO, while the stock traded in a range far lower than the initial offer price. She felt uncertain of the wisdom of another article, but didn't want to miss an opportunity to work with and learn from a journalist like Cliff. "Count me in," she said. "Let's discuss later."

Aviva turned slowly to take in the full extent of the newsroom, then walked over to her colleague and veteran *Barron's* columnist Michael Santoli. He had a common-sense market approach and imparted its nuances in a weekly column. "Got a minute to talk?" she asked.

They walked to a small, windowless conference room and sat face-to-face across the table under a flickering fluorescent bulb. Aviva laid out her misgivings about Cliff's idea to write a fresh bearish Facebook article.

Flattered that she'd sought his guidance, Santoli pondered her concerns carefully. Unbeknownst to any of his colleagues, he planned to resign soon from *Barron's* to work for Yahoo Finance, which was bulking up on talent under the leadership of its newly appointed CEO, Marissa Mayer. He gave Aviva his candid assessment. "Cliff is one of the best in the business—I don't like to second-guess his work. But in this case, I like your instinct. Perhaps he is too rigidly focused on valuation metrics and unwilling to imagine that the story can evolve."

Artfully, Santoli pivoted to pass along broader advice. "What you'll learn on Wall Street is that anyone who has correctly made a big call—whether they be a journalist, a hedge fund manager, an analyst, or even an economist—can easily become dogmatic in their viewpoint, which makes them difficult to argue against. Often, the people who've been dead right feel they've got the game figured out. What's remarkable is that consecutive great calls are very rare." He smiled and leaned over the table closer to Aviva. The flickering bulb threw shadows across his face as she turned an ear toward him. "So, bottom line: Never stop questioning and never stop challenging someone's thesis—*especially* those who have been right in the past."

When Aviva met with Cliff later that day in the same drab room, he confidently laid out his issues with Facebook. To Aviva, the passion Cliff put into his work reinforced why he was one of the best. The details of his bear case seemed unassailable. Yet after her conversation with Michael, she questioned whether Cliff's argument was also dogmatic and poorly timed. She'd come prepared to play devil's advocate. "Well," she said, "the bull case is that Zuckerberg figures out how to monetize the huge user base, especially through mobile. I read that at TechCrunch, Zuckerberg said, 'It's easy to underestimate how fundamentally good mobile is for us.'" She raised an eyebrow, awaiting his response.

Although her challenge took him aback, Cliff replied, "I'm not buying it. I'll only believe that when I see it. Even at $15, it would still be a $45 billion company, so there's already a lot of good news priced in. And the fact that they had to shell out a billion dollars for Instagram—because a *start-up* with 13 employees figured out mobile pictures before they did—bodes poorly. A *billion* dollars and not a nickel in revenue!"

Aviva was persuaded by Cliff's conviction but pressed the contrarian argument. She explained the long runway for the transition to mobile led by a younger demographic. She also argued the importance of Zuckerberg's pledge not to sell any stock for over a year, demonstrating his long-term focus.

Cliff pursed his lips. "Well, it's not much of a surprise that Zuckerberg pledged not to sell his stock—he would have a hard time selling without a seriously negative reaction in the market. But as you know, one of Facebook's first investors, Peter Thiel, sold off most of his stock last month at 20 bucks the moment the lock-up expired. That must tell you something."

Aviva nodded in acknowledgment as Cliff discussed several

widely respected analysts who shared his bearishness. She felt the argument slipping from her and acquiesced, fully grasping Michael Santoli's sage warning that the hardest person on Wall Street to argue with is someone who has been right. She saw how Cliff needed to get this story out, perhaps to relive the glory he felt before Loony-Life struck. "Sounds like you have a lot of new details. Is there anyone you want me to interview, maybe someone with a bullish angle?" she asked, wondering why he'd even asked her to help with the article. She was suddenly impatient to end their meeting.

Cliff shook his head. Months of frustration with Loony-Life, along with his conviction on Facebook, made him sound edgy. He straightened his horn-rimmed glasses. "There are 40 analysts who cover the stock, most with much higher price targets. If investors want the bull case, they don't have to look too hard. I don't buy into it so I'm not going to put it in print. As far as I'm concerned, it's faith-based investing—I'm going by the numbers. For now, all I'll need are a few comparative charts to other tech stocks."

On September 24th, *Barron's* devoted its cover to Cliff's brutal takedown of Facebook, with a large "$15" for his price target. The article was scathingly critical and reflected his bearish conviction, leaving barely a bone for investors to pick at for hope.

After the Facebook article, Aviva focused entirely on her own column, reporting on small-cap equities. She immersed herself in every aspect of her job: the in-depth research and speaking to institutional holders, analysts, and corporate executives. She wrote with a flair that she felt would impress even her old journalism professors if they read her articles, as she hoped they would.

On a crisp October morning, Aviva made the journey to Midtown on her Vespa. Helmet in hand, she strolled into the newsroom with Loony-Life the furthest thing from her mind. Sitting down at her desk, she started up her computer and opened her email. Her eyes widened in shock. She ripped off her coat and gloves, flung them aside, and grabbed the phone with her heart racing.

"Dad!" she cried the instant he picked up on the other end. "One of the trackers turned back on! It's transmitting from northwest China. Whaddaya think is going on? How's it possible?"

Still waking up, Stew Goddard said cheerfully, "This is good news. You know, it was a long shot, but I had my fingers crossed. The trackers were battery-powered for over three months, but I also hooked them up to the computer's power to recharge. I doubted they'd make it through refurbishing, so I didn't want to give you false hope."

"You're a genius. Gotta run. I love you, bye."

Aviva scanned the newsroom for Cliff and found him standing by the coffee machine. She tried to contain her excitement to avoid drawing the attention of the entire staff. In a hushed voice, she whispered, "Cliff, you won't believe this—a tracker turned back on. It looks like it's transmitting from a school in northwest China!"

Even though he'd been blasé about the trackers earlier, his subdued response baffled her. "That's what we hoped for, but at this point, I don't expect to follow that angle. Loony-Life's last SEC filing had extensive disclosures on the computer donations." He shrugged. "The disclosures were vague enough that the donated computers could have been refurbished."

Aviva flushed. She couldn't believe Cliff sounded so

apathetic. "But that's not what they claimed," she said. "They claimed they bought *new* computers *at cost* from the company. Who's going to be held accountable for that?"

Cliff looked resigned. "It's implied, but the filing didn't say 'new.'" He was ready to investigate the company's accounting, but if the tracking boiled down to just detecting a misrepresentation, he hardly wanted a part of it. "Anyway, at this point, suppositions will not fly with the editors. We can only print what can be proven, and we still can't prove a thing—even with the tracker, it's still conjecture. You're correct that it's suspicious, but it's too easily explained away." He sighed. "Only the SEC can discover what's truly going on internally."

"Nothing we've done has prompted the SEC to investigate. It's just not enough until they wake up and realize this is more than some fishing expedition," Aviva said sharply, no longer concerned about who could overhear her comments.

"I've already written a few follow-ups on Loony-Life's accounting. That's the best I can do. You see where the stock is trading—nobody cares. When you've been here as long as I have, you'll know where to draw the line."

Aviva stood speechless. Cliff himself had taught her that stock prices couldn't be relied on as efficient. She could hardly accept that he was now pointing to this stock's trading strength to dodge the story. She collected herself and said harshly, "So, nobody is held accountable because the stock is strong. *Perfect.*" Spinning abruptly on her heel, Aviva walked to her desk without waiting for Cliff's response. Before she could waver, Aviva typed a letter with her findings and enclosed a map of the computer tracking, originating in downtown Manhattan. She addressed it to Robert Khuzami, director of the SEC's Division of Enforcement.

On the way to yoga class, she stopped at the post office to mail the package and wondered if the effort was futile. She considered Goldman Sachs's fraudulent CDO, Abacus, conceived at the behest of John Paulson's hedge fund in order to short the mortgage market prior to the financial crisis. Neither Paulson nor the Goldman executives were charged. Paulson walked away with windfall profits while counterparties and insurers suffered massive losses. Only one low-level Goldman bond trader, Fabrice Tourre, took the fall for the whole scheme.

Aviva gazed at the name Robert Khuzami and puzzled why he hadn't done more to hold executives accountable for Goldman's deceit. A decade earlier, Khuzami had gained a stellar reputation in the New York U.S. Attorney's office for prosecuting complex white-collar fraud and organized crime in the securities industry. Yet she noted the confounding dichotomy between the aggressive prosecutions of Milken's cohorts from the 1980s junk bond era, and later Enron's executives, versus the lack of notable recent charges. Without much hope, she mailed the envelope.

The next day, Aviva marched up the floating staircase that connected *Barron's* to the *Wall Street Journal*. In silent protest of Cliff's unwillingness to take action and in search of a better job fit in a more collaborative newsroom, she dropped off her résumé with the HR department.

As she crossed the *Journal's* cavernous newsroom, the steady buzz and focused faces gave Aviva a sense of energy. She noted the quicker pace, the journalists much younger than her current colleagues at *Barron's*. As she passed by the Heard on the Street cluster of desks, her acquaintance Hugh McLaggen—a graduate of the London School of Economics who had settled in New York to cover healthcare and industrial companies—hopped up to greet her.

Aviva glanced pointedly at the half-dozen all-male faces of his colleagues and said jokingly, "Looks like you could still use some female perspective."

Hugh surveyed his environs, glancing from his section to the more gender-balanced newsroom floor. He gave a smooth chuckle. "Granted, we are somewhat underrepresented with respect to the fairer sex," he said in his posh accent. "For some reason, it always seems women are more lacking in skepticism. We Heard columnists are, as you know, *exceedingly* skeptical."

"Don't forget grouchy," a disheveled, heavyset colleague interrupted, then added in a high-pitched phony English accent, "*Exceedingly* grouchy."

Aviva was amused by the banter and refrained from volunteering how skeptical and perhaps grouchy she too could be.

"On the other hand," Hugh said as he ushered Aviva away, "we're always on the lookout for fresh talent."

While they walked toward *Barron's*, he continued, "My grouchiness is merely a consequence of too much corporate chicanery and too few hours in the day for writing about all of it. The *Journal's* retail audience desperately needs balance when a stock is valued on hype, dodgy accounting, or an over-promising CEO. As you might expect, I get tremendous push-back but I'm always poised for a kerfuffle—it's essentially part of my job description."

Aviva beamed as she listened to those words in an accent she found so delightful. She realized the *Journal* was indeed the place for her. Strolling back down to *Barron's*, Aviva day-dreamed of the first article she'd write if hired.

Chapter 27

TRUMPED-UP RESEARCH

Stan charged into Ethan's office waving a document. "We have a problem. The fuckin' analyst from Janney Montgomery Scott just went rogue and downgraded our bonds to sell."

Ethan grabbed the report with his stubby fingers and slowly swiveled in his chair. "I know this analyst," he said, his voice simmering with the dangerous steam of a slow boil. "Marvin Roffman. I once spoke with him when he needed *my* help with research. Now our stores are 'ugly and dreary'? This is *totally* unfair."

Stan repressed a smile at Ethan's rebuke. "You know it's bullshit. Our business is finally picking back up. The new iPad has been a hot seller, and every time I turn on CNBC they're talking about 'green shoots' in the economy."

Together they plotted a counterattack on the analyst. Stan circled slowly around the desk as he pointed out questionable projections in the research analysis. "He may know retail, but he doesn't know shit about accounting."

"Let's get this analyst's boss on the phone," Ethan fumed. "How much business have we given them?"

Stan delighted in the impending showdown. His goal was to keep the game going, to stymie suspicion and criticism. "Yeah, that's Edgar Scott. I've spoken to him a bunch of times. The past few years, they probably pocketed over half a mil in underwriting fees alone. They're a dinky regional firm, so that's big money for them."

"Good. Let's get Edgar on the phone to discuss this clown, Roffman."

As he connected to Edgar Scott, Ethan spoke amiably at first, dishing out compliments for the quality of the firm's work. Smoothly, he tried to convince the Wall Street pro that his analyst's report was unfair and untimely. Ethan concluded that in the wake of the deep recession, business was picking up strongly.

Mr. Scott countered that his analyst had been covering retail for 16 years. The negative research derived from concerns of weak earnings conversion to cash flow, which ought to concern bondholders.

Ethan's temper unleashed, and his tactics switched from flattery to bullying, threats, and lies. "Get a new analyst to cover our stock!" His face turned a deep red. "This guy should be *fired*—he has no idea what he's *talking* about. If he doesn't understand our accounting, he needs a new *goddamn* profession." Veins bulged from his neck. "And he says our stores are ugly and dreary—that's out of line. I have our general counsel sitting right here, and he thinks we'd have a pretty good lawsuit against that sort of slander. Our customers come in for the best prices, not a five-star luxury resort."

Ethan knew he had an edge to strong-arm and intimidate the president of the small regional firm. He went straight for the jugular. "Let me ask you: Do you know how much money you've made off my company? You know how many other firms want that business?"

Across Ethan's desk, Stan nodded approvingly.

Chapter 28

A FOND FAREWELL

The job transition within Dow Jones & Company's publications materialized swiftly for Aviva. As she prepared to embark on her dream career at the *Wall Street Journal*, Aviva anticipated working and writing in sync with Hugh McLaggen and the Heard on the Street crew. She was hired to fill an opening covering internet, telecom, and retail stocks.

On Aviva's last day at *Barron's*, Cliff met with her in the conference room in a parting gesture of reconciliation. "I want to tell you how proud I am of you."

Aviva smiled humbly in appreciation.

"I've been meaning to tell you my favorite tale. Better late than never, hmm?" he said with a generous smile. "It's about why we do what we do."

"I'm all ears."

"In the summer of 1920," Cliff began, adjusting his tie and clearing his throat, "Clarence Barron was in his office at the *Wall Street Journal*, sitting at his grand mahogany desk. He could sense the energy of Manhattan all around him, alive with jazz, bridges and buildings under construction, and automobiles now a common sight on the streets. The end of World War I was a turning point that ushered in a sense of power and achievement in America. It was a new era, you could say."

Aviva nodded, hiding her amusement at Cliff's mock formality behind an expectant smile.

"But in this city brimming with optimism and hope, Clarence Barron remained cynical. He viewed himself as a crusader fighting to educate and inform the investor class. He was passionate about making sense of the modern world and, at age 65, he had no intention of slowing down."

"Sounds like your hero," Aviva said. "Maybe even your role model?"

"Yeah, I guess. I've never tried to hide that. We do carry on something he started. Anyway, Barron was cynical with good reason—there was something suspicious happening in his hometown of Boston."

Aviva's eyes widened. "Go on."

"Well, the story I like to tell goes like this: One day in the newsroom, a young reporter in a drab suit slammed the phone receiver on the hook, left his cigarette smoldering in an ashtray, and hustled across the newsroom into Barron's office." Cliff's eyes were bright with the excitement of telling a story he loved. "Gasping, he relayed the breaking news to Barron that the Boston police had arrested his nemesis. He'd been charged with mail fraud by federal authorities and larceny by the state of Massachusetts."

Intrigued by the story and Cliff's energy, Aviva said, "Ah, his nemesis..."

"Yes, his nemesis: *Charles Ponzi*." Cliff adjusted his glasses. "Of course!"

"Barron immediately got up from his desk, the buttons of his vest straining over his ample girth. He bellowed, 'Arrested? Thank heavens! High time they got him,'" Cliff declaimed in the raspy Boston Brahmin accent Barron was known for, and Aviva smiled with glee. He continued his imitation, "'People in my own hometown throwin' money at a two-bit conman.

Nothing but robbin' Peter to pay Paul.'"

Noticing Aviva's wide grin, he asked, "Am I embellishing too much?"

"Lord, no. I love the way you tell stories. Especially the Boston accent."

"I confess, I practiced last night," Cliff admitted with a sheepish smile, pushing his glasses higher. "So. The reporter congratulated Barron on his work exposing Ponzi as a fraud. But Barron was still bewildered by the magnitude of the $20 million scheme. How had people believed what was *clearly* too good to be true? Would the banks that lent him money fail? And how could over half the policemen in Boston have invested with this charlatan? For many of them, it was their life savings." Cliff paused. "I like to think how Barron must have grieved, even in that moment of triumph."

"You would," Aviva said lightheartedly. "But I think he savored the moment as well."

"Maybe, maybe. Well, for months, Barron had observed droves of Bostonians lionizing Charles Ponzi for his investing prowess. Money flowed into his firm from far and wide as word spread of Ponzi's genius. In the end, it was Clarence Barron who helped bring down the scoundrel. The *Boston Post* had recruited Barron weeks earlier to help investigate the legitimacy of Ponzi's firm. He wrote a series of articles for the paper detailing his findings. Interestingly, he did come across something unexpected: There was a theoretical legitimacy to Ponzi's claim of huge profit margins by arbitraging postal reply coupons between countries."

"That does sound unexpected," Aviva agreed.

"Ah, but Barron calculated that Ponzi needed at least 160 million coupons to profit enough to pay off investors, and the postal service had only issued 27 thousand in total. Barron also deduced that the laborious effort required to redeem each coupon individually would undoubtedly annul the arbitrage value."

"I never knew the details," Aviva said. "I had so much to read in school, I sort of skipped a few thousand things."

"Me too, but since I started here, I've become the resident historian." Cliff loosened his tie and proceeded with the story. "So, to reinforce to the *Boston Post's* readers that Ponzi's investment returns defied logic, Barron calculated the compounding effects of his promised payout. Extrapolating from Ponzi's wild promises, reinvested returns would amount to a gain of 2,463% in the first year and 65,684% in the second. He facetiously mused how the Allies could pay off their war debt by earning $16 billion in three years with a mere one-million-dollar investment."

Aviva chuckled. "You know those numbers cold, don't you?"

"Sure do—don't double-check them," Cliff joked. "In one last blow to Ponzi's credibility—the coup de grâce, if you will—Barron revealed an inexplicable finding from his investigation. If Charles Ponzi was doubling investors' money every 90 days, why then did he have all his own savings in regional banks earning 5% instead of investing alongside his customers?"

"Wow. That's what did it, huh?"

"With all that evidence, you would think so, but not quite. Barron's articles created a run on Ponzi's firm, with investors clamoring to redeem their money. The scam was over, he figured. However, in a bewildering turn of events, once Charles Ponzi repaid the initial group of panic-stricken customers, many others felt more convinced of Ponzi's legitimacy."

"Now that sounds like a familiar story."

"Tell me about it. We're here because investors don't always get it right—especially when there's some corporate chicanery." After a brief pause, Cliff resumed. "Episodes like Ponzi's scheme are why Barron refused to retire. Ponzi, the smooth-talking Italian immigrant, had seemingly boot-strapped his way to success. He appeared to be the living, breathing embodiment of the American Dream. Barron's mission was apprising everyone of the truth—which, as we know, is always fraught with pitfalls."

"Indeed," Aviva said softly as she looked away.

"To Barron, it was vital to expose a conman for what he was, especially when the people treated him as a pillar of the community. But he was getting old, and he knew the need for exposés would continue as long as there were people to swindle and money to extract."

Aviva pressed her lips together and nodded. "Even to this day."

"For sure," Cliff said. "That's when it hit Barron. He had been bothered that the printing presses worked only five days a week for the *Wall Street Journal*—the inefficiency of it. Exposing Charles Ponzi gave him the spark to fulfill an idea: a weekly financial newspaper to print on the weekends when the presses were idle. A newspaper with reporters schooled in accounting and statistics, with the know-how to investigate financial machinations."

"You've told me his words, which I'll never forget: 'Reporters with the skill to *expose* what's bad and *exploit* what's good!'" She added the emphases just as Cliff had done on the occasions she'd heard him quote it.

"You got it. I can just picture him thundering away, patting the beads of sweat on his forehead with his handkerchief." Cliff mimicked the action with a make-believe handkerchief. "He recruited the best young reporter at the *Journal* to work as the lead investigative journalist, to follow the money and deeply scrutinize investment ideas for his new publication. Months later, at the dawn of the Roaring Twenties, *Barron's National Financial Weekly* was published, with Clarence

Barron as its editor-in-chief."

Cliff looked her in the eyes and concluded, "Aviva, whether it's here or upstairs at the *Journal,* we aspire to fulfill Clarence Barron's vision: to be staunch truth-seekers. To quote Barron one last time, 'We are in a field to defend the public interest, to illuminate the path and the financial truth for investors, to protect the funds that should support the widow and orphan.'"

Aviva's expression softened as she held her mentor's gaze. With glistening eyes, she said, "Why didn't I know that whole story? I love it. Thank you."

She stood and hugged him for what felt like the last time. When stepping back to shake hands, both shared a knowing, hopeful smile. Perhaps their common past would lead to them meeting in the field again—or at least the elevator.

Chapter 29

RIOTS TO RECOVERY

Greece seemed a million miles away when Stavros first stepped out of Kennedy International Airport, the frigid winter air scraping his face. The enduring economic plight of his country—still on edge in 2012, almost two years after riots overtook Greece—was behind him. On his way to his cousin's house in Astoria, Queens, his first sight of the Manhattan skyline overwhelmed him. Still, the opportunity to work in New York felt like a good trade-off for the warmth and age-old beauty of Athens. Already, he planned to overstay his travel visa.

With its large immigrant population, Astoria bore some familiarity. Greek was spoken and his home cuisine served on almost every street corner. Classical Eastern Orthodox churches with bas-relief carvings and stained-glass windows graced streets otherwise filled with bleak structures. Relatives and new friends were eager to listen to stories of struggles and riots past. Over drinks after pickup games of soccer, he'd recount the upside of austerity: Budget cuts led to dropped charges for first-time offenders arrested during the protests.

In no time, he'd found a job at Loony-Life's New Jersey warehouse. From its earliest days in Brooklyn, the company paid workers off-the-books whenever possible. Skills that Stavros mastered as a stevedore operating a forklift translated well to his new position. Just a few months into the job, Stavros was handed a wide range of responsibilities. He managed a few underlings, men he recruited from the neighborhood, to move a steady flow of pallets loaded with crates and boxes.

Stavros watched the news to help his English and learn more about how Americans viewed Greece. When he would call his sister, Maria, he would always laugh when explaining how pundits were preoccupied with the fear of America's financial markets going the way they did back home. The economy felt so vibrant, he failed to ever grasp the similarities. Yet, ironically, these same pundits seemed to prescribe the same concept of austerity which had been so devastating to Greece's economy.

Stavros had always known he would return to his homeland eventually, but he didn't realize how much he would miss Athens. He felt in his bones that city's connection to history, its ancient architecture, the charm and culture that Queens couldn't rival. Living and working in America made him feel like a mercenary.

After nine months, working at Loony-Life served its financial purpose. Buttressed by the thousands he'd saved, he returned to Athens and his sister's home. Syntagma Square became a place to remember his father and mull Greece's mercilessly slow recovery. Interest rates on Greek ten-year bonds were steadily easing back down from their peak near 40%, when default seemed inevitable earlier in the year.

As he stretched out on a bench one mid-October afternoon, his phone buzzed with an international call from the United States. Stavros didn't recognize the number. The woman introduced herself as a reporter from the *Wall Street Journal* with questions regarding his work at Loony-Life. The memory of his father's words, "Be proud and never fear honesty," helped him resist the urge to hang up.

Chapter 30

SWORD OF DAMOCLES

Reporters at the *Wall Street Journal* are among the best in the industry. Many of them had framed metal plates, gifted from the editors, of their first article printed in the paper. Aviva sat at her new desk pondering a meaningful story for her first column. She figured it would have to be impactful for her editor to even consider getting framed plates. Loony-Life was in her crosshairs, and she planned to come out swinging in her *Journal* debut.

Aviva seized the opportunity to interview Jim Chanos for any updated concerns—the abrupt departure of Loony-Life's general counsel, just months after being hired, had caught his attention. She also spoke with Marvin Roffman, the lone negative analyst who'd downgraded the debt, to assess his cash-flow concerns. Additionally, she found a source in a former employee, a Greek man willing to discuss curious anomalies in the New Jersey warehouse where he had worked.

Reading Aviva's first column was one of Cliff's proudest moments. The blow of losing her to their sister publication stung at first, but any hard feelings seemed petty after witnessing his protégée shine. She had his back on the Loony-Life story, and she had dug even deeper.

Apart from Cliff's appreciation, however, Aviva's column

caused an uproar on two fronts.

First, in an interview, Ethan Atlas spewed venom as he couldn't help but break his policy to avoid rebuking a critic. He threatened to pull Loony-Life's ads from the *Journal* in retaliation for Aviva's possible improprieties in her reporting. He leveled a spate of accusations—compensating a source for information, leaking inside information to Jim Chanos prior to publication, and blatant manipulation of the share price with fabricated stories—then called on regulators to investigate.

Confident in her sources and methods, and undaunted by the bullying and character attacks, Aviva knew nothing would make her back down. She even took in stride the vile hate mail the incident spurred, joking to her colleagues, "If Ethan Atlas wants to make me famous, that's fine—I'll take all the 'fan mail' they can muster."

Nonetheless, in solidarity, journalists came to Aviva's defense, and the *Wall Street Journal* maintained unwavering support for her reporting.

On CNBC, Scott Wapner interviewed Bethany McLean, a natural choice considering the executive onslaught she'd endured while reporting on Enron. Wapner inquired, "What do you make of a CEO you're trying to cover who becomes combative in the way he treats your reporting?"

McLean stared into the camera and replied, "Shareholders of Loony-Life should think about running for the exits." Poised, yet stern, she added, "When a CEO becomes combative like this—attacking a journalist to discredit her by any possible means, rather than focusing on the numbers and the results that will prove the journalist and short sellers wrong—what that says to me is that he's unsure the numbers or the results are actually there."

Aviva absorbed the moment as she watched the interview. McLean's commentary corroborated her instinct that Ethan

Atlas's allegations sounded flailing and desperate. Feeling like she was on the right track, she sought out one last integral source.

In the second blow to Aviva's reporting, Janney Montgomery Scott fired their Loony-Life analyst, Marvin Roffman. A standard company statement attributed the analyst's dismissal to unauthorized communication with the press—for speaking with Aviva Goddard of the *Wall Street Journal*.

At *Barron's*, Cliff Ludwig and Alan Abelson sprang into action with an immediate sense that Janney Montgomery was using Aviva's reporting as a false pretense to fire Roffman. In Abelson's half-century of journalism, he thought the firing of an analyst for a negative research report—as he was inclined to believe—would rank high in portraying Wall Street's lack of integrity. They set out to account for details of the episode.

When Abelson spoke with Edgar Scott, he sensed that Scott's rambling explanation betrayed the original rationale for Roffman's firing. Aside from the unauthorized communication with the *Journal*, Mr. Scott chided his former analyst's rendering of Loony-Life as inappropriate in tone and manner of criticism. Specifically, Scott was displeased with the "intemperate, flamboyant language" his analyst used to describe Loony-Life's stores. Abelson thought the whole affair smelled putrid, especially when he discovered Ethan Atlas had confronted Mr. Scott about the downgrade.

In his Up and Down Wall Street column, Abelson never hesitated to speak truth to power. With Cliff's help, he wrote a withering takedown of Janney Montgomery Scott, highlighting Edgar Scott's wandering justification for the dismissal. "Janney stood behind their analyst—as far behind him as possible. Mr. Roffman had not lived up to Janney's unspoken motto: If you don't have anything nice to say, don't say anything." With Abelson's flair for subtle ridicule, he further remarked,

"On the surface, the termination seems like an act of unsurpassed spinelessness. However, superficial impressions are often misleading. It is necessary in such delicate and complex cases to probe beneath the surface. And when one probes beneath the surface, we can assure you, the firing of Mr. Roffman seems like an act of unsurpassed spinelessness."

From her new home at the *Wall Street Journal*, Aviva reveled at Abelson's wry humor and sardonic take on the incident. She felt the weight of responsibility for reaching out to Roffman and using his comments in her reporting, which then led to the pretext for the analyst's dismissal. With relief and admiration, she noted that Abelson had uncovered the true reason—Roffman had dared to criticize Loony-Life.

Ethan Atlas, however, read through Abelson's article with exasperation. "Why is he even writing about this?" he muttered, troubled that everyone was now conspiring against him. He had already instructed Stan to take any legal measures possible to shut down leakers and whistleblowers. Now he was furious to see revelations of his conversation with Edgar Scott come to light.

Instinctively, Ethan wanted to stash away the cash from his stock sales rather than repair the inventory. But the accounting hole made him feel as if the Sword of Damocles dangled overhead. He could only resolve it, he thought, with drastic action, yet he was comforted by the thought of his protector. Like a knight in shining armor, Carl Icahn had become his steadfast defender—for now.

Days later, on Loony-Life's earnings conference call, Ethan sounded upbeat. Employment numbers were accelerating higher on the eve of the upcoming presidential election, and he emanated enthusiasm for a significant turn in business and the economy. He summoned all his confidence and numerous investor-inspiring buzzwords to dangle prospects for growth: "We expect a big pick-up in same-store sales." "Recent sales of iPads have been red-hot and look to be white-hot this Christmas." "We're working on significant new growth initiatives that will be unveiled later this year." He fully expected analysts' questions to reflect the company's bullish prospects. Instead, he faced tough, detailed inquiries concerning issues raised by Marvin Roffman and Aviva Goddard in their recently published cautionary takes. One analyst pressed hard for Ethan to address Roffman's balance sheet concerns, and why the financial statements weren't included in the earnings report. Ethan dismissed the balance sheet issues as inconsequential, then indiscreetly murmured, "Asshole."

Listening a borough away in his Manhattan office, Jim Chanos nearly fell out of his chair. He rushed to the door and stuck his head out to see if any of his analysts were tuned into the call. Flabbergasted, he had to confirm he wasn't just hearing things.

Part III

Chapter 31

ALIBABA'S PRICED TO SELL

September 2014

In the two years since Cliff's articles on Facebook and Loony-Life were published, the lessons learned from both stocks were never far from his thoughts.

Facebook's recent emergence as the top-performing growth stock forced him to abandon his bearish stance as the stock climbed back over its $38 IPO price to a heady $65. Mobile monetization had kicked into gear. The recollection of his cover article with the featured "$15" price target made him cringe.

He found some solace in the wisdom of his venerable colleague Alan Abelson, who'd once related to him a reoccurring market observation: "Even after the market takes something to the moon, somebody will always declare it can soar even higher; and regardless of how far something falls back to Earth, somebody will always say there's room to get buried deeper. If they rounded up all these prognosticators with unattained targets, there would scarcely be a soul left on Wall Street." Yet for Cliff, these reassurances weren't enough to make him contemplate reporting on Facebook again.

Loony-Life remained a battleground stock, with Chanos

periodically knocking the company while Icahn maintained a steadfast defense. The stock price had simply defied gravity and reflected a back-and-forth struggle with a slight edge for Icahn. While the economy improved, Loony-Life's fundamentals, despite all evidence to the contrary, appeared to remain intact.

Outside of a series of skeptical follow-up articles pointing to red flags, Cliff was dissatisfied with his coverage of the company, which seemed incomplete. Yet he never regretted the decision not to write about the computer trackers.

Wall Street, aside from a few indomitable short sellers, had largely ignored his reporting on Loony-Life. Even without a smoking gun of fraud, Cliff felt chagrined the SEC never investigated the company's accounting. In a sense, he believed he had failed the readers of *Barron's*.

His latest assignment gave him a jolt of excitement he hadn't felt over the past two years: Alibaba, the Chinese e-commerce juggernaut, was set to debut on the New York Stock Exchange in the largest IPO in history. He hoped his reporting would captivate readers and rival the prominence of his original Facebook story and the importance of his Magnitsky investigative research.

For months, the approaching IPO had been the talk of the stock market. Alibaba's roadshow presentation was attended by a who's who of the hedge fund world, including Lee Cooperman from Omega Advisors, Dan Loeb of Third Point, and David Tepper from Appaloosa Management.

During a year of generally poor hedge fund performance, face time for hedge fund managers at the IPO roadshow was necessary to demonstrate their commitment, which helped bolster share allocations.

When Cliff analyzed Alibaba, the contrasts with Facebook were stark. He was impressed with its valuation, profitability, and share of China's e-commerce market. Overall, he thought the company was far more established and profitable than Facebook had been when it went public, and far from fully valued at the potential IPO price range.

Cliff understood, much like the roadshow attendees, that the deal's underwriters didn't want to experience another Facebook debacle. Therefore, Alibaba's bankers were expected to price the IPO at a reasonable discount to leave room for significant appreciation in aftermarket trading.

The crux of the bull case Cliff laid out was logical and straightforward: E-commerce accounted for 8% of China's consumption but should continue to capture more share due to poorly developed brick-and-mortar alternatives. Since Alibaba had 80% of China's e-commerce market, its enormous growth would march ahead unabated.

It seemed like an easy call for Cliff to recommend buying Alibaba at the IPO offering based on their e-commerce dominance and projected earnings multiple relative to other Chinese internet stocks. He expected it to price in the high $60s, and even informed readers that the stock could reasonably trade well into the $80s. To be prudent, he suggested not paying higher than $80 after the IPO opening for trading.

Cliff also recommended buying shares of Yahoo. They owned a 24% stake in Alibaba and intended to sell over a quarter of their shares in the IPO, retaining at least a 16% stake.

The compelling story Cliff outlined for Yahoo was the discount to its sum-of-the-parts, including its core business, the value of its Alibaba stake, its stake in Yahoo Japan, and net cash on the balance sheet. He assumed if Alibaba traded at $80, Yahoo ought to at least hold its value at $42, as the Alibaba stake alone, if sold untaxed, would be worth $40 per Yahoo share.

Almost two years after Aviva's departure from *Barron's*,

Cliff still reflected on their work together. He was always cheered to see her in the elevator on her way to the *Journal*, and he regularly read her column on retail, telecom, and internet companies. Cliff still missed Aviva's fresh perspective, sense of humor, and high-spirited personality in the older, male-dominated *Barron's* newsroom. He wondered what her point of view would be on Alibaba and Yahoo in her column analyzing the upcoming IPO. He assumed his former protégée would follow his bullish lead and recommend that investors buy stock in both companies.

Chapter 32

GO BIG OR GO HOME

The morning of Alibaba's IPO was the most anticipated trading day since Facebook's debut two and a half years earlier, and the NYSE was abuzz. The largest global IPO in history, selling as much as $25 billion in stock, was set to open in a frenzy of press coverage. The company chose a stock symbol, BABA, that rolled off the tongue.

Amid a year of market strength, the hype of the IPO day aligned perfectly with other events that heralded a market top: Apple's iPhone 6 was released to long lines and the S&P 500 climbed to an all-time high. One acerbic market pundit, Doug Kass, sensed a market peak and dubbed it the "Ali Blah Blah top."

On the morning of the IPO, an intense atmosphere enveloped Glacial's trading desk. Strategies had been in the works for weeks, and the targeted stocks set up well going into the offering.

To break the tension, Mitch provided some early morning levity. "Tommy, you're going to have to say something interesting because you need a nickname," he said to the new trainee, whose eyes widened. "We had this guy on the desk who we called Bud Fox—he was another one of our trainee disasters. Five months we worked with him before we put him in front of a computer to trade. He was a fearless paper trader, but the first time he took a real position in a stock where he was down some decent dough, he started hyperventilating. No kidding."

Goldie added, "I've never seen anyone breathe like that outside of getting punched in the stomach—he actually gasped for air."

"We really gave the kid a chance, but poor Bud was like a fish out of water—literally," Steve said.

"Goldie fired him after that. It's always something. That chair has seen a lot of asses." Mitch snickered while Tommy silently gulped.

Brandon felt guilty for laughing along. After all, Bud did try to help him, albeit with inside information. In fact, like his *Wall Street* namesake, the information Bud relayed turned out to be remarkably prescient. However, Brandon's bearish options trade went awry when the competitor was acquired. *Things always have to be done the hard way,* Brandon surmised of the affair. Still, he had to throw in a positive word for Bud. "Come on, he was a good guy. He had that Midwestern optimism."

Mitch grinned through his bushy beard. "Yeah, but trading isn't for optimists—it's for masochists." Not one other trader cracked a smile at Mitch's quip. At that moment, his remark stung and left his fellow traders nodding in agreement.

Never hesitating to dish out snark, Sneaks added, "Bud was *optimistic* he didn't deserve to get fired because he was all buddy-buddy with us. But Goldie gave him the Heisman while showing him the door."

"That's right," Goldie said, re-enacting the stiff arm. "He should have listened to his idol, Gekko: 'If you want a friend, get a dog,'" he added quickly, ready to move on to the day's business. Yahoo remained the primary target, as the stock hovered near its high owing to the Alibaba stake.

As a senior partner, Goldie knew how critical the day was to the firm. A year earlier, he'd made the tough decision to slash Eli's buying power in response to his reckless, hubris-driven trading based on stock calls from his Goldman sales trader—calls Eli followed "like a Muppet," as Goldie had characterized him. Eli's reaction to Goldie's slight was no surprise: He lost his shit and resigned on the spot. Before storming off, he'd vented his indignation to the entire desk in a wild rant. "You guys have done nothing but suckle off the teat of my Street contacts. For years I've showered you all with money." For good measure, he'd chucked a half-filled coffee cup at the wall on his way out.

The traders were simultaneously appalled and amused by Eli's teat metaphor, especially since all his industry contacts were men.

"You see?" Goldie had held his index fingers to his temples and revealed his long-held psychological assessment. "The dude's fucked in the head. He never had the humility to make it as a trader anyway. And you certainly don't have to second-guess that decision when someone acts that insane on the way out the door."

Despite the loss of Eli's connections, the desk was relieved to see him—with his penchant for drama and lack of camaraderie—clear out. They had traded profitably on their own ideas long before Eli showed up, and they planned on doing so long after he left. Yet a year later, perhaps coincidentally, the desk was struggling. Now they had no choice but to go big where they perceived an edge.

Goldie stood up, straightened his spine, and opened the morning meeting in his usual confident voice. "Guys, there's a lot riding on this, but today is our day. Let's face it, it's been a tough year for us with the market right at the high and QE sucking out volatility. Every day feels like *Groundhog Day* with Yellen stuffing us with jelly donuts. But today the tide turns. Alibaba's IPO and Apple's iPhone 6 release, plus the Fed winding down its balance sheet expansion, could signal a market top and usher in a real pullback.

"As we've discussed, Yahoo is the number one idea to be short today. I've worked through the numbers with Brandon, and the market needs to discount the sum-of-the-parts far more than where it's trading now at $42.50. Even if allocations for BABA are tight and the stock is strong, there's still no good case for owning Yahoo at this valuation after the deal. Even though *Barron's* says to buy Yahoo in their sum-of-the-parts analysis, they fail to realize that *some of the parts* are terrible—like Yahoo's entire fucking core business." Goldie slowly shook his head with a look of pity. "Traders who follow that misguided analysis are sheep headed to slaughter."

The previous weekend, Brandon had been surprised to read Cliff Ludwig's bullish take on Yahoo. He dismissed the call straight away. Convinced of the strength of his viewpoint, he emailed his take on Yahoo to Jim Chanos, the first such missive in the two years following his disastrous phone call. The unease over pitching Facebook as a short play still lingered, though he was content and even a bit pleased, in retrospect, that he'd dared ask Chanos for a job. Now he had a bulletproof short target to share.

Goldie grabbed a bottle of water, then continued. "For a more informed point of view, Brandon's friend Aviva Goddard wrote a great article in the *Journal* that advised selling Yahoo. Her article fit right into our thinking that the stock will sell off after Alibaba goes public."

Brandon was amazed to read Aviva's column, where she boldly advised investors to dump Yahoo's stock because, thanks to Alibaba's IPO, "its magic carpet ride is over."

Goldie stopped to sip water as Brandon raved to the desk,

"Aviva made a great case for Yahoo to go lower. Who would want to own an Alibaba proxy stock when today you can buy Alibaba directly? Investors only bought Yahoo to own Alibaba, so once they can own the real thing, nobody will want the proxy with all its baggage. Now let's hope she's right."

"She is—not a doubt in my mind," Goldie said. "There's no real upside. Yahoo, at $42.50, has way too much optimism already baked in. I'll bet it sees $38 in short order. Like I've said before about proxy shorts: This idea is one hundred percent likely to work today." Goldie enunciated slowly to stress the point, then scanned the room for a glimmer of doubt in the eyes of his colleagues. There was none.

He folded his arms and added, "Experience on Wall Street is being able to discern the same mistakes investors make over and over. This is the mother of them all." Goldie pointed at Tommy to ensure the trainee was paying attention. "I'll also highlight one more stock. JD.com has made a nice run from the $27s to the $30s the last few days in anticipation of the deal. I really like the short idea. This is a $50 billion company as the purported 'Amazon of China'—also looks way hyped up and should head back to Earth after the deal. As for trading Alibaba, if it opens in the $70s, that would be ridiculous and a huge buy; they'd also destroy Yahoo if it did. But in the low $80s, it's probably still good for a few points to the upside. Cramer and *Barron's* both like it there." To emphasize its importance, Goldie repeated, "Guys, a lot is riding on this day—let's get it right. There will be plenty of opportunity, so stay sharp."

Since the debacle two years ago, investment bankers had taken pains in the IPO process to "avoid another Facebook." Underwriters placed shares in strong hands, allocating fewer shares to hedge funds that were more likely to flip the stock on the first day. Also, bankers had to price deals at an attractive level, even if this meant insiders left money on the table. This relieved pressure to flip shares. Lastly, they shunned listing any high-profile IPO on Nasdaq in favor of the NYSE.

By ten thirty, the NYSE started to update a range for where Alibaba would open. "There's the first indication, $80–$83," Dominick said eagerly.

"That'll be going higher." Brandon sounded displeased. "There's 30 mil to buy, paired on only a half million. They'll need to take this higher to find some sellers."

"There goes the dream of buying it in the $70s," Goldie said ruefully. "But this is perfect. Yahoo's trading huge volume here at $42.25. When they ratchet up the indication, this could get going higher, too. I'm trying to be patient putting on a sizable short."

The nervous anticipation on the desk was palpable. Sensing the anxiety, Mitch emptied his stress ball collection as he tossed them one by one around the office. "Chillax, men," he encouraged.

"BABA up to 45 mil to buy, paired on a mil. There goes the indication, $83–$86. Oh wow, the volume in Yahoo is off the charts, and there she goes up." Dominick flung his hand toward the ceiling to help encourage Yahoo higher.

"Do you hear this guy on CNBC from the NYSE?" Brandon squinted. "He's trying to explain the matching process to Bob Pisani. This is a joke. He says there's huge demand for BABA at the indicated level with very little supply. He's describing the search for sellers—just stupid. This is going to open much higher now that sellers can back away." Brandon figured that anyone who worked on Wall Street would understand the perverse logic at play: The higher a stock goes, the more people want to buy it, especially when told that sellers are scarce. For an instant, he recalled Loony-Life's march higher, and his stomach dropped. To fight through the mental distraction and refocus on Alibaba, he shouted at the TV, "Pisani, the only way they're gonna shake the tree is to indicate some weakness."

"Well, that's not happening—now indicated $87–$90. Yahoo is running here, $42.75—this is perfect." Goldie jumped out of his chair, pumped his fists, and released a powerful primal scream from his small frame. "Come on!"

The traders were so captivated and focused on the trading action that no one even flinched at Goldie's blaring shriek.

While the desk continued to work into a large Yahoo short position, the strength of Alibaba's indication made the concept of shorting Yahoo uneasy, as both were moving briskly higher. Alibaba's indication advanced to $90–$92, while Yahoo rallied through $43.

Despite Alibaba's opening trade indicating higher than expected, the desk stuck with their conviction that Yahoo would fall once Alibaba started trading, as the Facebook proxies did when that deal opened.

The NYSE indication tightened as the floor specialist explained how they were paired on 40 million at $93, and there would still be two million to buy, which would be good for buyers at the cross.

Brandon crushed a stress ball and continued his nervous blather, with hardly anyone listening except for Tommy. "I'll tell you what's interesting," he said, "we all clamored to buy Facebook and Twitter on the opening cross, but not one of us is remotely interested in buying BABA up here—I think that's telling. This stock is probably going to open way too high. I can't imagine who's buying this in the $90s, and conversely, who's not selling their $68 stock in the $90s. At $90, the market cap is $225 billion. That seems *very* aggressive."

As he puzzled over where the sellers were, dread ran through him when he realized the date. Only one week until the end of the quarter. At once, he surmised that all the big-shot hedge fund managers wouldn't want to be obvious flippers of the stock when they could hold for a week into the quarterly 13F reporting date.

Brandon had underestimated how effectively Morgan Stanley managed the deal. His faith in the desk's strategy was shaken as he realized the underwriters must have taken extra precautions to avoid another Facebook debacle. Brandon stared wide-eyed across at Goldie as he laid out his disturbing revelation. He added the obvious connection, "There might not be any real sellers in BABA for the Yahoo trade to work."

Calmly, Goldie dismissed this insight. "Don't worry about it, dude. Stick with the plan."

Brandon had voiced his doubts, but there would be no audible at the line of scrimmage—the play was set. Shoulders slumped, he accepted the incoming fight in the trenches for the one strategy they had committed to. They would either live or die by it. The strategy was the desk's trading dogma—they *must* have faith in it.

In the moments before Alibaba's stock opened, Yahoo started to break to the downside, back to $42.25, to the traders' relief. After the NYSE prepared participants for the opening trade, Alibaba finally opened at $92.70 and promptly ran seven points higher to a peak of $99.70, while Yahoo just as swiftly dropped under $42.

"Oh my God, the BABA quick flip was worth at least five points. What a goddamn miss," Sneaks said, dismayed.

"That's okay. Fuck the flip. This Yahoo's gonna work," Goldie said quickly. "The stock is finished. Don't cover any—they're gonna kill it."

Mitch sauntered away from the desk. "That's it. I'm maxed out on my Yahoo short position, so I'll be doing a handstand over here by the wall. I have some bids in—*much* lower."

In an instant, he flipped onto his hands, his cargo shorts

and sandals lifted toward the overhead TV as his heels hit the wall. Brandon glanced over his shoulder at him with incomprehension and envy, struck by Mitch's cool attitude at such a pivotal moment. Brandon's stomach churned. He could barely take his eyes off the screen and fought a pressing urge to make a run for the bathroom.

Mitch's nonchalant break proved premature as Yahoo changed direction and raced higher to $43. With Alibaba sitting in the high $90s—Yahoo's stake alone worth well over $40 per share—it appeared *Barron's* had the correct call. As blood slowly pooled in Mitch's head and the desk remained short over 195K shares of Yahoo, the strength in both stocks led to moments of fear, uncertainty, and doubt.

"Shit, from the groaning, it sounds like I need to come back to the desk," Mitch said.

Promptly, Goldie offered commentary. "No, no, stay there. BABA just dropped four bucks to $95 in a heartbeat—bought some as a hedge. Whoa, it's still dropping. Yahoo is breaking back down again. I believe this time, it's officially over, Johnny."

With a feel for Yahoo's impending collapse, Steve cocked his head upward, hands around his mouth, and bellowed, "Release the hounds!"

Still upside down, Mitch chanted Snoop Dogg's chorus: *"Drop it like it's hot, drop it like it's hot, drop it like it's hot..."*

Shouts of "Pound it!" and "Crush this thing!" sounded around the desk as they tried to coax Yahoo lower.

Moments later, when Mitch casually strolled back to his seat, he beckoned to his screen, "That's right—come to Papa."

"Thar she blows!" Goldie exclaimed triumphantly as Yahoo tumbled down.

Over the next thirty minutes, Yahoo sank to a low of $38.60, a 10% top-to-bottom move. As it broke $39 to the downside, where many shorted shares were covered, Brandon uttered, "Mortimer, we're back!" more in relief than celebration, before finally seizing the opportunity to make a bathroom run.

"Lobbies?" Steve chimed in with the one word the traders were always delighted to hear. A raucous whooping greeted this clearly rhetorical question. Tommy hustled off to pick up a round of lunchtime lobster rolls from Cucina Café in the MetLife Building. After a tough year for the desk, the rolls tasted especially blissful.

As soon as the closing bell sounded, Brandon perched on a windowsill and zoned out, hypnotically staring up Park Avenue. Rectangular islands of flora floated in a sea of asphalt. Cars crawled by like endless lines of marching ants. Pinheads of light flicked on and off, green, yellow, then red. Flows of humanity crowded and dispersed on cue.

Steve stretched his back, then ambled over to Tommy for a recap. "You see, Alibaba opened too high, and if you didn't buy the opening and make the quick flip, there wasn't any money to be made in it. Aside from that quick opening move up in BABA, we caught the only big trades: short Yahoo and JD.com."

Tommy nodded vigorously as Steve added, "I know that looked easy when the desk made a score and our plan worked perfectly, but the game is still a lot harder than it looks. In this case, we had the conviction to stay short, but for a moment, my instinct was to cover Yahoo and maybe even get long."

"Ah, if every instinct you have is wrong, the *opposite* has to be right." Sneaks smirked.

"Okay, Jerry," Steve said, chuckling half-heartedly.

"This whole day was amazing," Tommy said. "It definitely looks way more fun when you guys get the trade right. And thanks again for the lobster roll—it was awesome."

"I have to call Aviva." Brandon turned from the window

with refreshed mental synapses. "She totally trumped the call from *Barron's* for Yahoo to go higher. Got to give her kudos for sticking her neck out and getting Yahoo right."

He strode back to the desk and dialed deliberately. Aviva's upbeat greeting sounded especially genuine, buoyed by her Yahoo call. She continued, "It was set up to be a classic proxy stock decimation, which, from what I've heard on the Street, works one hundred percent of the time," quoting Brandon's words back to him. Floored to hear his old line, he sat stunned and thoroughly dazzled.

Chapter 33

BLAST FROM THE PAST

Cliff quietly relaxed at his desk as the small electronic ticker displayed the closing trades: Alibaba at $92, up $24; Yahoo at $39.90, down $2.55. Despite his regrettably bullish call on Yahoo, he was content with his Alibaba reporting. He slid paperwork aside and grabbed his battered calculator, punching in numbers to figure out how Aviva had called the stock move correctly. He leaned back in his chair and ran through the numbers mentally, with an arm stretched over his head and eyes staring blankly at the ceiling tiles. If Yahoo's sales were fully taxed, then his valuation discount hadn't been conservative enough, he concluded. Drained and tired, Cliff nodded and half smiled to himself at Aviva's correct take on the trade. Getting the Yahoo narrative wrong felt more tolerable since Aviva had gotten it right.

Suddenly, a roaring sound wave swept over him, and all thoughts of Yahoo were wiped from his mind. He turned toward the clamor but was slow to process the commotion—his colleagues were shouting and hooting in his direction.

A few seconds later, he finally grasped the fragments.

"Loony-Life…"

"FBI raided offices…"

"Stock halted…"

"Computers and documents seized..."

"You nailed it!"

Paul hustled up to Cliff, shoved the press release at him with a flourish, and clutched him in a bear-hug. With a shaking hand, Cliff skimmed the release and said unsteadily, "Looks like they found the smoking gun. I knew it had to be there—I just couldn't get the right look inside to find it."

Paul recognized the magnitude of the news and beamed. "There's no doubt your reporting led the regulators right to their front door. You could not have done your job better. This is an incredible moment—enjoy it."

Cliff sat in his chair and spun around to focus on the press release:

> The FBI, in conjunction with the SEC and under the supervision of the Department of Justice, has conducted a raid of Loony-Life's corporate offices in New York and the company's warehouse in Red Bank, N.J. The FBI seized computers and documents to further an investigation into fraud that stemmed from a whistleblower accusation and other corroborating sources.
>
> In conjunction with the investigation, CEO Ethan Atlas and COO Stanley Atlas were arrested and face indictment by the U.S. Attorney for the Eastern District of New York on charges of conspiracy to commit accounting fraud, wire fraud and money laundering. The SEC is also evaluating possible violations of the U.S. Foreign Corrupt Practices Act for a scheme to bribe Chinese government officials in order to facilitate business in China.
>
> Following a year-long investigation, the FBI and SEC have determined that the two executives conspired to alter the books and records of Loony-Life

over a five-year period by inflating inventory numbers and falsely booking OEM rebates on the fictitious inventory.

The SEC has also determined that earnings per share were dramatically overstated through a series of accounting irregularities. This includes a scheme to inject cash back into the company via an offshore account through Loony-Life's subsidiary in China. The investigation is ongoing.

Cliff stood up, a look of astonishment spreading on his face as he reread the release. His phone rang. He recognized the excited voice of his former *Barron's* colleague Erin Arvedlund on the other end. "Cliff! I'm sure you saw the news on Loony-Life."

"I just saw—it's unbelievable," Cliff responded, almost subdued.

"I wanted to call with my congratulations. I'd bow down before you if I were there, like you did for me after Madoff's arrest." They both laughed at the flashback of Cliff's genuflecting in front of Erin as he applauded her skepticism of Bernie Madoff's operation. "You did an awesome job red-flagging Loony-Life. It only took two and a half years, but you must feel vindicated."

"Yeah, only two and a half years." Cliff chuckled. "You're not going to believe it, but I was thinking of you and your reporting on Madoff when I wrote the original article. The news today hasn't sunk in yet—I'm still numb, but I feel completely vindicated. What went through your mind when news of Madoff's Ponzi scheme broke?"

"I'll never forget listening to CNBC from home, jumping off my sofa and screaming, 'They finally got him!'" Erin paused. "It took a while to understand the scope of the scheme. I was vindicated, but it was heartbreaking to see the investor losses and the betrayal of the faith they had put in that man. As you know, the seven years that elapsed after my story were sometimes painful. In my gut, I knew *something* was wrong, so it gnawed at me as time went by with not a word from anyone about his money management operation. I was dumbfounded."

Cliff cleared his throat. "I can relate. For over two years, I've questioned my reporting. I can't imagine seven years in limbo."

"It's never easy feeling like Cassandra in this business," Erin said. "Again, my congratulations; you deserve it. But I'll let you go. You must have people lining up at your desk with champagne." Her voice was warm and genuine, and Cliff smiled as he hung up.

He hadn't noticed Aviva entering the newsroom. As a journalist, Aviva knew the importance of containing her emotions, but as she approached Cliff, the delight of success bubbled over. The time to reflect on the harm to shareholders and employees of Loony-Life could wait. She skipped across the floor with her hands high in the air. Editors and reporters reached out to slap high fives as she glided through. Aviva stopped in front of Cliff and leaped for joy. He could muster no words as they hugged, his eyes welling up. He wanted to say so many things but just held her tightly. Finally, he whispered, "You made a heck of a call on Yahoo." Aviva laughed through her tears.

"My heart was pounding so fast as I ran down those two flights of stairs," she said breathlessly.

After a few seconds, he stepped back with an inquisitive look. "Did you pass along the information about the refurbished computers? Were you a 'corroborating source' for the SEC?"

She shrugged with a coy expression. Cliff understood, bowed his head, and simply said, "Thank you."

Aviva gave a tiny curtsy and grinned. "And the FBI." Then with a wink and a whisper, "Just in case."

Chapter 34

ISN'T IT "MEMORY LANE"?

On the desk, the traders lazily decompressed at the end of the day after the Alibaba IPO. The relief was palpable. The bliss from capitalizing on the trading opportunity led to a loose atmosphere, but Dominick sat stone-faced. He'd been withholding bad news for days, waiting for the right moment. The highly profitable session set up an opportunity. "Gentlemen, gather round. I have news to report," he called out loudly.

Mitch turned down the blaring music as the traders approached Dominick. None of them imagined anything could take the wind out of their sails, yet his stoic demeanor gave them pause. Brandon popped over, a puzzled expression on his face. He'd been on the phone with Aviva to congratulate her on the Yahoo article, but she had brought the call to an abrupt and confusing end. He would have to call her back later to make sure everything was okay.

Dominick sighed. "You know I've been working for the last two years on our Facebook IPO grievance with Nasdaq. Well, they rejected our claim for recompense. Some technicality."

Most eyes fell on Steve. He had lost the most in the Facebook IPO and would have stood to recover over half of the firm's losses. Steve lowered his head and said, "Never really thought I'd see those losses recouped. Not even close."

"Sorry, Steve," Dominick said. "After we met all their criteria for an accommodation, I thought the two years of back and forth would have produced *something*. But now, it's officially not happening."

"Quarter mil out of our pockets right to Greifeld's bonus." Sneaks turned to Dominick. "What bullshit technicality did they come up with?"

Without another word, Dominick handed out copies of the rejection letter. After two years of paperwork, he almost couldn't believe Nasdaq's excuse and wanted everyone to read it for themselves.

As he scanned the notice, Brandon knew it was over. The outcome was hardly a surprise, nevertheless he was vexed. "What the hell?! They're first telling us this now—after two friggin' years?"

Dominick rolled his eyes and shrugged. Sneaks crumpled the copy and slam-dunked it into the garbage.

Mitch mockingly read aloud, "'Due to your firm's status as an LP and not a broker-dealer, your claim needs to be filed through the firm's clearing broker instead of directly to Nasdaq.' Case closed. Nasdaq won. Fuck off."

They knew there was no way to refile the way Nasdaq wanted, so without another grumble, the guys headed back to their seats. Mitch turned Whitney Houston back up and shimmied as he strained to sing along to "I Wanna Dance with Somebody."

Back in his seat, Goldie exclaimed derisively over the music, "Oh, look who's on CNBC—it's Gundlach! Taking a little walk down 'mammary lane' should be a better way to cap off the day." CNBC had dubbed Jeffrey Gundlach the "new bond king." He'd ostensibly dethroned the former bond king, Bill Gross.

Goldie strolled around the desk. "Tommy, catch this story. This dude, Jeffrey Gundlach, had a huge falling out with his former employer, TCW. It ended up in court, where all this dirty laundry came out. In order to show some sort of character flaw, TCW presented the contents of Gundlach's office." Goldie winked at Sneaks. "Let's recount for young Tommy what one of the most respected money managers had stored among his files."

Sneaks chimed in, "I got it right here. Are you ready for this?" He grinned mischievously. "Ten pornographic videos including *A Trip Down Mammary Lane*; *Swallow My Pride: Volume 2*; *Dr. Fellatio: Volumes 1–4*; and, my personal favorite, *Weapons of Ass Destruction*."

"Whoa, he sounds like a fun guy to work with," Tommy said, laughing.

Goldie added, "I wish that were it, but there was more stuff: straps for restraining, a sex slave kit, and a special one for the ladies—one ball gag! What bond trader wouldn't need one of those?" He laughed blithely. "But meanwhile, he's still über-respected in bonds. His track record in stocks is hit or miss, but he did make a prophetic call that Apple would go to $425 when it was in the $600s."

"Icahn swooped in down there," Mitch chimed in, then lowered his head.

Steve hastened to add, "Unfortunately, Gundlach followed up his Apple call with a call to short Chipotle in the $300s. He met his Waterloo for guru status after the stock doubled. He's—"

Quick to take a swipe, Sneaks interrupted, "That same short Chipotle call took Einhorn down a peg as well—something dumb about competition from Taco Bell."

"Einhorn definitely got Finkled on that one," Goldie added, using a familiar desk vernacular.

Steve spun back to Tommy and continued, "I was just saying, though, he's a super-smart guy. It was unfortunate that he had all that shit in his office, but in this business, when you get fired, they escort you out the door, leaving everything behind. They don't want you to take customer info or anything sensitive if they can help it."

Goldie chuckled. "Yeah, coulda happened to anyone." Imitating George Costanza, he said, "Had I known that sort of thing was frowned upon at work... Gotta plead ignorance on this one." After speaking over the entire interview, Goldie said to Tommy with unintended irony, "I give him shit, but ignore him at your own peril. He's legit one of the smartest dudes on Wall Street. Next time he's on, listen to what he's got to say. He's always got some good insight."

Mitch interjected, "Hey, guys, did you see this?" He looked around and saw blank faces. "I hope it's okay—I know I'm breaking the desk rule—but I just saw Loony-Life is halted. No earnings news is expected." Everyone's eyes turned to Brandon.

The desk had ignored Loony-Life for two years since Brandon's losses. It was disregarded to the point that it had informally brought the number of desk rules up to two: No crying and no discussion of Loony-Life.

Brandon waved Mitch off dismissively. "That stock could be halted for a $100 takeover, or the company might be charged with accounting fraud. Who the heck knows? That's why it's never been worth getting involved again." As he scanned for the news, he said, "Oh, wait, on the squawk box: FBI raid. Great. The stock's a zero, and um, about two years too late for me." He flung a pen across the room and winced as it hit the wall far closer to Greenspan's portrait than intended.

"FBI raid! Booyah!" Mitch whooped. "Bring on the liquidation sale for a new 70-inch flat panel TV, just in time for football season."

"Holy shit, that's fucked up. FBI raid—the stock's gonna

be wallpaper," Goldie exclaimed. "We had the right idea—just slightly fucking early. That stock'll go from $60 to zero faster than a Tesla goes from zero to sixty."

The color drained from Brandon's face as he ran a hand through his hair. "It really doesn't bother me a bit," he said unconvincingly. "Just confirms my cynicism. Yet another fuckin' scam. God bless anyone who hung in there short for the last two years. That would take the cojones of Cohodes." Shaking his head in resignation, he added, "And we all know—I ain't got that kind of testicular fortitude."

The desk delighted in schadenfreude when investors on the Street lost money from a stock gone awry. "Who's getting fleeced on the long side?" Mitch asked gleefully.

"Let me check the institutional holders. Icahn Capital, of course, still in there," Brandon noted. "I think he'll be okay, though. He's up a couple of bil this year on his 'no-brainer' Apple call. Um, also a few small hedge funds, but looks like mostly index funds."

"That's a shame. At least some douchebag touts on Twitter are gonna take it up the bunghole. Of course, we'll no doubt see the shorts take a victory lap." Mitch rolled his eyes.

"Can anyone explain to me the Loony-Life story?" Tommy looked around, nonplussed. "You know, the desk rule."

Mitch quickly looked at Tommy, winked, and held up his index finger. Even two years later, he'd rather wait until Brandon was off the desk to explain the story.

CNBC broke the Loony-Life news, and Herb Greenberg was thrust on air to comment. "I have to say, while doing my reporting on Loony-Life, I always believed there were serious accounting issues, but the magnitude of the fraud outlined by the SEC and FBI is truly stunning. Right when you think you've seen it all, there's something new that you can't believe is happening. This scheme," he said, gesturing pointedly with the press release clutched in his hand, "represents not only pre-meditated fraud but a carefully orchestrated plan to defraud investors. You know, it doesn't surprise me at all that sophis-ticated hedge fund investors fell for this accounting fraud—it was hard to detect. Although there were many red flags, some-times they don't amount to much in other companies, which is why they often get ignored by Wall Street. It's just amaz-ing. I *personally* met with this company's management. They looked me straight in the eye and *flat-out lied.*"

A pause. Greenberg choked up before emphasizing his next point. "It truly bothers me to see people get hurt, completely betrayed by a company they believed in. I would tell investors that this won't be the last company to use accounting shenani-gans or engage in fraud. I've spent my career red-flagging com-panies that play accounting games, and it's hard to keep up." The desk followed his every word though they already knew well the lesson of his lecture. "Don't be fooled by companies that hide in plain sight. It's a brilliant investor relations strat-egy that only works until it doesn't. Certainly, neither side has a monopoly on being right, but most investors ought to avoid stocks that become a battleground between shorts and longs because of accounting issues. There are plenty of other great companies to invest in." Greenberg looked down at the press release one last time and shook his head. "A fraud this blatant, persisting for so many years, can only be perpetrated with the assistance of a wide range of enablers. They all bear some re-sponsibility, and for the good of the financial markets, they too need to be held to account."

Chapter 35

REALITY HITS HOME

With the commotion of the breaking Loony-Life story, Brandon scarcely remembered the Yahoo short call he had emailed to Jim Chanos. Later that day, he glanced at his inbox and immediately felt gratified to spot Chanos's reply. Unexpectedly, Chanos mentioned Loony-Life; although he shouldn't have been surprised, Brandon was still jolted. It immediately brought back uncomfortable memories of their last conversation.

Chanos left little doubt in the email that he was still short Loony-Life shares. He praised the SEC and the FBI for successfully gathering solid evidence to halt fraud in its tracks and indict the culprits in the executive suite. "Fraud is challenging to prosecute," he wrote. "Usually, regulators and law enforcement are like financial archeologists, unearthing facts after many years have passed, long after the dust has settled." With no direct criticism of Carl Icahn, Chanos mentioned that investors had ample opportunity to recognize the red flags and divest.

As he glanced at the rest of the email, Brandon spotted the word "Yahoo" in the next paragraph. His eyes widened. Chanos commended the insightful call to short Yahoo and expressed appreciation for Brandon's reasoning. He went on to illustrate why he agreed Yahoo was a short, but by a markedly different logic than the case Brandon had made.

Chanos explained that his fund, Kynikos, had done extensive research on Alibaba and found their accounting opaque, even by Chinese standards. He derided Alibaba for its lack of transparency, huge capital expenditures, and use of off-balance-sheet entities. He doubted that if presented with the prospectus, buyers of the deal would even recognize its bright orange cover.

Brandon was left in wonder at the sophisticated short argument. For a second, he chuckled. So far, the only concern bandied about on the Street was Alibaba's unusual Cayman Island corporate structure.

By the end of the email, Brandon's smile turned into a stare of bewildered amazement—Chanos had invited him to interview for an opening as an analyst at Kynikos. "I haven't forgotten about your past interest, if it still holds," he wrote.

It could not possibly have wavered, Brandon thought.

He also hadn't forgotten what Chanos had mentioned two years earlier about traders and analysts. To debunk the notion that the skill sets of the roles were too different to move between them, he'd always rooted for industry professionals to make the transition successfully—and found himself consistently disappointed.

Recently, Brandon had followed the career change of Meredith Whitney, the acclaimed analyst of the financial crisis. She'd made a stunningly prescient bear case on financial stocks, especially Citigroup prior to its implosion. After only a year of managing her own hedge fund, she was off to a rocky start. This didn't inspire confidence.

A week later, Brandon arrived at Kynikos for an interview. Dressed in a gray suit primarily reserved for weddings and bar mitzvahs, he stood frozen in front of the door, taking in the moment. He was about to meet his hero, the man he thought the smartest in the industry, and interview for a job at his fund. Even with Brandon's extensive experience, he couldn't help thinking, *I'm not worthy.* As Chanos greeted him, Brandon tried his hardest to wipe the goofy grin off his face, and realizing he was failing to do so made him more anxious in front of his idol. This could be the meeting that changed everything for him, if he could only stop smiling like an idiot.

After a brief tour of the office, he met the head of the analyst team and several other analysts. Amidst a short dialogue about Micron and DRAM prices, it dawned on Brandon that he did know an analyst who'd successfully transitioned to trading: Dan Niles. Niles had used his sharp skills, honed as a tech analyst, to shift into trading within a hedge fund. Perhaps Brandon could transition the opposite way and use his trader instinct for timing to flourish as an analyst.

With this new vision of success, he felt his confidence rally for the interview he'd aspired to since that Metro-North ride years ago. Brandon reminded himself to maintain eye contact as he was grilled on the extent of his finance and accounting skills, his eagerness to study and dissect corporate filings regularly, and his ability to detach from the stock market's daily moves.

Somewhere toward the middle of the interview, his anxiety swelled and his wool suit felt uncomfortably warm. When asked if he knew how to spot corporate fraud in SEC filings, he realized he was out of his depth. His eyes strayed toward the ceiling as he labored to recall the first time Chanos outlined the red flags he uncovered in Enron's SEC documents—but his mind went blank. For a moment, he considered responding,

"I've always been suspicious when I find related executives," but he didn't want to embarrass himself with such a feeble response. Instead, he grimly shook his head.

It didn't take long for his interviewers to expose the finance skills he'd acquired years earlier as long-forgotten, and for them to note that the investing tactics he used as a trader were far different from what Kynikos valued. Deep into the interview, the questions seemed to ease—perhaps from an unspoken understanding that his knowledge was not up to snuff. Even before the session ended, Brandon sensed that his dream, perhaps always misguided, was over.

Before he left, Brandon could hardly believe his luck as he followed Chanos into a conference room and nervously searched for something interesting to say. Worried his mouth was too dry to speak, he went straight for a water dispenser and gulped down a paper cup of water as he admired an enormous painting of a red flag raised high atop a flagpole blowing in the wind. He was struck by the befitting symbolism of a red flag embodied in a work of art. Aside from the apparent depiction of the firm's endeavor to root out warning signs, he thought of how capitalizing on red flags was more art than science.

Feigning casualness, he strolled over to a bookshelf to peruse for a recognizable title. *The Match King*, *Red Capitalism*, *The Demon-Haunted World*, *The Seven Signs of Ethical Collapse*, *A World Lit Only by Fire*, *7 Deadly Scenarios*, a few from John Kenneth Galbraith... *It would help if I had read any of these*, he thought. A basket of apples on the cabinet below the bookshelf caught his eye, and he turned to motion curiously at them.

Chanos chuckled. "They were a gift from a friend who appreciates my work—*this time*. Read the card."

Brandon peered at the attached note and read, "You did good work this time on that Loony company. Atlas is one rotten apple. —CI"

Brandon affirmed the card's sentiment with a steady nod, then whispered in a parched voice, "Icahn?" When Chanos smiled broadly, Brandon's jitters eased as he grabbed a shiny red and green McIntosh and said, "Classy move." To his delight, they went on to talk for what felt like minutes but approached two hours. They joked about how Herb Greenberg would appreciate the painting of the red flag. Enron came up, as did Chanos's recently disclosed short position in Valeant, a pharmaceutical roll-up. He outlined a convincing case for the Valeant short, noting how their accounting of acquired drugs neglected to amortize those costs in operating cash flow. On the other hand, Brandon knew Bill Ackman has staked out an outsized long position and publicly decried the premise behind Chanos's short call, and felt apprehensive of the hedge fund battle brewing.

Toward the end of the conversation, Chanos revealed a story about Yahoo and Alibaba. "Our research gave us a considerable interest to short Alibaba, but we were unsure about a borrow of the shares." Chanos explained further that they figured shorting Yahoo was equivalent to a cost basis of being short Alibaba a lot lower, and Brandon had demonstrated a more refined discounting mechanism for them. "In fact, your math for shorting Yahoo as a proxy for Alibaba turned out to be far more accurate than our own." Brandon wasn't sure he'd ever be able to take the smile off his face.

When he arrived home that evening, Lily was anxious to hear how his interview had gone. With no detail spared, he recounted the spirited conversation on the subject of stocks, the basket of apples from Icahn, the enormous red flag painting—Lily insisted the art must symbolize the Bolshevik Revolution in a way Brandon failed to grasp—and the golden fried cheese curds Chanos shared from his recent trip to his home state of Wisconsin.

The kids had gone to bed and the two of them retired to the front porch to savor the last of the summer warmth. "Do you think you'll get the job?" she asked over the din of crickets.

"I doubt it," he said with no hesitation. Gently, he laid his hand on hers. "But I'm not sure I'd want it even if I did." Already he had resolved that being in the thick of the trading action was an ingrained part of his life not easily shed. Plus, as an analyst, he'd often have to miss evenings with Lily and the kids, and he'd probably be too tired for morning fishing trips with Dylan and Ella.

The following weekend, a letter from Kynikos arrived in the mail. Fully expecting a rejection, he tore open the envelope. The formal missive confirmed what he already knew—he'd never work with his industry hero. An unexpected moment of emptiness consumed him. Brandon walked toward the forest at the edge of the lawn. Birds were singing, and a cottontail rabbit scurried over dead leaves. The echo of a distant hunting rifle had him take stock of a handful of wild turkeys pecking away under the old maple. Suddenly, a delighted laugh caught his attention.

"Come play with us, Daddy!" cried Ella from across the lawn.

In an instant, the setback was forgotten. He jogged back through the yard and scooped up a Wiffle ball from where it had landed on the grass. A breeze gusted toward left field while he pitched the ball to Dylan, who slugged it as Ella ran around imaginary bases. They shouted and laughed when she beat the tag at home plate.

Later, on the porch with Lily, Brandon reflected on the trader's life: the never-ending entertainment and drama on the desk he'd helped build, and the free time it allowed him to spend with his family. Trading had never been his ideal job, but Brandon realized he was happy with it anyway. *The desk will always figure out a way to survive by adapting to the times,* he thought. Next to him, the cover of *Barron's* stared up from the side table. The game plan on how to trade the feature story on Monday morning took over his thoughts.

Chapter 36

SECRETS AND LIARS

Holly Walsh had been a secret keeper from a young age. She grew up with the secret that her family was poor, a circumstance her mother, Faye, had insisted stay guarded.

In 1980, Holly's father, Murray, was diagnosed with the incurable disease ALS, otherwise known as Lou Gehrig's disease. On advice from his broker at Merrill Lynch, Pierce, Fenner & Smith, Murray took most of his life savings and purchased a single-premium deferred annuity from the University Life Insurance Company of America to provide for his wife and two children after his death.

"There's nothing safer than annuities," the broker had assured him. With the extraordinarily high interest rates of the day, the annuity compounded annually at 15.5%, and the value was set to almost triple over seven years. Critically, the accrued benefits were payable tax-free upon death.

Murray believed his family's financial burden was satisfied when he succumbed to the disease three years later. At the time, Holly was eight. She was a shy child, too young for her world to take on such misfortune, but circumstances were set to grow even gloomier. The annuity payout the family had expected was held in limbo. The issuer's parent company, Baldwin-United Corp., had just filed for bankruptcy protection, which thrust annuity policyholders at its subsidiary into jeopardy.

Desperate for funds to support her family, Faye jumped at the first offer to cash out the annuity. Two years after her husband's death, she signed over the rights to the bankruptcy settlement. She received 75% of the original investment as a loan, with interest on the loan covered by the remaining 25%. The complex structure contained full loan forgiveness at the end of the term. Had she held out for a couple more years, she would have received back the original principal invested plus most of the income due—almost three times the amount she ended up getting.

Without Murray's income, the Walsh family struggled and never recovered financially. In the years that followed, her mother's constant fear of poverty left a scar on Holly's impressionable mind. Faye, pugnacious and proud, refused to admit they were poor. Young Holly and her brother played along with the masquerade, but the truth of their situation eventually became clear. When the siblings planned for college, the family's exact financial condition could no longer be avoided. Only then did Faye recount to her kids the troubling details of their father's investment mishap.

As an adult, Holly read about the incident of Baldwin-United that so fractured her childhood. She learned of the young analyst at Gilford Securities who warned about the company's accounting irregularities well before its bankruptcy—and came to admire his search for honesty on Wall Street. *The whole issue*, she thought as she read, *could have been sidestepped: the annuity, all our financial problems, everything*. She vowed that day to better understand financial markets to never experience the same troubles her family had lived through. As time passed, she continued to follow the Gilford analyst's career closely.

Holly had secrets at work, too. Billy, her son, was conceived during an affair with her boss, Ethan Atlas. She was naive at the time and thought it romantic, but soon realized how Ethan had taken advantage of the power imbalance between them. After Billy was born, she was forced to rely on Ethan for financial reasons—both for child support and her paycheck. So, she remained his assistant. Their affair ended shortly after she gave birth, and no one at work ever suspected the child was his.

For years, Holly searched for a way out. She would have done anything to get away from Ethan and Loony-Life. When she came across documents related to his money transfers to China, she saw her chance for escape. With her boyfriend, Fred, she hatched yet another secret, a plan to profit from the information and make enough money to provide for Billy and her mother without Loony-Life and Ethan's support.

She passed the information on to a respected reporter, Cliff Ludwig. Once he seemed interested in the story, she bought puts on Loony-Life. When Cliff's groundbreaking article on Loony-Life's accounting issues was published on the cover of *Barron's*, Holly went to work the following day with her heart racing but her demeanor composed. She watched in amazement as a windfall of profits accumulated in her account in the significant stock downdraft that followed the article. That same day, she saw Ethan and Stan Atlas conferring, then read the press release they'd crafted. She rushed to contact Fred to sell the puts, but the stock had already been halted. For weeks she held on to the options in the vain hope the stock would turn back lower. They eventually expired, worthless.

After Cliff's article fell flat on Wall Street, Holly questioned whether the suspicious issues were truly part of a bona fide scheme. For a time, she was saddened to think she'd misjudged Ethan. His claim of making huge charitable gifts with his stock sales was widely accepted. To determine the veracity, she tried listening in on his and Stan's closed-door conversations, but to no avail. If anything, all the article had done was increase Ethan's secrecy. Her suspicions felt vindicated once Jim Chanos disclosed his Loony-Life short position. The former Gilford analyst she had followed and trusted for more than a decade gave her the resolve to fight anew.

Once Holly realized her original plan to buy puts had been crude and hastily executed, she vowed to take a more thoughtful approach to bring down Ethan Atlas and Loony-Life. For months, she and Fred plotted together, debating the best course of action. They eventually decided to take her findings to the SEC. Holly started to assemble a package of information, but she received a phone call before she was ready to contact them.

"Holly Walsh?" The voice on the other end was female and unfamiliar.

"Speaking," replied Holly warily. She kept her voice pleasant but cool at the sight of an unknown number.

"My name is Aviva Goddard. Last year, I worked with Cliff Ludwig on a story for *Barron's* about Loony-Life. I was wondering if we could meet somewhere and talk."

The next day, Holly met Aviva in a quiet corner booth at the Parkway Diner in Little Neck, Queens. As she and Aviva talked, a bond began to form between the two women. Through dinner and late into the night over coffee, Holly unloaded her secrets to Aviva, including her true motives for calling Cliff.

Within days, Aviva accompanied her to meet a representative from the SEC's Division of Enforcement. They placed a high priority on Holly's allegations in conjunction with the package of evidence Aviva had sent earlier to the SEC. The two women met with the FBI soon afterward. Over the next year, Holly's list of secrets grew, as did Aviva's. Unable to write about Loony-Life while the investigation continued, Aviva and

Holly grew closer. The reporter became a close confidante for Holly as she navigated through challenges at work and in life. Thanks to this friendship, Holly felt the weight of a lifetime's worth of secrets gradually lift from her shoulders.

On the afternoon of September 19, 2014, Holly still kept many secrets, but the events that unfolded that day took her by surprise.

Holly sat jarred when the FBI stormed into Loony-Life's offices as she watched Ethan Atlas cuffed and led away. From the sour ending of their affair to the past year spent working with the SEC and FBI, she'd come to see him as sinister. However, she still wished she hadn't been at work to witness his arrest, especially when she recognized the two agents who led the raid and supervised the removal of the company's computers and documents. Although the agents didn't acknowledge her, she was uncomfortably aware of her every movement and expression, certain that anyone who saw her would immediately be able to read her part in bringing this raid down upon them. She knew it was a secret that would be out before long—the FBI had made it clear her role as an informant would likely be discovered by Ethan and Stan once evidence was presented against them. She'd already spent many sleepless nights and phone calls with Aviva imagining how the disgraced executives would retaliate.

But while Holly sat at her desk watching the commotion that day, the courage that had summoned her to follow the righteous path manifested, as difficult as that path had been to navigate. At that moment, she felt pride in her integrity and closed her eyes tightly. She knew more trying times lay ahead and wanted most of all to believe in herself. She had done the right thing; that was undeniable.

In need of fresh air, Holly stepped out of the office, crowded as it was with agents and her bewildered colleagues. In the lobby, she halted in her tracks when she suddenly found herself face to face with Stan Atlas, who was being frog-marched out of the building in cuffs. She stared, frozen, at the odd smile on his face. He was grinning ear-to-ear, clearly relishing the moment as if it were his finest rather than the moment all his schemes came crashing down. All she could think to attribute it to was some relief that the fraud was over.

But this was a fine day indeed for Stan, one he had long prepared for, and the smirk on his face was the only outward indication of the cogs turning in his brain. He improvised nothing; like a chess player, he was thinking three steps ahead for his next move and considering every possibility.

After the article about Loony-Life had been published in *Barron's*, Stan had taken extra precautions. He knew it would take government investigators ages to go through the byzantine accounting on the tens of thousands of scarcely relevant documents he'd maniacally printed and stored in the empty warehoused boxes; in fact, he was counting on it. The paperwork would demonstrate that the boxes had a purpose, however flimsy it might be, and he could blame the confusion on underlings for mistakenly counting them as inventory. The investigators would also find nothing incriminating on his work computer—the second set of books only resided in his head. Just as he'd made his auditor's work difficult to accomplish in a reasonable amount of time, he planned to make it nearly impossible to sort through Loony-Life's files with the manpower the government investigators would allocate.

Stan had two scenarios planned for his dealings with the investigators. Plan A: With righteous indignation, he would play dumb, a complete incompetent, and imply that any errors were from his poor accounting knowledge while portraying an unimpeachable integrity with only the shareholders' best interests at heart. Plan B: He would cop a deal with the prosecutors to avoid prison in return for his help with sorting through the mess, while incriminating Ethan. He reasoned that the Feds would rather the satisfaction of a quick deal than spend years examining mountains of paperwork. Ultimately, he knew investigators would follow the money to catch the biggest fish, and it was Ethan who had made the big bucks from selling shares. Stan would use to his advantage the fact that his take was small potatoes by comparison.

In the end, both plans came into play. Stan played dumb for as long as possible, but his innocent guise only irked the FBI and SEC investigators, who didn't buy into his story.

The months that passed under federal investigation were far more intimidating than Stan could ever have imagined. Thoughts about the case and the accusations he faced consumed him. When he wasn't strategizing with his lawyer, he was contemplating their next conversation. The constant stress and significant weight loss he endured were punishments in and of themselves.

When his lawyer told him in no uncertain terms that the investigators had enough evidence to suggest that he was the architect behind the accounting fraud, Stan knew Plan A had failed; it was time to turn to Plan B. He offered to cooperate fully in return for leniency. At a minimum, he recognized the opportunity in the advice of his counsel: "The first co-conspirator to talk gets the best deal with the Feds."

When a gaunt Stan flipped from declaring his innocence to complete cooperation, the federal authorities had difficulty believing he was telling the truth. The lead investigator, Marcus Ferry, summed up their thoughts to Stan in a tirade. "You've been bullshitting us for months—your credibility is in the toilet bowl. How the fuck are we supposed to believe a word you say now that you want to cooperate?" He stared deep into Stan's downcast eyes. "By the last count, we've uncovered 445 boxes of documents sitting in your warehouse in Red Bank. What the fuck is with that?"

At once, a wave of relief poured over Stan, and he did everything possible to suppress a grin. His plan had worked. His interrogator was handing him an opening—they needed Stan's help. Stan had suspected that even the best prosecutors would need someone on the inside to help guide them through the accounting complexities.

"I'm prepared to come entirely clean with you," he replied to the scowling agent. "I've got nothing to hide anymore."

Ferry raised a skeptical eyebrow. All Stan had done for months was hide the truth.

Stan had to stop himself from rolling his eyes. "I mean it," he said earnestly. "I'll tell you every fuckin' detail of the train wreck at Loony-Life. To be honest, I just want to stay out of prison. Period." Stan folded his hands and formulated his words carefully. "Nobody can tell you where the bodies are buried like I can. I can tell you things you'd never figure out on your own. I'll tell you where money is hidden, how to sort through the convoluted accounting system, how we fooled the auditors, and how we laundered money through foreign banks. Best of all, I'll tell you how Ethan Atlas orchestrated it all."

Agent Ferry remained stone-faced. "Come on, Marcus," coaxed Stan. "You don't want to have to tell the victims and class action attorneys to wait years for compensation until it's all sorted out. Right now, as far as I can tell, we need each other to make this work, and I'm ready to come clean. What do you say?"

Ferry left the room to discuss the offer with his colleagues. Stan leaned back in his chair, and even his lawyer by his side let a smile take shape on his face.

Stan and the FBI cut a deal that very day.

Chapter 37

CONSPIRACY

Unlike Stan, Ethan had not planned ahead for the unraveling of Loony-Life's fraud, except for the cash he'd secretly stashed in overseas banks.

He seethed as he sat handcuffed in the back of a patrol car outside of Loony-Life's offices. He'd never be worth a quarter of a billion dollars again, he thought to himself, but he was ready to live on the $14 million he had stockpiled abroad. First, he had to get out of this mess.

When Ethan met with federal investigators, he denied involvement in any attempt to defraud investors and fully blamed Stan as the mastermind behind the scheme. No one doubted Ethan's claims that he could never have pulled off such an audacious accounting scheme with his limited knowledge of accounting. Still, prosecutors had in their possession recorded conversations and records of wire transfers that implicated him in the conspiracy.

When Ethan learned that Stan had agreed to cooperate with the investigation and had taken full responsibility for doctoring the books but only at Ethan's direction, he felt cornered. He knew the Feds had their smoking gun—and it was Stan himself firing away at him. Ethan could barely bring himself to feel surprised. Faced with grim prospects, he vowed to do whatever possible to avoid prison.

At that instant, like the illumination that came when Salome's final veil dropped, a seventh epiphany struck Ethan: He had believed the link he forged between the Wall Street perception he'd cultivated and the company's reality to be meaningful and lasting. But instead, he now realized it was all superficial and fleeting—much like his trust in Stan.

Ethan looked back on his desire to please Wall Street and how he'd worried so much about the company's stock, and saw that all of it was hollow. At times, the satisfaction of burning the shorts and naysayers had coursed through his body like a drug. The importance of the company's deteriorating balance sheet had paled as the stock price became the barometer of his success. Although he knew it wasn't about the money, per se, his self-respect had ebbed and flowed with fluctuations in the stock price and his net worth as a shareholder. Now he could no longer fathom how this had ever made sense. His job was to manage a business, yet he'd become too caught up in managing Wall Street.

Little good that epiphany did him now.

The $14 million he had stashed abroad seemed like all the money in the world. Getting to that cash was more important now than anything else other than also avoiding prison. This, combined with pressure from the federal investigation, sparked his decision to abandon his family and flee the country rather than face the weight of the charges brought against him.

With the help of several phony passports, Ethan traveled covertly to Europe to withdraw his cash in preparation for living abroad indefinitely, and in due course, he fled to Namibia. The country, chosen for its lack of an extradition treaty with the United States, was the home of Ethan's acquaintance Kobi Alexander, founder and former CEO of Comverse Technology.

Like Ethan, Kobi had gone on the lam to avoid fraud charges, including securities fraud and wire fraud, brought by the U.S. Department of Justice.

Kobi embraced Ethan when they met at a hotel. "Namibia is a beautiful country. It's a suitable place to spend the rest of your life, if necessary, as I intend to do." Ethan's lack of a plan left him uncertain of the duration of his stay abroad, but he found immense comfort in Kobi's guidance.

After months of conversations, Ethan's lawyers convinced him to return voluntarily to the U.S. to face charges. Unlike his fellow fugitive, Ethan couldn't adjust to life in Africa on the run. He felt an overwhelming sense of innocence in the entire affair; after all, he had attempted to right what he and Stan had done wrong.

Upon returning, he agreed to meet Stan in a sauna at a club on Long Island—their first meeting since Stan became a witness for the prosecution. Each had been stewing to have his say with the other. Once they got it off their chests, they both expected this would be their last conversation.

Stan spoke, but not before he unwound the towel from his waist and flashed his naked body to show he was not wired. The trust they once shared was gone. "You know it was Holly who fucked us," he said.

"No, it was that reporter from the *Wall Street Journal*—she fucked us," Ethan said with disgust. "I read her articles. How could she write about misdeeds at the company and then send information to the SEC to fulfill her reporting? That bitch went over the goddamn line to fuck us and come out the hero."

"Oh, please. The problem is you left us wide open. You turned a blind eye to Holly, that's for sure."

Ethan stood up and jabbed his finger in Stan's face. "What's for sure is *you* betrayed me. My own flesh and blood threw me under the bus. For a scheme that was *your* idea."

"You're the one who exposed us to accounting fraud by trying to 'fix' things." Stan waved Ethan's hand away. "Nobody knew about my idea."

Sweat rolled off Ethan's face. "You know, I'm not saying I never did anything wrong, but at least I tried to save the company by undoing your inventory mess—with money out of my pocket!"

"You had to do it your way—that's what got us caught." Stan paused and gritted his teeth. "We would have had years more time if you'd listened to me. One day—far in the future—Loony's business would have gone south like so many electronics stores before. We could have gone bankrupt and claimed to be the victims of a brutally competitive retail environment, meanwhile wiping our books squeaky clean. That's it. That was our out. No fraud, none of this bullshit, just another failed business. Don't you get that? There's not one executive in jail from all the failed banks during the financial meltdown. Not one! Hundreds of billions wiped away. And we know what shady bookkeeping and misrepresentations they made." He put his palms together in admiration of the blatant deceit. "AIG said that under no circumstances would they lose any money after they were already knee-deep in collateral calls. So, who's coming after a failed electronics company?"

"I tried to save the company. That's all," said Ethan, his voice ice cold.

"You wanted to be a hero on Wall Street. You were trying to save the stock."

Ethan sat down. There was no use in trying to argue the point.

Sensing his advantage, Stan pivoted and spoke as if he were omniscient, without a trace of doubt in his voice. "It was revenge, Ethan, plain and simple. You should have left your wife once Holly became pregnant. But your boy will be fine—she'll get 20% of the SEC's take." In Stan's belief system, the altruistic whistleblower didn't exist; there was always a motive.

Ethan sat befuddled with his elbows on his knees while he contemplated his affair with Holly and the child that was born. Gone was the confident tone in his voice. "Revenge? Why revenge? I gave her plenty of money to raise my son."

"Nickels and dimes, that's what you gave her," Stan said. "She still needed to work, for Christ's sake. Holly wanted her share. She saw all the stock you were selling, snooped around to see where it was all going, and wondered why she wasn't getting more. Then she called *Barron's* and the Feds. That's what I call revenge."

"Give me a break. She found some other guy, and I still gave her plenty of money." He added uncomfortably, "So, the Feds must know. She has this misconduct claim against me. Total bullshit."

"You bet the Feds know. And you know what? They see a mess coming they'd rather avoid." Stan knew Ethan was hooked. If he could help reel in the big fish for the prosecutors, it would mean a more lenient sentence for himself. He had to play both sides against the middle. He flipped his best card. "'The CEO on trial fathered the child of the whistleblower!' The Feds want those headlines even less than you do."

"So, what are you saying?" Ethan asked as Stan smiled.

He would spell it out for Ethan one last time. "I'm saying it puts them in the mood to cut a deal."

EPILOGUE

December 2016

Aviva flexed her fingers, sore from holding a Sharpie for so long. Next to her, Cliff stifled a groan.

"This wasn't what I had in mind when I decided I wanted to be a writer," she joked, shaking her cramped hand. Cliff reached over and patted her on the shoulder.

"That's the price of fame, I guess." He winked. "We'll survive."

She took a deep breath as she noticed the line moving forward again. Their short break was over. "Here they come," she murmured as she forced a smile on her face.

Her grin quickly grew genuine when she saw Holly standing in front of her, holding a shiny hardcover copy of Cliff and Aviva's new book, *Unboxed: The Loony-Life Story.*

"You made it!" Aviva rose to hug Holly over the signing table.

Holly smiled. "Of course! I had to be here for your big night. I certainly don't miss driving around the city though."

After Ethan pleaded guilty and was sentenced to eight years in prison and $150 million in fines and restitution, Holly left the city to start a new life. The SEC penalized her for taking part in a scheme to manipulate the shares of Loony-Life for personal gain. Instead of the usual 20% whistleblower claim,

Holly's award was capped at the lower amount of 10% or $10 million of recovered funds. She took the $10 million gratefully and bought a farm in upstate New York, where she and her family ran an animal sanctuary for rescued and unwanted farm animals.

Aviva and Holly remained close after Loony-Life's demise, and Aviva spent many long weekends and even a few holidays at the farm. Holly had been an instrumental source for Aviva and Cliff when they wrote their book, and Aviva was glad to see her here now.

"Looks like a great turnout," said Holly, glancing around at the long line of people waiting to have their books signed. "Think I could get a couple of autographs on this thing?"

Aviva laughed. "Holly, it's you who should be signing these copies. Without you, we'd never have had a story, and Loony-Life might still be in business."

Holly's smile was tight. In a deal with prosecutors, she had withdrawn her misconduct complaint against Ethan in return for his agreement never to contact her or Billy until he was 18. But the thought of him still made her stomach churn.

Aviva wrote a heartfelt note to Holly on the front page, and Cliff did the same. After Holly left, with promises to see them at the after-party, Cliff and Aviva got back to their line of fans.

The queue eventually dwindled, and they dropped their markers to make their way together to the reception area. The publisher had gone all out for the party after their book debuted that week on the *New York Times* Best Seller list (Aviva's colleagues insisted it was, in fact, a *Wall Street Journal* best seller). Greeted by a server offering champagne, they both gratefully accepted a glass.

Aviva gestured to the packed room. "Did you ever expect this when we wrote that first article?"

"I didn't expect anything, really," said Cliff. "Except maybe a good story and for investors to see the warning signs and divest." He clinked his glass to hers in a brief toast to their shared success.

"Oh, by the way," he said as though commenting on the weather. "Did you hear that Stan Atlas was released from house arrest a few weeks ago?"

For his cooperation in the legal case against Loony-Life, Stan received leniency from the judge: six months of house arrest, three years of probation, 1,200 hours of community service, and a $10,000 fine. He was also permanently barred by the SEC from any involvement with the accounting of publicly traded companies.

Aviva furrowed her brow. "He's not off the hook though; he's still got years of probation, doesn't he?"

"Three years," said Cliff in that same casual tone. "But now that he's off house arrest, he can travel abroad. Rumor has it, he's headed for a vacation. In Panama."

"Panama," Aviva blurted, astonished. She recalled some of the details of her original research with Cliff for their first Loony-Life article, details on offshore accounts and shell corporations. "That's certainly... interesting."

Cliff left her shortly after to find his wife, and Aviva's eyes scanned the room, resting briefly on her family, who had all flown in from Oregon, and Hugh McLaggen, standing among a cluster of her *Journal* colleagues. She even spotted Brandon with his wife, Lily, and waved when she caught his eye.

No, she thought, reflecting on her question to Cliff, *I'd have never guessed that writing about Loony-Life would end with a best-selling book and this party.* She had only pictured success like this in her wildest dreams, and even then, not seriously.

Her phone vibrated in her purse and she automatically reached for it, wondering if one of her friends or a family member from out of town had gotten lost on the way to the venue.

"Hello?" she answered without even a glance at the screen, not realizing the call was forwarded from her work phone.

"Aviva Goddard? At the *Wall Street Journal*?"

Aviva ducked away from the noise and bustle so she could hear better. "Yes," she responded slowly. She didn't recognize the voice on the other end of the line, but his nervous tone, tinted with hope, was all too familiar to her.

The stranger continued, "I just read your book, and I—" he stammered, clearly anxious, "I have some information I think you might be interested in hearing."

If anyone had glanced at Aviva at that moment, hunched over her phone in the darkest corner of the room, they'd have seen the furrow in her brow and intensity of her eyes as she listened to the caller tell her about a particular Panamanian shell corporation. Her mind was in overdrive as she thanked the caller and hung up. She placed her phone back in her purse, straightened, and headed back to the party with a fresh smile on her face.

THE END

ACKNOWLEDGMENTS

Six years is a long time to spend writing a book, and I didn't do it alone. Every word of encouragement, constructive criticism, advice, and imparted knowledge from the many people who were so generous with their time helped make *The Trading Desk* possible.

The journalists I spoke with were so kind and helpful in providing insight into their methods, scope, and mission. In part, *The Trading Desk* is my homage to financial journalists for the inspiration I've found from their work.

Among this group of journalists, I must give a special thank you to Miriam Gottfried for her patience and insight through my numerous inquiries, as well as for inspiring me to write this book; Bethany McLean for her encouragement, her cameo in the story, and for allowing me to co-opt some of her illuminating wisdom; Erin Arvedlund for the stellar anecdotes, for making a cameo in the story, and for the resource of her superb book on Madoff; Roddy Boyd for imparting invaluable knowledge of investigative journalism; Bill Alpert for sharing deep wisdom and historical perspective; Gretchen Morgenson for the helpful insight and candor; Michael Santoli for his always spot-on perceptiveness and for making a cameo in the story; Linette Lopez for her candor, coolness, and her inspirational, unrelenting persona; Jesse Eisinger for granting me permission to use a sentence about the "moral order" from *The Chickenshit Club*, a book that was also a helpful resource; Peter

Eavis for setting me off in the right direction; Charley Grant for providing uniquely valuable insight; and Herb Greenberg for a list so long it would embarrass us both.

I owe my gratitude to Jim Chanos for his guest appearance in the book and for far exceeding my expectations whenever I needed ideas and information.

Thank you to Sam Antar. There was nothing more helpful for understanding how a devious conman thinks than having it imparted unabashedly from the mind of one of the all-time best.

A special thank you to my old friends and colleagues at Monarch Financial/WFP for their support: Jason Auerbach, Matt Auerbach, Jerry Efremides, Stefan Magel, Alex Scribner, and Dennis Seff.

A huge thank you to Raymond Wapner. When I gave up after six months of writing, Raymond unwittingly motivated me to get back to work after reading the early story and enthusiastically remarking on the parts he enjoyed. This made all the difference.

Thank you to Scott Goldman for always being amenable and optimistic when asked to read parts of the book.

I'm grateful to my editing contributors for their expertise and help in elevating my manuscript into a novel: Tenyia Lee, Kerri Miller, Peter Kelton, Jeanie Lyubelsky, Nathan Hassall, Oliver Corlett, and Charlie Mouaikel. I especially owe a huge debt of gratitude to the incomparable Emily Krempholtz for all the editing and writing assistance. In addition to being a deep source of ideas and a great help in vastly improving the book, Emily came up with the premise for the epilogue and collaborated on writing.

To the memory of special friends and family: Aviva Bershaw and Murray & Faye Rosen. Also, in remembrance of Billy Micciulli and Fred Gabler, my friends who worked at Cantor

Fitzgerald and died on September 11th.

To the memory of Alan Abelson, whose column in *Barron's* engaged generations of investors. The paragraph I quoted from his reporting about "an act of unsurpassed spinelessness" in a parallel incident from 1990 is probably the best-written of this entire book.

Special thanks to Simone Dinnerstein, Dan Niles, Scott Wapner, Doug Kass, Marc Cohodes, Michael Cohn, and Ivan the K.

I'm grateful to Simon Rosen, Esq., for the legal expertise and making every journey an entertaining one.

Throughout the writing process, I often issued pleas for feedback. For answering the call and taking the time to read and discuss the manuscript, I owe my great appreciation to Jerry Rosen, Danny Ben-Ari, Vicki Bryan, Joseph Colaprico, Brian Ducey, Julie Rosen, John Cortapasso, Eric Stine, Jerry Kessler, Will Qi, Emily Berger, Anthony Sabia, Curtis Watkins, Val Siretsanou, Stephanie Weiner, and "Big Al" Ginesin.

Many people on FinTwit helped me far above and beyond what I could have deserved or expected. In 2015, when the book was in a nascent stage and especially terrible, those who read it provided enough encouragement and ideas to make its completion possible. I'm incredibly grateful to the complete strangers who took significant amounts of time and effort to offer feedback and constructive criticism. I hope we won't always be strangers. Standing invitation to meet for drinks on me to @Wmboot, @Friedoystercult, @BarbarianCap, @FourFilters, @RyeNotBerben, @michaelswimelar, and @eLearnabunch.

Thank you to @DonutStocks for graciously allowing me to co-opt a tweet from his thread on fraud at Wirecard.

Thank you to Helene Meisler (@hmeisler) for the clarity of her long-time pinned tweet, "Nothing like price to change sentiment."

A thank-you with great admiration to my favorite author Tom Robbins, in whose writing I always found creative inspiration. I must acknowledge a tribute to one of Robbins's literary creations tucked within the pages of this book. Anyone who has read *Skinny Legs and All* would perhaps have recognized the reference.

I have benefitted immeasurably in all ways, including my use of the English language, from my dear wife, Lucia. Fortunately, she continually motivated me to improve the book. I also have her to thank for the way she mercilessly and liberally slashed or reconstructed much of my ill-conceived and wordy prose.

Finally, I'm eternally grateful for the enduring support of my children, Zack and Petra. Their patience and encouragement through my endless stories about the book, along with their belief in me, helped me to believe in myself.